T0311574

Money and the market

In this volume of essays Kevin Dowd presents a strong case that state intervention into financial and monetary systems has manifestly failed, and that we would be better off if governments stopped interfering with financial markets and central banks were abolished. Instead, he argues that financial markets should be left to regulate themselves; market forces would then deliver an efficient and stable financial system, safe and strong banks and sound money. *Money and the Market* fall into three parts:

- Part 1 deals with the theory of free banking and begins with a presentation of the case in its favour. This is followed by essays examining the arguments advanced for government deposit insurance, capital adequacy regulation, banking clubs, the role of the invisible hand in the evolution of the monetary system, and asks whether we can blame *laissez-faire* for the instability we observe in contemporary financial markets.
- Part 2 explores the monetary regime under *laissez-faire* and examines how fully automatic monetary systems might operate to stabilize the price level. Further essays look at Irving Fisher's 'compensated dollar' and at currency boards to replace central banks.
- Part 3 examines a variety of diverse policy issues from a free market standpoint – international capital controls, monetary policy in the twenty-first century, the future of gold, the bailout of Long-Term Capital Management in 1998 and the Financial Services Act in the UK.

This collection will be of considerable interest to students, researchers and policy-makers in the monetary and financial area.

Kevin Dowd is Professor of Financial Risk Management at the University of Nottingham Business School and adjunct scholar at the CATO Institute in Washington.

Foundations of the market economy

Edited by Mario J. Rizzo, *New York University* and
Lawrence H. White, *University of Georgia*

A central theme in this series is the importance of understanding and assessing the market economy from a perspective broader than the static economics of perfect competition and Pareto optimality. Such a perspective sees markets as causal processes generated by the preferences, expectations and beliefs of economic agents. The creative acts of entrepreneurship that uncover new information about preferences, prices and technology are central to these processes with respect to their ability to promote the discovery and use of knowledge in society.

The market economy consists of a set of institutions that facilitate voluntary co-operation and exchange among individuals. These institutions include the legal and ethical framework as well as more narrowly 'economic' patterns of social interaction. Thus the law, legal institutions and cultural and ethical norms, as well as ordinary business practices and monetary phenomena, fall within the analytical domain of the economist.

Other titles in the series

The Meaning of Market Process
Essays in the development of modern Austrian economics
Israel M. Kirzner

Prices and Knowledge
A market-process perspective
Estaban F. Thomas

Keynes' General Theory of Interest
A reconsideration
Fiona C. Maclachlan

Laissez-Faire Banking
Kevin Dowd

Expectations and the Meaning of Institutions
Essays in economics by Ludwig Lachmann
Edited by Don Lavoie

Money and the Market

Essays on free banking

Kevin Dowd

Routledge
Taylor & Francis Group

LONDON AND NEW YORK

First published 2001 by Routledge

Published 2013 by Routledge

2 Park Square, Milton Park, Abingdon, Oxfordshire OX14 4RN

Simultaneously published in the USA and Canada
by Routledge

711 Third Avenue, New York, NY 10017

First issued in paperback 2014

Routledge is an imprint of the Taylor & Francis Group, an informa company

Typeset in Times
by Curran Publishing Services Ltd, Norwich

British Library Cataloguing in Publication Data
A catalogue record for this book is available
from the British Library.

Library of Congress Cataloging in Publication Data
Dowd, Kevin
Money and the market: essays on free banking/Kevin Dowd
p. cm. – (Foundations of the market economy series)
A collection of 16 essays written between 1986 and 2000, with 14
previously published, they are a sequel to his *Laissez-faire banking*
(1963).
Includes bibliographical references and index.
1. Free banking. 2. Money. 3. Free enterprise. I. Dowd, Kevin. Laissez-
faire banking. II. Title. III. Series.
HG1811.D682 2000
332.1--dc21   00–032180

This book has been sponsored in part by the Austrian Economics
Program at New York University.

ISBN 978-0-415-24212-7 (hbk)

ISBN 978-0-415-75842-0 (pbk)

Contents

Tables

Preface

This book is a collection of essays on financial *laissez-faire* (or free banking) and its opposite, state intervention in the financial services sector and the monetary system. These essays were written between 1986 and 2000, and are a sequel to my earlier book, *Laissez-Faire Banking* (1993). Of the sixteen essays included here, fourteen have been published before in various places and two are published here for the first time. Those that appeared before have been lightly edited, but are substantially the same as they were before – with dubious judgements, falsified predictions, and so on, mostly intact.

I would like to thank the various publishers and copyright holders for permission to reprint my articles here: Blackwell publishers and the Royal Economic Society (chapters 2, 9 and 10), the *Journal of Financial Services Research* (chapter 3), the Cato Institute (chapters 4, 12, 14 and 16), the Ohio State University Press and the *Journal of Money, Credit, and Banking* (chapters 5 and 10), John Smithin and Routledge (chapter 6), *Critical Review* (chapter 7), Natwest Bank (chapter 13), and Sheffield Hallam University's *Review of Policy Issues* (chapter 15).

It is a great pleasure to thank many friends and co-workers for all manner of contributions, both direct and indirect. To begin with, I thank Alan Jarvis, Heidi Baytazo, Robert Langham, and the rest of the team at Routledge for various inputs to the book, Susan Curran for editing, and Maureen Jackson for help with the typing. I thank Alec Chrystal and Jimmy Hinchliffe, who co-authored one chapter each, and contributed to the book in many other ways besides. Thanks also to Charles Goodhart and Mervyn Lewis for encouragement and good advice which often went over my head, and to Chris Tame, Jim Dorn and the Cato Insitute for their steadfast moral as well as other support over many years. I also thank many co-workers in the field: Jeff Friedman, George Selgin, John Smith, Larry White and the many other people acknowledged in individual chapters throughout the book, as well as friends in the UK and Eire: Dave Cronin, Tony Courakis, David Goacher, Chris Humphrey, Ian Gow, Dave Owen, Denis Smith, and John Whittaker. I particularly thank Mark Billings,

Dave Campbell, Dave and Pat Chappell, David and Yabing Fisher, Barbara Hollman, Duncan Kitchin, Anneliese Osterspey, Alan and Ruth Rawling, Sheila Richardson, Stan and Dorothy Szynkaruk, and Basil and Maggie Zafiriou for their encouragement and friendship over many years. As ever, however, my biggest debts are to my family – to my parents, to my brothers Brian and Victor; and, most of all, to my wife Mahjabeen and my daughters, Raadhiyah and Safiah, for their love and support, and for all that they have had to put up with over the years. It is really high time that I promised them (and everyone else) no more books on free banking. I would therefore like to dedicate this book – hopefully my last on the subject, at least for a few years – to them.

Kevin Dowd
Sheffield
March 2000

Permissions acknowledgements

Chapter 2, 'The case for financial *laissez-faire*', was first published in the *Economic Journal* vol. 106, no. 436, May 1996, pp 679–87, and is reproduced by permission of Blackwell and the Royal Economic Society.

Chapter 3, 'Bank capital adequacy versus deposit insurance', was first published in the *Journal of Financial Services Research* vol. 17, no. 1, February 2000, pp. 7–15, and is reproduced by permission of the *Journal of Financial Services Research.*

Chapter 4, 'Does asymmetric information justify bank capital adequacy regulation?', was first published in the *Cato Journal* vol. 19, no. 1 (Spring–Summer 1999), pp. 39–47, and is reproduced by permission of the Cato Institute.

Chapter 5, 'Competitive banking, bankers' clubs, and bank regulation', was first published in the *Journal of Money, Credit, and Banking*, vol. 26, no. 2 (May 1994), pp. 289–308, and is reproduced by permission of the *Journal of Money, Credit, and Banking.*

Chapter 6, 'The invisible hand and the evolution of the monetary system', first appeared as Chapter 7 of *What is Money?* edited by John Smithin (Routledge 1999, pp. 139–56).

Chapter 7, 'Are free markets the cause of financial instability?' first appeared in the *Critical Review,* and is reproduced by permission of the *Critical Review.*

Chapter 8, 'A proposal to end inflation', was first published in the *Economic Journal* vol. 104, no. 425 (July 1994), pp. 828–40, and is reproduced by permission of Blackwell and the Royal Economic Society.

Chapter 9, 'Reply to Hillier', was first published in the *Economic Journal,* vol. 106, no. 436 (May 1996), pp. 635–6, and is reproduced by permission of Blackwell and the Royal Economic Society.

Chapter 10, 'Using futures prices to control inflation: reply to Garrison and White', was first published in the *Journal of Money, Credit and Banking,* vol. 32, no. 1 (February 2000), pp. 142–5, and is reproduced by permission of the *Journal of Money, Credit, and Banking.*

Chapter 12, 'Money and the market: what role for government?', was originally presented at the Cato annual monetary conference in 1992 and published in the *Cato Journal*, vol. 12, no. 3 (Winter 1993), pp. 557–76. It is reproduced by permission of the Cato Institute.

Chapter 13, 'Two arguments for the restriction of international capital flows', co-written with Alec Chrystal, was first published in the *National Westminster Bank Quarterly Review*, November 1986, pp. 8–19. It is reproduced by permission of the Nat West Bank.

Chapter 14, 'Monetary policy in the twenty-first century: an impossible task?' is based on a presentation to the 1997 Cato annual monetary conference, and was first published in the *Cato Journal*, vol. 17, no. 3 (Winter 1998), pp. 327–31. It is reproduced by permission of the Cato Institute.

Chapter 15, 'Reflections on the future of gold', was first published in Sheffield Hallam University's *Review of Policy Issues*, vol. 1, no. 2, (Summer 1994), pp. 45–55, and is reproduced by permission of the *Review of Policy Issues*.

Chapter 16, 'Too big to fail? Long-Term Capital Management and the Federal Reserve', was published as Cato Institute *Briefing Paper* no. 52, on 23 September, 1999, and is reproduced by permission of the Cato Institute.

1 Introduction

The essays in this book share a common concern with the impact of government intervention in the financial and monetary areas: not just the banking system, but the financial services industry more generally, as well as the issue of money and the control of inflation. Some of the essays investigate what unregulated financial systems would look like; others examine some of the justifications given for particular forms of state intervention, such as deposit insurance and capital adequacy regulation; while still others look at rules to govern the issue of currency in the absence of discretionary monetary policy; and the remaining essays look at a variety of monetary and financial policy issues from a free banking perspective.

My outlook is essentially very simple, even simplistic. I believe that markets generally work and governments generally fail: the invisible hand of the market is better than the visible hand of the state. This is not to say that market solutions are 'perfect', but I have often been impressed by the ability of markets to find ingenious solutions to complex problems that no economic planner could ever have found. Over the years, I have also been struck again and again by the way in which the invisible hand strikes back and superficially plausible justifications for government policies tend to unravel under close scrutiny. Add to that many years of observing government in action – sometimes at very close quarters – and I developed a strong sense of the pervasiveness of government failure. Indeed, the only time government seems to achieve its objectives is when the powers of the state are hijacked by powerful special interest groups who use them for their own ends, and this strikes me as more an argument against government intervention than for it.

Much of my research has been, in effect, no more than a continuing effort to think through these issues as they apply to the financial and monetary system. To be frank, I have always been baffled by the resistance of most economists to the idea of free banking: I have never understood how most of them can be content to argue for the principle of free trade in general, and then argue against free banking, which is after all no more and no less than free trade in financial services. If free trade is good, then what is wrong with free banking; and if free banking is undesirable, how can they advocate free trade? Do they support the principle of free trade or don't they? At the same time, government interventions in this area – financial regulatory systems, deposit insurance, bank bailouts and so on – seem to have a track record at least as dismal as government interventions elsewhere. The personalities and circumstances may change, but the underlying issues stay much the same, and the same old mistakes are repeated again and again. Everything changes, and everything remains the same. Not surprisingly, the fundamental remedy for many of our problems also remains the same as it always was: to work with market forces, rather than against them, and establish free banking.

The theory of financial *laissez-faire*

These essays fall quite naturally into three main main groups. The first of these deals with the theory of financial *laissez-faire*: what financial *laissez-faire* might look like, arguments for and against state intervention, the historical evidence on the relatively unregulated financial systems of the past, and so forth. The opening chapter in this section – Chapter 2, 'The case for financial *laissez-faire*' – originally appeared as part of a controversy on the theme of 'Should we regulate the financial system?' in the May 1996 issue of the *Economic Journal*. It begins by setting out a vision of a *laissez-faire* financial system: how banks would arise and issue currency under *laissez-faire*; how they would compete for business and be as safe and sound as their customers demand; and how the banking would be stable, even though individual banks would inevitably experience difficulties from time to time and might even be run out of business. It then discusses the ways in which state intervention into the financial system – in particular, lender of last resort policies and deposit insurance – can undermine the stabilizing mechanisms on which the *laissez-faire* system depends and lead to a weaker and less stable banking system. It also suggests that these speculations about free banking are entirely consistent with the empirical evidence from less regulated financial systems of the past. Finally, the chapter addresses some specific criticisms of financial *laissez-faire* made by the other participants in the *Economic Journal* controversy: George Benston and George Kaufman, who argue for a lender of last resort and deposit insurance; and Sheila Dow, who argues, among other things, that *laissez-faire* would be unstable.

The next two chapters deal with arguments for and against specific interventions into the banking system. Chapter 3, 'Bank capital adequacy versus deposit insurance' was first published in the *Journal of Financial Services Research* in 2000. This chapter deals with the highly influential justification for deposit insurance provided by the work of Diamond and Dybvig (1983). To analyse this issue, they set out a theoretical framework in which financial institutions arise to provide individual agents with the opportunity to make liquid investments, but are prone to self-fulfilling fears of failure. If individual investors think their financial institutions will fail, they will run on them, and in so doing actually cause the institutions to fail: their fears of failure become self-fulfilling. The banking system is thus inherently unstable, and Diamond and Dybvig suggested that this instability could be remedied by a government guarantee or some form of deposit insurance.

Chapter 3 attempts to question this analysis by presenting a theoretical counter-example: a model environment similar to that of Diamond and Dybvig, but in which banks arise that are stable without any form of government guarantee. I argue that my model is more plausible than theirs: their model makes every individual identical *ex ante* and leads to strange-looking financial institutions that we do not observe in the real world, whereas my model allows individuals to be different and leads to financial institutions that look much more like real-world banks. Unlike theirs, my model also provides a natural role for bank capital – bank capital is a device to give investors rational confidence in their bank – and so helps explain why bankers have traditionally placed so much importance on their capital. The moral of the story? Banks do not need deposit insurance, provided they have adequate capital.

Should the government then 'help' banks to maintain adequate levels of capital? This takes us to capital adequacy regulation – the imposition by regulators of minimum acceptable capital levels for banks – which attempts to shore up the financial strength of the banking system and counter the moral hazard problems created by lenders of last resort and deposit insurance systems. Capital adequacy regulation is without doubt one of the most important features of modern systems of central banking and financial regulation. Yet, despite its importance, there have been relatively few attempts to provide it with a theoretically solid foundation. Most writers merely argue that we need capital adequacy regulation to counter the moral hazards created by other state interventions (e.g. Benston and Kaufman), or else argue for it on vague paternalistic grounds (for example, Dewatripont and Tirole 1994). To my knowledge, the only clear attempt to justify capital adequacy regulation from first principles is by David Miles (1995). He suggests that an information asymmetry between bank managers and deposits can lead to a market failure, and that state intervention in the form of capital adequacy regulation can correct this failure: the regulator would assess the capital the bank would have maintained in the absence of the information asymmetry, and then force the bank to maintain that level of capital. Miles' work is important because it provides the first rigorous attempt to justify capital adequacy regulation by reference to the (alleged) failure of *laissez-faire*. Naturally, I could not resist the urge to respond to such a challenge, and the result is Chapter 4, 'Does asymmetric information justify bank capital adequacy regulation?', which was first published in the Spring–Summer 1999 issue of the *Cato Journal*. In replying to Miles, I argued that his justification for capital adequacy regulation is inadequate. It fails to provide a convincing rationale for the distinctive regulation of banks – to explain why banks should be subject to this form of regulation but other firms should not be, as we both agree. In addition, the premise of Miles' argument – that depositors cannot assess bank capital strength – is both implausible and empirically falsified. Finally, Miles' suggested solution is not feasible in his model anyway (that is, the invisible hand has its revenge). *Laissez-faire* wins again, I think.

I then turn to consider a different line of attack against free banking. This comes from work in the 1980s by Gary Gorton and Donald Mullineux in the US and Charles Goodhart in the UK concerning what might be described as the microfoundations of banking regulation. Though their arguments differ considerably – Gorton and Mullineux use a contractual theory approach and Goodhart relies on the theory of clubs – these writers all maintain that information problems in financial markets pose problems that unregulated markets cannot properly handle, and argue that 'regulation' arose spontaneously to meet these problems. The emergence of banking regulation and central banking was therefore a natural response to problems inherent in financial markets, and the free banking view of them as damaging intrusions to financial markets should be rejected. Chapter 5, 'Competitive banking, bankers' clubs, and bank regulation', was my attempt to respond to these arguments, and was first published in the May 1994 issue of the *Journal of Money, Credit, and Banking*.

I readily concede that information problems play a large role in financial markets, and I also concede that these can sometimes lead banks to form 'clubs' or other hierarchical arrangements that restrict (that is, regulate, if you will) the freedom of member-banks. However, this spontaneous 'regulation' does not provide a justification for real-world systems of central banking and state-imposed financial regulation, because the two types of regulation – spontaneous and state-imposed – differ in a number of important ways (for example, 'spontaneous' regulation is very limited in scope and is still under the banks' collective control, and so on). A second problem with the spontaneous regulation argument is that the alleged benefits of regulation are in reality economies of scale; this type of argument therefore implies that banking is a natural monopoly. The problem, of course, is that the empirical evidence clearly indicates that banking is not in fact a natural monopoly. In any case, arguments for spontaneous regulation are also refuted by the abundant evidence that the relatively unregulated banking systems of the past developed little or none of it; and there is a plausible argument that the nineteenth-century US cases often cited as examples of 'private' regulation only arose in response to the branching and other amalgamation regulations that prevented US banks from appropriating economies of scale in more natural ways. In short, the free bankers appear to have been right all along: central banking and financial regulation did not arise to counter market failures, and cannot be justified by market failure arguments.

Chapter 6 looks at *laissez-faire* from a very different perspective. This chapter, 'The invisible hand and the evolution of the monetary system', first appeared in John Smithin's edited collection of essays, *What is Money?*, which was published by Routledge in 1999. Instead of looking at the desirability of *laissez-faire* using neoclassical analysis, it examines *laissez-faire* using a conjectural history: it investigates how it might plausibly evolve from some initial primitive state, driven by private self-interest in the absence of any form of government intervention. A conjectural history provides a simple but useful way of explaining how *laissez-faire* might work, and also provides a useful benchmark to examine our current system. If we start off in barter, say, we go through the standard Mengerian analysis of the evolution of commodity money; we then take the analysis forward to look at the development of coinage, the evolution of banks and bank currency, the changing role of the unit/medium of account, the evolution of currency convertibility, and the eventual development of a fully mature *laissez-faire* monetary system, based on an indirectly convertible commodity-basket standard. We can then examine this system in more detail – what it looks like, how it functions, and so on – and investigate its efficiency and stability. To my mind, this system is as efficient and stable as we could reasonably wish, and certainly a vast improvement over our current system, with its proliferation of different currencies, gyrating exchange rates, bank weakness, financial instability, and the like. If we could choose, why on earth would we not choose the patently superior system?

The last chapter in this section considers another important question: whether free markets can be blamed for financial market instability. The theme of this chapter was originally suggested by Steve Horwitz, and Jeff Friedman subsequently invited me to address it in an essay in the *Critical Review*. In doing so, they gave me an opportunity to think through more systematically issues I had been discussing for years with Dave Campbell, a very close friend who is now professor of law at Cardiff University. I wanted to get at the inappropriately polarized way in which many people tend to debate these issues: on the one hand, there are leftist critics, who tend to look at how financial markets appear to operate – how they appear to produce excessive volatility, and so on – and then reach for interventionist 'solutions'; on the other hand, there are free-market economists who all too often respond by denying point-blank that there could be anything much wrong at all with financial markets, more or less regardless of the empirical facts. These two sides tend to talk right past each other, and I felt there were merits and faults on both sides: the critics are right about there being problems with financial markets, but are far too ready to invoke the *deus ex machina* of state intervention to resolve them; the free-marketeers are right to be sceptical of interventionary 'solutions', but far too ready to defend the indefensible in existing financial markets.

The root of the problem, I concluded, was that both sides were too ready to identify the existing world financial system with *laissez-faire*. To investigate this issue further, the chapter compares a hypothetical *laissez-faire* system to the system we actually have, and, in effect, tries to drive a massive wedge between the two. One system has an excessive number of different currencies, is prone to currency crises and inflationary instability, and so on, and the other is not. The differences between the two systems are extremely significant. Free-market economists should therefore not feel under any obligation to defend the status quo. However, some speculations about the future also lead to the conclusion that these differences are likely to disappear over time as market forces become even stronger and existing currency regimes are forced to accommodate them. Maybe some of us may yet live to see financial *laissez-faire*.

The monetary regime

The second group of essays deals in more detail with this same subject: the monetary regime under *laissez-faire*. My own starting point is a long-held belief that a *laissez-faire* system would provide sound money, because I believe that the public fundamentally want sound money and that market forces would find some way of ensuring that they got it. I also take sound money to mean price stability: that our target price index (for example, the RPI/CPI) should remain stable over time. I have always believed that aggregate price-level movements are not only bad, but often very bad, particularly when they are difficult or impossible to predict in advance, and that our currency unit should provide a stable value-yardstick on which the private sector can safely rely as it goes about its business.

We come then to the all-important question: what rule(s) of currency issue would ensure that the currency would maintain its soundness? I struggled with this question for a long time, and my attempt to answer it is provided in Chapter 8, 'A proposal to end inflation', which was published in the *Economic Journal* in July 1994. (For pedagogical and diplomatic reasons, the suggested rule was couched there as one for the central bank to follow, but the mechanics of the rule apply equally to a free-banking system.) The idea can be thought of as a generalization of the gold standard. Under the gold standard, the currency issuer(s) buys and sells gold at a fixed nominal price, but the resulting price level is only as stable as the relative price of gold against goods and services in general. However, we can make the price level more stable by pegging the price of a broader basket of goods (and perhaps, services), rather than the price of a 'basket' only of gold. The broader the composition of the basket, other things being equal, the more stable the resulting price level. Given our objective of price-level stability, we would ideally like to choose that broad basket of goods and services whose price is reflected in the price-index we are seeking to stabilize. The problem is to make this idea operational, given that the basket in question is not transactable – and that people cannot buy and sell this basket the way they can buy and sell a 'basket' of gold.

The suggested answer is to replace the physical basket by an appropriate financial derivatives instrument, and the particular instrument proposed is similar to a financial futures contract based on (that is, has a payoff contingent on) the realized value of the RPI/CPI. The central bank would buy or sell this contract on demand at a fixed price, at regular intervals, and rely on market forces to ensure that the quantity of money was consistent with zero expected inflation. The system would also exhibit negative (that is, stabilizing) feedback in the face of incipient deviations from equilibrium: if prices were expected to rise, private agents could expect to make a profit by buying these contracts from the central bank, the supply of base money would fall, and expected prices would drop; and if prices were expected to fall, agents could expect a profit by selling these contracts to the central bank, the supply of base money would rise, and expected prices would rise. In equilibrium, the expected price level would be on target, and the realized, actual, price level would equal the expected price level plus or minus an unpredictable random error. This error should be fairly small, so the resulting price level could reasonably be described as fairly stable. The rest of the chapter then goes through various technical conditions and compares the proposed rule to alternatives.

This proposal got a very mixed reaction. The most amusing was that of another old friend, John Whittaker, of the University of Lancaster, who commented drily that he knew there was something wrong with it, but could not quite put his finger on what it was. However, some others were more confident that they could. One of these was (the, sadly, late) Brian Hillier, who published a critical comment on it in the May 1996 issue of the *Economic Journal*. Brian tackled it by building a version of the Lucas tree model and claiming that this showed that the arbitrage mechanism I was relying on did not work. He also claimed that my monetary rule was unsustainable in an unpleasant monetarist arithmetic world where fiscal and monetary policies were inconsistent in the long run and the fiscal policy was effectively set in stone. Chapter 9 is my response, which was also published in the same *Economic Journal* issue. The argument about the arbitrage process boils down to whether the discount rate used by private-sector arbitragers would move closely with the short-term market interest rate, and I felt I was right on this issue, based on what I knew of the discount-rate practices of City firms trading comparable instruments. His second argument was correct but irrelevant. *If* fiscal and monetary policies are inconsistent in the long run, *and* if fiscal policy is not going to be changed, then the monetary policy *must* eventually give way. This logic is cast-iron and applies to *any* monetary policy or monetary policy rule. However, I also think it misses the point: the key issue is surely how my rule *compares* to alternatives, and the unpleasant monetarist arithmetic logic gives us no indication of the relative merits of the alternative rules on offer.

My proposal was also criticized by Roger Garrison and Lawrence H. White in the November 1997 *Journal of Money, Credit, and Banking*. My 'Reply' to them came out in the February 2000 *Journal of Money, Credit, and Banking* and is reproduced here as Chapter 10. They argued that the feedback process in my scheme would not ensure that the central bank and/or money supply were adequately disciplined, and they also made various criticisms of the ways the market for my financial instruments would operate. Frankly, these arguments – theirs or mine – are not easy to follow, and the reader with the intestinal fortitude for these debates can read up the detailed arguments later on. Suffice it for now to say that I think my feedback mechanism is sound, but Garrison and White seem to be right on some (and wrong on other) market organization arguments. That said, I am still fairly confident that the proposal itself is fundamentally sound and that any problems with the 'details' can be rectified. However, this area is conceptually very difficult – too much mental effort and the brain hurts – and I am reminded here of Gladstone's comment that the study of monetary economics was the surest source of insanity he knew of.

The next two chapters look at two very different ways of trying to implement sound-money rules. The first of these is Irving Fisher's 'compensated dollar' scheme, considered in Chapter 11, 'The "compensated dollar" revisited'. This chapter was written in 1994 but has not been published before. The 'compensated dollar' scheme was widely discussed about ninety years ago, but relatively few modern economists seem to have looked closely at it, even though most profess some familiarity with it. I do not think they do themselves any favours by neglecting it. Fisher's work is an apt illustration of Jürg Niehans' observation that since the early part of the twentieth century, monetary economists have forgotten more about the economics of commodity money than they have acquired. Fisher's scheme is a natural precursor to all modern schemes that seek to make use of price indices in one form or another; it is relatively easy to analyse using the mathematics of difference equations, which Fisher did not use; and I think Fisher makes instructive mistakes which we can learn from and, hopefully, avoid ourselves.

Fisher hoped that his scheme would deliver a more stable price level than the contemporary gold standard. The idea was that the currency issuer would operate on an adjustable-peg gold standard: if prices were too high, the issuer would decrease the price of gold in accordance with a specified formula; and if prices were too low, the issuer would increase the price of gold in accordance with that formula. This formula was designed to ensure negative feedback, so prices would return to their target value. There is much more to the scheme than just that, of course – as always with such schemes, much depends on the 'details' – but in the end I believe the scheme is fundamentally flawed. One flaw is that it makes the short-run price level depend on a difference equation, but does not guarantee that this difference equation will stabilize the short-run price level; another flaw is that it does not ensure that the long-run price level is stable either, even if short-term deviations from it are stable; and finally, the scheme leaves the issuer open to successful speculative attack in certain circumstances: speculators can therefore blow it out of the water. However, it is easy to criticize, especially when one has the benefit of superior mathematical technology, and even the weaknesses in his scheme are still very instructive. In my opinion, Fisher still has a lot to teach us and all modern monetary reformers should study him properly.

Chapter 12, 'Money and the market: what role for government?' looks at a very different approach to establishing sound money, and in a very different context: it looks at monetary reform in the former communist countries. It was originally presented at the Cato annual monetary conference in 1992 and published in the Winter 1993 issue of the *Cato Journal*. The question in the sub-title was less rhetorical than it might sound; given the mess left by communism after it collapsed, and the absence of suitable legal and other infrastructures in all these countries, I felt it made little sense to advocate a completely hands-off approach by the government. Instead, the only option was to advocate a programme to establish a sound currency and then lead over time to eventual government disengagement from the monetary system. The package itself was fairly straightforward: the immediate stabilization of the currency to end inflation; the abolition of the central bank and the establishment of a currency board to issue currency, but with a predetermined 'sunset clause' to ensure that the currency board would itself eventually be abolished; the currency itself to be pegged, initially at least, to a strong western currency such as the mark; financial liberalization, including the abolition of existing legal tender restrictions and exchange controls; and thoroughgoing liberalization in other sectors to lay the foundations of a sound market economy. I thought then and still think now that the former communist countries should borrow extensively from the West, but should try to avoid some of the mistakes that western countries have made, particularly in the monetary and financial area.

Policy issues

The final part of the book is a selection of essays on miscellaneous policy issues of one sort or another. The first of these, Chapter 13, 'Two arguments for the restriction of international capital flows', was one of my first papers and was published in the *National Westminster Bank Quarterly Review* in November 1986. It was written with another friend, Alec Chrystal (who was then professor of economics at the University of Sheffield), shortly after I returned from Canada. At the time, there was considerable controversy over the impact of international capital market integration, and there were a number of calls to try to halt it. Some of the most vociferous came from the UK Labour Party, then still socialist, which was proposing to re-introduce exchange controls in the UK and establish a National Investment Bank to 'invest in Britain' and counter the 'excessive' tendency of UK financial institutions to invest abroad. We argued that these proposals were based on mistaken views about capital outflows being harmful to domestic investment, the underlying premise here being that domestic investment has to be financed out of domestic saving. Of course, this is nonsense in an open economy. In any case, the Labour proposals would almost certainly have had only a minimal impact because they would merely have created a huge market in swaps. Instead of UK and overseas agents trading assets and in so doing subjecting themselves to the Labour taxes, they would simply swap cashflows and produce essentially equivalent portfolios without exposing themselves to tax liabilities: a swap market would arise which would reduce the Labour controls to all but a minor inconvenience. We also looked at the proposed National Investment Bank and pointed out some problems with the idea: inconsistencies between its objectives, the scope for and dangers of political interference, and the likelihood that the Bank would, like similar institutions before and since, merely pick up bad investment projects that could get no other funding.

We then examined a second set of proposals by James Tobin and Rudy Dornbusch to increase the costs of transactions in international financial markets to – as Tobin put it – 'throw sand in the[ir] wheels' and reduce their 'excessive efficiency'. Apart from the obvious objection that the benefits of making markets less efficient are counter-intuitive, to put it diplomatically, the chances are that financial markets would find ways round such restrictions anyway, as with the earlier swap examples. This is perhaps just as well, because restricting capital flows would make it even harder for the real economy to adjust to shocks – and be counterproductive, if our objective is to protect the real economy against shocks.

The next chapter looks at a very different monetary policy question: the likely impact of future IT and financial-market developments on the ability of central banks to conduct monetary policy. This chapter is based on a presentation to the 1997 Cato annual monetary conference, the paper from which was published in the Winter 1998 issue of the *Cato Journal*. The starting point is the observation that financial markets are imposing ever tighter constraints on central banks, and are steadily reducing the effectiveness of the monetary policies they pursue. However, as we look into the future, long-run factors –

technological ones in particular – are likely not only to reduce the effective-ness of monetary policy even further, but to destroy it altogether. The point is that the central bank's leverage over the monetary system – its ability to influ-ence interest rates, exchange rates, and so on – hinges on the demand for central bank ('base') money, but this demand is already declining, and new developments threaten to reduce it to a level where that leverage disappears. Moreover, if the demand for base money falls, central banks will have to reduce the supply correspondingly if they are to avoid major inflation. This means that they will have to 'buy' their money back (that is, hand over valu-able financial instruments in exchange for their own currency). Their seignorage revenues – their revenues from money creation – would become negative, and many central banks (and possibly all of them) would need bailing out if they are to avoid bankruptcy. To make matters even worse, the declining demand for base money will make price and interest rates more vul-nerable to shocks and, in particular, to changes in the technological, legal and other factors that influence the demand for currency. The implications are alarming. For example, if the domestic demand for base money in the US declined to negligible levels, the dollar price level in the US would become entirely dependent on the non-US demand for US dollars, and therefore become hostage to whatever factors affected that demand. Any factors that sig-nificantly reduced that demand – the successful remonetization of the former Soviet Union, the legalization of hard drugs, or whatever – could then have major consequences for US inflation. In short, discretionary monetary policy is going to become impossible. However if managed currencies become impossible, the only alternative is to put the issue of currency on a fully auto-matic basis: to reconvert currencies and tie them firmly to commodity-based anchors. The days of inconvertible fiat money are numbered.

Chapter 15, 'Reflections on the future of gold', first appeared in the Summer 1994 issue of the *Review of Policy Issues*. It examines the curious fact that a considerable proportion of the world's stock of gold is held by central banks for what is, effectively, no sensible purpose at all. This will not make me popular with gold bugs, but the fact is that central banks hold gold only because they held it in the past, and the reasons they held it in the past – because we were on a gold or gold-exchange standard – no longer apply and are unlikely to apply at any foreseeable time in the future. The central banks' stocks of gold are therefore an expensive anachronism. If this is the case, then it is only a matter of time before central banks get rid of their gold stocks, and some are already moving in that direction. When that happens, I believe it will happen fairly quickly, because central banks will race to dump gold before the bottom drops out of the market. These actions will become self-fulfilling, and the price of gold will fall sharply. I am aware that this scenario might sound far-fetched to some people, but would also suggest that there is a partial historical antecedent in the late nineteenth century, when silver was demonetized and the world moved to a gold standard. When I wrote the paper, I stuck my neck out further by speculating that the price of gold would fall by about 40 per cent, and by suggesting that this would be enough to put perhaps 70 per cent of the current gold mining industry out of business. The prospects for the industry therefore seem pretty bleak. However from a social point of view, what is the point of spending so much to dig gold out of the ground when so much of it already lies unused in the vaults of the world's central banks? Of course, time will tell whether my predictions are right. Who was it who said that forecasting wasn't easy, especially forecasting the future?

Chapter 16, 'Too big to fail? Long-Term Capital Management and the Federal Reserve', is an assessment of the role of the Federal Reserve in the Long-Term Capital Management (LTCM) fiasco, and was published as a Cato Institute *Briefing Paper* in September 1999. LTCM was a large and very prominent hedge fund that mismanaged itself to the brink of failure in September 1988. (Of course, LTCM was also unlucky, but the point of risk management is to ensure that survival is not left just to good luck; any fool can gamble.) As LTCM rapidly deteriorated, the Federal Reserve organized a rescue package, and the firm was taken over, recapitalized, and put on its feet again. Not surprisingly, the management of LTCM came in for a lot of criticism, but my concern was the public policy angle: was the Fed intervention justified? I felt it wasn't. To begin with, LTCM would not have failed anyway: another consortium also made a bid for it, and the management of LTCM would have had little choice but to accept that offer if the Fed had not been involved. All the Fed intervention achieved was a better deal for LTCM's investors and managers – an achievement that hardly justifies a Fed intervention. However, even if LTCM had failed, I doubt there would have been the dire consequence on world financial markets that Fed officials feared: the markets would have taken a hit, to be sure, but letting LTCM fail would have sent out a very strong message that no firm, however big, could expect to be rescued from the consequences of its own mistakes, and this message would have strengthened financial markets in the longer term.

The Fed intervention had various detrimental consequences: it encouraged calls for more regulation of hedge funds, which would be pointless at best and counterproductive at worst; it implied a massive and very open-ended extension of Federal Reserve responsibilities, without any public discussion or Congressional mandate; it implied a return to the discredited old doctrine of 'too big to fail' – that the Fed will rescue large financial firms, precisely because they are large – which merely encourages irresponsible risk-taking by them; and, perhaps worst of all, it did a lot of damage to the credibility and moral authority of US policy-makers in their efforts to encourage other countries to persevere with the difficult process of economic liberalization. How can the US tell the Russians and Japanese to let big financial institutions fail, if they are afraid to do the same themselves?

The final chapter – 'Paternalism fails again: the sorry story of the Financial Services Act' – is a hitherto unpublished analysis of the biggest financial scandal in UK history, and was written in 1993. It looks at what happens when public choice meets paternalism. It is co-authored with Jimmy M. Hinchliffe, a very talented Ph.D. student at Sheffield Hallam University, and has the benefit of his extensive fieldwork on the subject (in particular, of Jimmy managing to persuade a number of the industry people involved to speak openly, often after a fairly liquid Friday lunch). It recounts the story of how minor scandals in the early 1980s led Parliament to legislate to give ordinary retail investors cast-iron protection on their life insurance, private pensions and other long-term financial investments, and how the industry captured the new regulatory system and then fleeced millions of investors as the regulators and the Government stood by and watched. The story of the Financial Services Act is a classic example of public choice theory in action, in which the principal parties involved – the Government, policy-makers, regulators, and the industry – each put their own interests first, and an ostensibly paternalistic regime became a smokescreen, behind which investors were blatantly exploited by the industry, with the open connivance of the regulators who were supposedly there to protect them.

What does this costly failure say about the policy-making process in the UK? Not a lot, apparently. The Government acted because 'something had to be done', and they never considered their alternatives properly. So they commissioned the distinguished lawyer, Gower, to report, and then everything got out of hand. Gower himself was appalled at the legislation supposedly inspired by his report, and we ended up with a monstrous regulatory system that was extremely costly, unaccountable, and almost totally ineffective. But once set up, it was also very difficult to change, and the Government did not really know what to do with it. Instead, it chose to pass the buck and argue that the outcome would have been even worse if the Government had adopted the opposition's advice and set up an SEC-type system instead. Perhaps they were right, but governments should not seek to avoid responsibility for their own disastrous mistakes by arguing that their opponents' proposals would have been even worse. As George Bernard Shaw once observed, 'there is plenty of humbug in hell'.

Part 1

The theory of financial *laissez-faire*

2 The case for financial *laissez-faire*

The argument for financial *laissez-faire* (or free banking) is essentially very simple: if free trade is generally desirable, what is wrong with free trade in financial services? If nothing is wrong with it, the whole panoply of government intervention into the financial sector – the central bank, government-sponsored deposit insurance and government regulation of the financial system – should presumably all be abolished. If there is something wrong with *laissez-faire*, on the other hand, then what exactly is the problem with it? Why does this problem justify intervention? And why does it justify the particular interventions we have, such as a central bank?

Most economists take a patently untenable position on these issues. For the most part, they accept the general principle of free trade, but they deny that it applies to financial services. Yet relatively few could give a coherent defence of this position or even have thought that much about it. They oppose free banking more or less instinctively, as if its failings are obvious. The response, of course, is that what is obvious is not necessarily true: the history of science is full of cases where the 'obvious' turned out to be wrong. It therefore behoves us, as academic economists, to explore these issues more carefully and beware of assuming that we already know the answers before we start.

Before getting into detail, I would like to make three general points. First, if free trade is good, as most of us agree, there must be at least a prima facie case in favour of free banking. If the principle of free trade applies in general, we must presume it to apply to any specific individual case, unless we have clear reason to believe the contrary. The onus of proof is on those who oppose free banking to demonstrate its undesirability. Most professional economists have the wrong priors on this issue. Second, while I accept that free banking seems strange at first sight, I believe this reaction mainly reflects the way we have been conditioned to think. Our education leads us to take certain things for granted, and the need for central banking is one of them. After all, why else do we initially react so strongly to what is no more than the application of the generally accepted doctrine of free trade to financial services? Finally, there is a great deal of empirical evidence on the free banking issue, and this evidence is supportive of the predictions of free banking theory, and, in particular, of its claim that unregulated banking is stable. Economists therefore cannot maintain that free banking has never been tried, or that it has been tried and 'failed'. The evidence also supports the predictions made by free banking theory that intervention generally weakens the financial system and causes the very problems it is ostensibly meant to cure. By contrast, the evidence is also inconsistent with opposing theories that have been suggested as providing justifications for central banking.

The free banking position

A laissez-faire *financial system*

So what would a free banking system look like, and how would it operate? Imagine a hypothetical *laissez-faire* economy with an underlying 'imperfect' economic environment: information is scarce and asymmetric, there are non-trivial agency and co-ordination problems, and so on. These problems give rise to a financial system characterized by the presence of intermediaries that enable agents to achieve superior outcomes to those they could otherwise achieve (e.g. by cutting down on transactions and monitoring costs). Perhaps the most important intermediaries are banks. These invest funds on behalf of client investors, some of whom hold the bank's debt liabilities and others its equity. Most bank debts are deposits of one form or another, and most of these can be redeemed on demand. Many deposits are also used to make payments by cheque. The equity holders are residual claimants, and their capital provides a buffer that enables a bank to absorb losses and still be able to pay its debtholders in full. The banking industry exhibits extensive economies of scale, but not natural monopoly, and there is typically a small number of nationwide branch banks, with a larger number of specialist banks that cater to niche markets.[1] The industry is competitive and efficient by any reasonable standard.

We can think of this banking system as operating on a convertible, commodity-based monetary standard (e.g. a gold standard).[2] Bank liabilities are denominated in terms of the economy's unit of account (such as the pound), and underlying the system is some rule that ties the unit of account to a unit of the 'anchor' commodity on which the monetary standard is based.[3] The price level in this system is then determined by conditions in the market for the 'anchor' commodity.[4] Bank currency is convertible – the banks must redeem their currency when required to – and so the amount of currency in circulation is determined by the demand to hold it. If banks issue too much currency, the public simply return it to the banks for redemption, and the excess currency is automatically retired.

The stability of financial **laissez-faire**

But how stable is the system? With no lender of last resort or state-run deposit insurance system, depositors would be acutely aware that they stood to lose their deposits if their bank failed. They would therefore want reassurance that their funds were safe and would soon close their accounts if they felt there was any significant danger of their bank failing. Bank managers would understand that their long-term survival depended on their ability to retain their depositors' confidence. They would therefore pursue conservative lending policies, submit themselves to outside scrutiny, and publish audited accounts. They would also provide reassurance by maintaining adequate capital. The greater a bank's capitalization, the more losses a bank can withstand and still be able to pay off depositors in full. If the bank's capital is large enough – if the bank is adequately capitalized – the bank can absorb any plausible losses and still repay depositors, and depositors can be confident their funds are safe. The precise amount of capital is determined by market forces. The better capitalized a bank is, other things being equal, the safer and more attractive it is to depositors, but capital is also costly, and depositors need to pay shareholders to provide it (e.g. by accepting lower interest on deposits). Competition between banks should then ensure that banks converge on whatever degrees of capitalization their customers demand (and, by implication, are willing to pay for): banks will be exactly as safe as their customers demand. If bank customers want safe banks, market forces will ensure they get them.

The conclusion that banks under *laissez-faire* would maintain high levels of capital is also consistent with the empirical evidence. For example, US banks in the antebellum period were subject to virtually no federal regulations and yet had capital ratios in most years of over 40 per cent (Kaufman 1992: 386). US banks were subject to more regulation at the turn of the century, but even then their capital ratios were close to 20 per cent, and capital ratios were still around 15 per cent when federal deposit insurance was established in 1933 (ibid.). The evidence is also consistent with the associated prediction that *laissez-faire* banks face low probabilities of failure. Thus US banks appear to have been fairly safe in the period before the Civil War (Dowd 1992c: ch. 11), and for the period afterwards, Benston *et al.* (1986: 53–9) report that bank failure rates were lower than the failure rates for non-financial firms. Losses to depositors were correspondingly low (Kaufman 1988). Failure rates and losses were also low for other relatively unregulated systems such as those in Canada, Scotland, Switzerland and various others (see e.g. the case studies in Dowd 1992a).

Nor is there any reason to expect banking instability arising from the ways in which banks relate to each other, either because of competitive pressures, or because of 'contagion' from weak banks to strong ones. It is frequently argued that competitive pressures produce instability by forcing 'good' banks to go along with the policies of 'bad' ones (e.g. Goodhart 1988: 47–9). The underlying argument seems to be that if the bad banks expand rapidly, they can make easy short-term profits which pressure the managers of good banks to expand rapidly as well, with the result that the banking system as a whole cycles excessively from boom to bust and back again. However, a major problem with this argument is that it is not in a bank's interest to engage in aggressive expansion of the sort this argument envisages.

A bank can usually expand rapidly only by allowing the average quality of its loans to deteriorate, and a major deterioration in its loan quality will undermine its long-run financial health and its ability to maintain customer confidence. A profit-maximizing bank will not choose to undermine itself this way, even if other banks appear to be doing so. Indeed, if a bank believes that its competitors are taking excessive risks, the most rational course of action is for it to distance itself from them – perhaps to build up its financial strength further – in anticipation of the time when they start to suffer losses and lose confidence. The bank is then strongly placed to win over their customers and increase its market share at their expense, and perhaps even drive them out of business. The bank would have to forgo short-term profits, but it would win out in the long run. There is no reason, then, to suppose that competitive pressures as such would force free banks into excessive cycling.[5]

Then there is the contagion argument that the difficulties of one bank might induce the public to withdraw funds from other banks and threaten the stability of the financial system. The conclusion normally drawn from this argument is that we need a central bank to prevent 'contagion' by providing lender of last resort support to a bank in difficulties. However, this argument ignores the earlier point that good banks have a strong incentive to distance themselves from bad ones. If the good banks felt there was any danger of contagion, they would take appropriate action – they would strengthen themselves and curtail credit to weak banks – to help ensure that contagion did not in fact occur. Indeed, as discussed already, they would position themselves to offer the customers of weaker banks a safe haven when their own banks get into difficulties. A serious danger of contagion is therefore inconsistent with equilibrium. Instead, we would expect the difficulties of a weak bank to trigger a 'flight to quality' in which customers transfer their accounts to stronger banks, and this expectation is borne out by the evidence that tells us that runs occur in response to news that a particular bank or group of banks has sustained major losses that call into question its ability to repay its debts (Kaufman 1988). When runs occur, the typical scenario is a flight to quality, with substantial inflows of funds to the stronger banks, and there is little evidence that runs are contagious (Benston *et al.* 1986: 53-60; Benston and Kaufman 1995; Dowd 1994a: 297). The contagion hypothesis is implausible and empirically rejected.

The impact of state intervention

There is also the issue of what happens to this system if the government intervenes in it. There is no space to consider here all the ways in which governments intervene, but two specific interventions are particularly important: the establishment of a central bank to provide lender of last resort (LLR) support to the financial system, and the establishment of a state-sponsored system of deposit insurance, both intended, according to their proponents, to stabilize the banking system. The establishment of an LLR is meant to provide liquidity to banks that cannot otherwise obtain it. Since good banks can always obtain loans to maintain their liquidity, an LLR therefore protects bad banks from the consequences of their own actions. It therefore directly encourages the very behaviour – greater risk-taking and the maintenance of weaker capital positions – that a sound banking regime should avoid. It also undermines the discipline of the market in another, less obvious way. Since an LLR in effect tries to keep weaker banks open, its very existence reduces the incentives for good banks to adopt the virtuous strategy of building themselves up in anticipation of winning weaker banks' market share. That strategy depends on the weaker banks facing ruin and cannot promise much pay-off if the LLR is going to bail them out. In these circumstances, even the (otherwise) good banks may decide to take greater risks and let themselves go. Ironically, the LLR can then produce the very instability that proponents of central banking often claim would arise under free banking. In fact, someone who observed this instability might easily attribute it to the market itself, and falsely believe that the banking system actually *needs* the LLR support that is, in reality, undermining it. A major *cause* of banking instability – the LLR – could easily be mistaken for its *cure* – and, unfortunately, often is.

A system of deposit insurance has comparable effects. Once we introduce deposit insurance, depositors no longer have any incentives to monitor bank management and managers no longer need to worry about maintaining confidence. A bank's rational response is to reduce its capital, since the main point of maintaining capital strength – to maintain depositor confidence – no longer applies (see Chapter 3). Even if an individual bank wished to maintain its capital strength, it would be beaten by competitors who cut their capital ratios to reduce their costs and passed some of the benefits to depositors by offering them higher interest rates. The fight for market share would then force the good banks to imitate the bad. Deposit insurance consequently transforms a strong capital position into a competitive liability, reduces institutions' financial health and makes them more likely to fail. It also encourages more bank risk-taking at the margin: if a bank takes more risks and the risks pay off, then it keeps the additional profits; but if the risks do not pay off, part of the cost is passed on to the deposit insurer. The bank therefore takes more risks and becomes even weaker than its capital ratio alone would suggest. These claims are borne out by the evidence: thus the claim that banks reduce their capital ratios is confirmed by the observation that US bank capital ratios more than halved in the ten years after the establishment of federal deposit insurance (Kaufman 1992b), and there is abundant evidence that US deposit insurance has increased failure rates and associated losses.

Benston and Kaufman

Benston and Kaufman (BK) agree with much of this analysis, but disagree on the central bank LLR function and on government deposit insurance. On the former issue, they argue that a central bank LLR is necessary to provide liquidity assistance and avoid banks with liquidity needs having to sell assets at 'firesale losses' (e.g. Kaufman 1992a: 106). However, I would object that this position depends on the unjustified assumption that free banking would not provide adequate liquidity. If a bank does not have good collateral, we agree that it should not get assistance; but if it does have good collateral, it presumably can get loans or liquidity provided other banks are free to provide them, and other banks would grant those loans if the terms were right; hence, there should be no need under free banking to establish a central bank to provide lender of last resort assistance. If banks cannot provide such assistance, it must presumably be because of legal restrictions, in which case the first and best solution is *not* to establish a lender of last resort, but to abolish the legal restrictions. Nor is a central bank-LLR a perfect substitute for the automatic support mechanisms of the free market. The LLR creates serious moral-hazard problems, as well as a need for system management and 'policy' decisions (and all their attendant problems) that does not arise under free banking. The record of historical central bank LLR operations does not inspire confidence either, as when much of the US banking system collapsed in the early 1930s because of the Fed's refusal to grant the very support it was established to provide. Benston and Kaufman have no convincing answer to these problems, and I fail to understand why they insist on trying to patch up a patently unsatisfactory system when a much better one is available.

Benston and Kaufman support government deposit insurance for a number of reasons. In large part, they support it because they believe that the alternative of private deposit insurance is seriously inadequate (e.g. because of the limited capacity or credibility of private insurers; cf. Benston *et al.* 1986: 83; Benston and Kaufman 1996: 693), but they also support it because they believe there would serious external effects in its absence, such as the danger of a run to currency (Benston and Kaufman 1995).

However, I believe these arguments miss the point. The relevant choice is not that between government and private deposit insurance, but that between government deposit insurance and the free-banking scenario outlined earlier, in which banks provide implicit insurance through strong capitalization. If bank customers demand safe banks – as we all agree they do – the free market would provide safe banks via appropriate bank capitalization, *not* through private deposit insurance. The reason is straightforward: providing depositor security through deposit insurance creates conflicts of interest between bank shareholders and the insurance agency, and handling these conflicts is costly; however, providing security through bank capitalization does *not* create such conflicts, and is therefore a more efficient means of ensuring depositor safety. Private deposit insurance would of course be allowed under free banking, but we would not expect to see it, and this expectation is confirmed by the evidence.

I readily accept their point that bank failures involve third-party effects, but would argue these effects merely reinforce my position. The third-party-effects argument is essentially an argument for the safer system, and we have already seen that the safer system is free banking. It is therefore an argument in favour of free banking and against deposit insurance. In any case, the danger of third-party effects is not unique to bank failures, and applies to the failures of most other institutions as well. So Benston and Kaufman must argue either that bank failures are 'special' in ways that other failures are not, or they must be consistent and advocate a policy of preventing all institutional failures, and not just those of banks. Yet they are unwilling to do either.

Sheila Dow

Sheila Dow takes a more hostile approach to *laissez-faire*. Part of her case against it is a version of her earlier argument that free banking produces excessive cycling (Dow 1993: 199; 1996: 702), from which she concludes that there is a need for the state or a central bank to 'stand above' the market process and take action to correct the excessive cycling to which *laissez-faire* is prone. Her argument is distinctive in that it rests on an underlying post-Keynesian view of the uncertainty attached to valuing bank assets, and not just on a herd theory of bankers following each other over the cliff. However, despite its distinctiveness, it is still open to the objections already made against the excessive cycling theory: it ignores the point that individual free banks *do* have incentives to go against the market trend, and thereby counteract it, because doing so enables them to increase their long-run market shares; and it is empirically falsified, because there is little evidence of such cycles under historical free banking systems. In any case, even if free banking does produce some cycling, it still does not follow that it produces excessive cycling to which some form of intervention is an appropriate solution. Intervention has costs of its own: it uses up resources, the parties involved have their own interests, and so on; it cannot therefore be treated as a costless process that is guaranteed to produce the result its advocates hope for. One must also keep in mind that the historical record suggests that real-world intervention has *desta-bilized* the financial system rather than stabilized it (see e.g. the readings in Dowd 1992a). Dow's post-Keynesian version of the cycling argument also has its own distinctive problems. If assets are so difficult to value, then how can we expect central bankers to know where the private bankers are going off the rails? If they don't know, how can we expect them to ameliorate cycles and not inadvertently add to them? Even if they do know, what can they do about it if they are as powerless over the cost and volume of credit as Dow seems to suggest they are?[6]

Dow also opposes free banking for another reason. She effectively argues that free banking is pointless because central banking would emerge spontaneously from it (Dow and Smithin 1994: 21), or at least would do so in cases where free banking was 'successful' and did not lead to some form of chaos (Dow 1996: 704). The Dow-Smithin argument is that the requirements of a credit-based economy produce a degree of centralization of power that is more or less tantamount to central banking. When a crisis occurs under free banking, there is a scramble for safe assets. This scramble focuses on the banking system's ultimate settlement asset. The issuer of this asset then has great power over the system and effectively becomes a central bank (Dow 1996: 704; Dow and Smithin 1994: 14–15). To give this argument empirical support, Dow and Smithin point to the role of the three big banks in making emergency loans, disciplining minor banks, and the like, in early nineteenth-century Scottish free banking (Dow and Smithin 1994: 25).

There are a number of problems with this argument. First, while it is true that crises do produce a scramble for safe assets, we would expect this scramble to take the form of a flight to quality, and the evidence confirms that it generally does; it does not usually take the form of a scramble for some ultimate settlement asset, whatever that might be. There tends to be recycling *within* the banking system, rather than a flight *from* it. Second, even if there was a scramble for 'ultimate' settlement assets, it still does not follow that such assets are issued by one institution only. To assume that there is only one key institution consequently begs the point at issue. One must also keep in mind that the experience of historical free banking suggests that there is always more than one 'big' bank; no bank ever spontaneously established its supremacy over all the others. To assume that there is only one key institution in the free banking system therefore also flies in the face of the evidence. Third, even if one accepts their logic, Dow and Smithin establish the existence of the wrong animal. At most they establish the possibility of a private bankers' 'club', a club that might impose 'rules' on and sometimes assist its members, but establishing the existence of full-blown central banking is an altogether different matter.

The powers of a private bankers' club would be (and historically were) extremely limited: membership would be voluntary in a way that 'official' regulations are not; club powers would be determined by the banks themselves, not by some outside agency, and as a corollary, club officials would be accountable to the banks rather than to outsiders; and, perhaps most important, the scope of club rules and the demands they would make on members would be far less those implied by modern central banking (see Chapter 5). Fourth and finally, even if one accepts their whole argument, they still have no substantial objection to free banking. If they are right, they merely establish that free banking would be pointless, but not harmful; but if I am right, then free banking is best and central banking is harmful. But whoever is right, we would never choose to suppress free banking in favour of central banking – free banking wins by Pascal's wager.

Conclusions

None of the critics of free banking has presented a convincing case that free banking is an exception to the general presumption in favour of free trade. Consequently, our initial prima facie case in favour of free banking still stands. However, we should also assess the competing theories against the evidence, and the evidence clearly indicates that historical free banking *was* in fact stable, just as free-banking theory predicts. The conventional view that free banking *could not* be stable must be rejected, and with it the conventional wisdom that tries to justify central banking and state intervention in the financial system.

3 Bank capital adequacy versus deposit insurance

Despite its major shortcomings as revealed in recent years, most economists still believe that government deposit insurance has a useful role to play in promoting the stability of the banking industry. This belief goes back to the view that banking is 'inherently' unstable, so government support is needed to reassure depositors who would otherwise be prone to run on their banks. The seminal statement of this view is Diamond and Dybvig (DD) (1983), who build a model that, with various modifications, has since become standard.[1] In their model, agents face individual liquidity risk, but aggregate liquidity needs are (at least partially) predictable. Agents therefore form an intermediary to pool their liquidity risks. However, this arrangement has a problem: the agents who do not need liquidity might 'panic' and demand payment prematurely, in which case the intermediary would face a damaging run. DD suggest that this outcome could be avoided if the government provided those agents with a guarantee (which DD interpret as a form of deposit insurance) that they would be paid in full. Agents would then have no reason to run and the intermediary would be safe.

This chapter presents a stylized version of the DD model that calls this conventional view of banking instability and deposit insurance into question.[2] The chapter addresses a shortcoming of the DD analysis, which models intermediaries as having only one source of finance, making the DD intermediaries more like mutual funds than banks. Indeed, these DD intermediaries are odd even as mutual funds, since the nominal value of their liabilities is fixed, yet they have no capital to absorb any shocks to their portfolios and thus maintain their ability to honour their deposits in full.

There is also a serious problem with the analysis itself. The proportion of agents who face positive liquidity shocks, t, needs to be stochastic to make the analysis interesting. However, if t is stochastic, the DD intermediary will not know the actual value of t until all the agents who want to withdraw early have already done so, in which case it is presumably too late to make payments conditional on t's realized value. The obvious alternative is to make payments conditional on expected t, but in this case the DD intermediary would have total liabilities that exceed its total assets whenever the actual value of t exceeds its expected value. The mere possibility that this might occur then undermines the intermediary's ability to provide credible insurance. The problem is not so much that the DD intermediary faces instability, as DD themselves suggest, but that it has no clear reason to exist in the first place.

An alternative involves bringing some other agent(s) into the model to provide liquidity insurance. If the new agents know that they face no consumption risk, then under plausible circumstances they will offer the DD depositors insurance against their own individual liquidity risk in return for adequate premiums. They provide insurance by setting up their own financial intermediary. This intermediary would issue demand deposits to the other agents, while issuing a residual claim, equity, to the new agents. The intermediary therefore resembles a real-world bank financed by both deposits and equity. Furthermore, provided it has enough equity, it can guarantee all its deposits against default risk. My model formalizes the notion of bank capital adequacy, while also suggesting that banking without deposit insurance is more stable than the DD model would suggest.[3]

Diamond and Dybvig reconsidered

A stylized Diamond and Dybvig intermediary with no aggregate consumption risk

Suppose initially that we have a large number of identical individuals, each of whom lives for three periods, 0, 1 and 2. In period 0, each individual is endowed with a unit of a good and decides how to invest it. He faces an investment technology which, for each unit invested in period 0, yields 1 unit of output in period 1 or, if left till then, $R > 1$ units of output in period 2. When period 1 arrives, each agent receives a signal telling him the period in which he wants (or will want) to consume, with some (the type I agents) wishing to consume only in period 1, and the others (the type II agents) wishing to consume only in period 2. The type Is will therefore liquidate and consume all the proceeds of their investment in period 1, but the type IIs have to decide whether to retain their initial investments until period 2 or liquidate their investments in period 1 and keep the proceeds till the next period. Storage from one period to another is costless and unobservable. An agent's type is not publicly observable, but the proportion of type I agents, t, is initially assumed to be fixed and known. I also follow Wallace (1988: 9) and assume that agents are isolated from each other in period 1, in the sense that those who collect their returns in period 1 do so at random instants during that period.[4]

Each agent maximizes the expected utility function:

$$E\{tU(c_1) + (1 - t)U(c_2)\} \tag{1}$$

where c_1 is consumption in the first period, and c_2 is consumption in the second period. Since the type Is would consume only in period 1 and the type IIs would consume only in period 2, c_1 and c_2 can also be regarded as the consumption of type I and type II agents respectively. To make the analysis explicit, $U(.)$ is assumed to take the following form:

$$U(c_i) = c_i^{1-\gamma} / (1 - \gamma) \tag{2}$$

where i equals 1 or 2, and $\gamma > 1$.[5] $U(.)$ thus exhibits constant relative risk aversion and has a risk aversion coefficient greater than 1. Agents seek to maximize their utility subject to the resource constraint:

$$tc_1 + (1 - t)c_2 / R = 1 \tag{3}$$

which tells us how total consumption is limited by agents' initial investments and returns in each of the two periods (see also Diamond and Dybvig 1983: 407).

One option is for agents to live in autarky. If they do so, our assumptions about endowments and investment technology imply that the type Is would consume 1 unit and have *ex post* utility $U(1) = 1 / (1 - \gamma)$ and the type IIs would consume R units and have *ex post* utility $U(R) = R^{1-\gamma} / (1 - \gamma)$. *Ex ante* (i.e. in period 0), an agent living autarkically would therefore expect the utility:

$$tU(1) + (1 - t)U(R) = t / (1 - \gamma) + (1 - t)R^{1-\gamma} / (1 - \gamma) \tag{4}$$

However, since agents are risk-averse, they would value an opportunity to insure themselves in period 0 against the 'unlucky' event of turning out to be type I. Given that the proportion of type Is, t, is known in advance, it ought to be possible for our agents to come to some arrangement to diversify this risk among themselves. Assuming it can be arranged at no cost, the optimal insurance arrangement is found by maximizing (1) subject to (2) and the resource constraint (3). The optimal consumption levels in periods 1 and 2 can then be found from (3) and the first-order condition:

$$U'(c_1) / U'(c_2) = R \tag{5}$$

which tells us that in any optimum, the marginal rate of substitution between consumption levels in the two periods should equal the marginal rate of transformation, R. The optimum consumption levels turn out to be:

$$c_1 = R^{(\gamma-1)/\gamma} / (1 - t + tR^{(\gamma-1)/\gamma}), \quad c_2 = R / (1 - t + tR^{(\gamma-1)/\gamma}) \tag{6}$$

where:

$$1 < c_1 < c_2 < R \tag{7}$$

The optimal insurance arrangement leads type I agents to have higher consumption than they would have obtained under autarky, while the type II agents get less than they would have under autarky; however, the type Is still end up with less than the type IIs because period 1 consumption has a higher opportunity cost (see also Diamond and Dybvig 1983: 407).

One way to provide this insurance is for agents to form a financial intermediary in period 0. Instead of investing their endowments in their backyard, agents would deposit them with the intermediary, and the intermediary would invest them on their behalf. When agents' types are revealed in period 1, the intermediary would pay out more to those withdrawing in period 1 than the one unit they would have received had they invested autarkically, with the remainder being paid out to those who withdraw in period 2, who would get less than the R they would have received under autarky. This solution also satisfies a self-selection constraint (i.e. it induces type Is to withdraw (only) in period 1, and type IIs to withdraw (only) in period 2). No type I agent would ever wish to keep his deposit until period 2, because he only benefits from consumption in period 1. At the same time, no type II agent would withdraw prematurely, because the return from premature withdrawal would be less than the return from withdrawing later.

This intermediary also operates in period 1 under a sequential service constraint (i.e. it deals with requests for redemption in period 1 in a random order, until it runs out of assets). This constraint arises because of agents' isolation in period 1: since agents collect their returns at random times within period 1, the intermediary must deal with their requests for redemption 'separately, one after the other' (Wallace 1988: 4). It follows, naturally, that any suggested arrangements must be consistent with the sequential service constraint.

The stylized Diamond and Dybvig intermediary in the presence of aggregate consumption risk

Unfortunately, the DD arrangement is not robust to uncertainty about t. Suppose we now assume that t is, say, a uniform random variable that can take any value between 0 and 1 with equal probability. The uncertainty about t means that contractual payments cannot now be made conditional on the realized value of t because, first, the sequential service constraint requires that depositors must be dealt with sequentially, and second, the realization of t cannot be known until all period 1 withdrawals have been completed. The intermediary does not know what to pay each depositor until they have all gone and it is too late to do anything about it. Consequently, it is not possible to condition any insurance arrangement on the realized value of t.

Suppose, then, that our intermediary were to offer agents insurance contracts along earlier lines, but with payments now conditional on t^e (which is equal to 0.5) rather than t:

$$c_1 = R^{(\gamma-1)/\gamma} / (1 - t^e + t^e R^{(\gamma-1)/\gamma}) , \; c_2 = R / (1 - t^e + t^e R^{(\gamma-1)/\gamma}) \tag{8}$$

Using (8) rather than (6) to determine payouts, the intermediary would pay out tc_1 to agents withdrawing in period 1, leaving $(1 - tc_1)$ at the end of the period. It would then make a gross return of $(1 - tc_1)R$ in period 2, from which it would have to pay out $(1 - t)c_2$ to those withdrawing that period. A little manipulation then shows that its net profit is:

$$\Pi = R(t - t^e)(1 - R^{(\gamma-1)/\gamma}) / (1 - t^e + t^e R^{(\gamma-1)/\gamma}) \tag{9}$$

Since $R^{(\gamma-1)/\gamma} > 1$, the net profit is positive if $t < t^e$ and negative if $t > t^e$.

But a new problem now becomes apparent: if $t > t^e$, the intermediary's promised payments exceed the return on its investments, and the intermediary cannot make its contractual payments; this means that it cannot offer credible insurance. (By contrast, the intermediary *could* offer credible insurance before, precisely because t was deterministic: the deterministic t meant that the intermediary knew its future payments and knew that it could make them.) A type II depositor cannot now be confident of the promised return if he or she waits until period 2 to redeem the deposit, so the depositor may rationally decide to 'play safe' by redeeming the deposit in period 1 and keeping it under the mattress until he or she consumes it in period 2. In other words, the self-selection constraint no longer holds, and type II investors may rationally decide to run on the intermediary in period 1. Indeed, if agents expect the type II agents to run in period 1, they would have no reason to leave deposits with the intermediary in the first place.[6]

The DD solution is for an outside party, the government, to guarantee the intermediary's payments to those withdrawing in period 2 (Diamond and Dybvig 1983: 413–6). Type II agents would then have no reason to run; the self-selection constraint would be satisfied and the intermediary could provide optimal insurance. However, this 'solution' is not feasible if we take investors' isolation seriously: if the deposit insurance guarantee is to work, the government must credibly promise that depositors who keep their deposits till period 2 will get repaid in full. Yet the only available resources are those the intermediary has already paid out to agents who have withdrawn in period 1, and the government can only get access to these resources if it has some means of overcoming the sequential service constraint – which in turn implies that the government has the means to overcome the period 1 isolation that gives rise to this constraint. If we take the isolation assumption seriously, the government has no way of providing credible deposit insurance – and the DD solution is not feasible (see also e.g. Wallace 1988).[7]

A 'real-world' bank

A more fruitful approach is to consider another way for investors to obtain the insurance they want. If depositors cannot provide such insurance themselves, the obvious alternative is for some other agents to provide it. Suppose, then, that we add a third type of agent to our model, a type III agent. This new agent is endowed with an amount K for each depositor, and also differs from the other agent-types in that he or she already knows in period 0 that he or she will want to consume (only) in period 2. (This latter condition makes it easier for the type III agent to commit to postponing consumption until period 2.) This agent too has the option of investing in his backyard, and if he does so, knows that there will be a return of KR (per depositor) in period 2. The issues involved are most easily seen if we initially suppose that the type III agent is risk-neutral, but I shall relax this assumption later.

The question is whether a type III agent would wish to use his or her endowment to provide aggregate consumption insurance to the other agents. To answer this question, we need to establish whether the agent could charge an insurance premium p for his services that would be high enough to induce him to sell insurance, but low enough to make it worth their while for the other agents to buy that insurance.

A risk-neutral type III agent

The analysis is very straightforward if our type III agent is risk-neutral. Suppose the agent sets up his own bank, and offers investors the same optimum returns as earlier, minus a charge p. (We assume for convenience that this charge is deducted from the deposit repayment.) The agent's return in period 2 would be the sum of the return on the agent's own capital, KR, the same net profit Π we had earlier, and the charge p. Given that (9) implies that the expected value of Π is zero, a risk-neutral banker would choose to set up a bank – that is, he or she would choose the uncertain return $(KR+\Pi+p)$ over the certain return KR – for any positive value of p. Any inducement, however small, will lead our type III agent to set up a bank.

A risk-averse type III agent

What happens if the type III agent has the same aversion to risk as the other agents? In this case, it is easy to show that by setting up the bank, the type III agent accepts a gamble on the realization of t, the expected utility from which is:

$$EU = \int_{t=0}^{t=1} p(t)U(KR + \Pi_t + p)dt \tag{10}$$

Assuming that t is distributed uniformly over the interval [0,1], we substitute (9) into (10) and rearrange to obtain:

$$EU = [1 / (1 - \gamma)] \int_{t=0}^{t=1} (\alpha + \beta t)^{1-\gamma} dt \tag{11}$$

where:

$$\alpha = KR + p - t^e R(1 - R^{(\gamma-1)/\gamma}) / (1 - t^e + t^e R^{(\gamma-1)/\gamma}) \tag{12a}$$

$$\beta = R(1 - R^{(\gamma-1)/\gamma}) / (1 - t^e + t^e R^{(\gamma-1)/\gamma}) \tag{12b}$$

We then integrate (11) and obtain:

$$EU = [(\alpha + \beta)^{2-\gamma} - \alpha^{2-\gamma}] / [\beta(1 - \gamma)(2 - \gamma)] \tag{13}$$

For the agent to accept the gamble and establish the bank, the expected utility in (13) must exceed his autarky utility level $(KR)^{1-\gamma}/(1 - \gamma)$. Some numerical simulations then suggest that, provided the type III agent has sufficient capital, there always exist values of p that would make the depositors and the type III agent better off with a bank than under autarky.[8] A bank would always be in everyone's interest, provided the type III agent has enough capital.

Capital adequacy

The analysis thus far presupposes that the bank is able to guarantee its promised payments, and we need to check that this is the case. To guarantee its payments, the bank must have enough capital to cover its losses in the worse-case scenario. The worst-case scenario in our model is where every depositor decides to redeem in period 1. Given that the bank would have to pay out c_1 to each depositor who withdraws in period 1, but would only make a return of 1 on each such deposit, the worst possible loss the bank could face is $c_1 - 1$ per depositor. The bank can therefore guarantee all its commitments only if the type III agent's capital per depositor, K, is at least as great as this maximum possible loss:

$$K \geq c_1 - 1 = [R^{(\gamma-1)/\gamma} / (1 - t^e + t^e R^{(\gamma-1)/\gamma})] - 1$$

$$= (R^{(\gamma-1)/\gamma} - 1)(1 - t^e) / (1 - t^e + t^e R^{(\gamma-1)/\gamma}) \tag{14}$$

(14) gives us a capital adequacy condition (see also Dowd (1993a: 366) or Eichberger and Milne (1990: 19)). Provided the bank's capital satisfies (14), the bank can always meet its commitments and depositors can be fully confident of being repaid.[9] The bank's contracts are then fully credible and there is no reason for a type II agent ever to run. Even if a type II agent expected all other agents to redeem in period 1, it would still be rational for the agent to wait until period 2

because the return would be higher. The agent would therefore wait. Other type IIs are just the same, so they would wait as well. A run would therefore never occur, and the only agents who would redeem in period 1 are the type I agents who should redeem in that period anyway.

Conclusions

An intermediated arrangement is feasible in a DD-like environment, provided there exists one or more additional agents who are able and willing to commit the resources needed to ensure that the intermediary can honour its obligations. This intermediary would be similar to a real-world bank and would issue demand deposits, which would be redeemable on demand and fixed in nominal value, and a residual claim, held by the type III agent(s), which would be similar to real-world bank equity. By contrast, the DD model predicts the existence of a peculiar type of mutual organization that we seldom observe in the real world, but does *not* predict the existence of banks as such. It therefore cannot provide a rationale for real-world banking regulation or government deposit insurance.[10]

My model also explains the function of bank capital: bank capital is a device to give depositors rational confidence in the bank. This explains why bankers have traditionally placed so much emphasis on bank capital, an emphasis that makes no sense in traditional DD models that deal only with mutual institutions. My model also suggests that there need be no bank stability problem provided a bank has sufficient capital. It is therefore not surprising that banks are the dominant form of intermediary and that intermediaries like the DD one rarely, if ever, arise.

4 Does asymmetric information justify bank capital adequacy regulation?

One of the more important developments in twentieth-century central banking is the rise of capital adequacy regulation: the imposition by regulators of minimum capital standards on financial institutions. Most bank regulators see capital adequacy regulation as a means of strengthening the safety and soundness of the banking system, and many see it as a useful – perhaps even necessary – response to the moral-hazard problems created by deposit insurance and the existence of a lender of last resort to assist banks in difficulties. If deposit insurance and a lender of last resort encourage banks to take excessive risks and run down their capital, then forcing banks to strengthen their capital positions is a fairly obvious regulatory response. As a result, the regulation of bank capital adequacy has come to be one of the most important concerns of any modern central bank. Indeed, much of the case for modern central banking now depends on the justification (or otherwise) for capital adequacy regulation.

Yet arguments for capital adequacy regulation are relatively sparse and not particularly convincing.[1] Perhaps the most important argument is one recently put forward by David Miles (1995). He suggested that an information asymmetry between bank managers and depositors could produce a market failure that provides a rationale for government (or central bank) intervention in the financial system. This intervention would take the form of capital adequacy regulation to force banks to maintain a stronger capital position than they otherwise would. The essence of the argument is that if depositors cannot assess the financial soundness of individual banks, then banks will maintain lower than optimal capital ratios, where the optimal capital ratios are those banks would have observed if depositors could have assessed their financial positions properly. Intuitively, if depositors can assess a bank's capital strength, a bank will maintain a relatively strong capital position because greater capital induces depositors to accept lower interest rates on their deposits; however, if depositors cannot assess a bank's capital strength, a bank can no longer induce depositors to accept lower interest rates in return for higher capital, and the bank's privately optimal capital ratio is lower than is socially optimal. Information asymmetry therefore leads to a bank capital adequacy problem. Miles' solution is for a regulator to assess the level of capital the bank would have maintained in the absence of the information asymmetry, and then force it to maintain this level of capital.

Miles' work is significant because it appears to be the first rigorous attempt to justify capital adequacy regulation by reference to the (alleged) failure of the free market. By contrast, standard justifications are either incomplete (e.g. the usual prudential or paternalistic arguments for capital adequacy regulation), or else argue that capital adequacy regulation is required to counter the effects of other *given* interventions such as deposit insurance (e.g. Benston and Kaufman 1995). This latter argument defends capital adequacy regulation given the presence of other interventions, but cannot defend it in their absence (i.e. from first principles, by reference to a failure of *laissez-faire*). Miles therefore attempts to fill an important gap in the central banker's intellectual armoury, and in so doing he throws down the gauntlet to free bankers who have argued that capital adequacy regulation is unnecessary under *laissez-faire*.

My purpose here is to pick up the gauntlet and defend the free-banking position.[2] In so doing, I wish to make three main points. First, Miles fails to provide a convincing rationale for the distinctive regulation of banks: he fails to explain why banks (or financial institutions more generally) should be regulated, but non-financial firms should not be. This is a problem for Miles, since he readily concedes that non-financial firms should not be subject to capital adequacy regulation. If non-financial firms should not be subject to such regulation, why should financial firms be treated any differently? Second, the premise of his argument – that depositors cannot assess banks' capital positions – is both implausible and empirically falsified. Third, Miles' solution (of capital adequacy regulation) is inconsistent with this premise, even if the premise is granted. Put another way, there are no plausible circumstances in which the free market 'fails' and Miles' capital adequacy rule improves upon the free-market outcome. Either way, regulation cannot improve upon *laissez-faire*.

The distinctive regulation of banks

Miles readily acknowledges the need to justify why there should be 'restrictions on the lending and financing activities of deposit taking financial intermediaries when there are no limits on the balance sheet structure of car companies, hotel chains or computer manufacturers' (Miles 1995: 1366). So the question naturally arises: what is 'special' about banks that might justify regulating their capital adequacy, given that we agree that non-financial firms should not be subject to such regulation?

Yet, having accepted to need to base a theory of bank regulation on factors that are specific to banks, Miles then has very little to say on what those factors might be. His formal analysis is too general, and his model has nothing in it to make his firm specifically a bank rather than some more general type of firm. There is little on the liability side of his firm's balance sheet that makes his firm a bank as such, and simply labelling the firm's debt as 'deposits' clearly does not restrict the model to apply to banks alone. Nor does the Miles firm have any distinctive bank-like features on the asset side of its balance sheet: whilst Miles' discussion of his firm's assets is couched in language suggestive of a bank, he actually identifies no specific factors that would make it difficult to interpret his firm more generally. Most firms have many imperfectly marketable assets, for example, so his assumption that the firm's assets are imperfectly marketable is still not enough to narrow it down to a bank. There is therefore nothing here that applies to banks, that does not also apply to many non-financial firms as well.

In fact, the only explicit difference between banks and other firms identified by Miles is that the average size of bank debt contracts (relative to the balance sheet) is small (Miles 1995: 1376, note 2). Even so, he still does not show how this factor makes banks sufficiently different from other firms to motivate bank-specific regulation. Instead, he merely suggests that this lower relative size gives bank debtholders (i.e. depositors) less incentive to overcome information problems than debtholders at other firms. Yet problems of monitoring incentives are not unique to banking, but apply more generally (e.g. with large public firms) whenever there is a large number of investors each of whom bears the cost of their monitoring activity, but recovers only a fraction of the gain it creates.[3] These monitoring problems also have natural market solutions: if we start off with a large number of small investors, each of whom faces the monitoring disincentives just described, there is presumably some gain from concentrating the monitoring function by having one or more large debtholders (or other investors) take a more junior claim than the small debtholders (or investors). Their junior status and the need to protect their investments give the big investors an incentive to monitor, and their knowledge that the big investors face this incentive alleviates the small depositors' monitoring problem.

Miles thus fails to explain what is special about banks that justifies bank-specific regulation. The justification for capital adequacy regulation that he puts forward must therefore apply to many non-financial firms as well as banks, or not at all.

Can depositors assess individual banks' capital strength?

So does it apply or not? I believe not. As noted already, a crucial link in Miles' analysis is his claim that depositors cannot assess the capital strength of individual banks. This link is crucial because it is the inability of depositors to assess the capital strength of any individual bank that leads banks to maintain less capital than they otherwise would, and thereby gives rise to a 'need' for capital regulation. Miles accepts that this assumption might appear 'unusual' (Miles 1995: 1375), but defends it on two principal grounds. First, he suggests that 'in practice it is not easy' for depositors to evaluate bank capital because doing so requires valuation of the banks' assets.[4] Second, he suggests that

> depositors cannot depend on stock market valuations of a bank to assess the value of shareholders' capital (or equity) backing their deposits; the stock market value may be increased by gearing up and stock market participants also face the problem of valuing the underlying assets (loans) of the bank.
>
> (Miles 1995: 1375–6)

Yet the depositor monitoring problem is not as difficult as Miles makes out, and depositors can and do manage to assess the capital strengths of individual banks.[5] To some extent, this problem is solved in practice by depositors relying on shareholders to value bank capital, and depositors can reasonably assume that their funds are safe if the shareholders give the bank a sufficiently high capital value. The point is that shareholders are residual claimants who can only be paid after all the depositors have been paid in full, should the bank default on its debts. Shareholders as a group therefore have strong incentives to value the bank carefully, and if they believe that the bank has a high positive net worth (i.e. is well-capitalized), then depositors can reasonably assume that their own funds (which have prior claim on bank assets) must be fairly safe. The typical depositor's monitoring problem is thus considerably simplified; and, in practice, it frequently suffices for the depositor to check that the bank maintains a fairly high capital valuation and watch for signs of trouble in the media. In addition, the bank management themselves also have a strong incentive to make monitoring easier for depositors (and shareholders). The bank must maintain their confidence if it is to remain in business, and one of the ways in which it maintains confidence is by making it relatively easy for depositors to satisfy themselves that their bank is sound. Thus, if a bank management believed that depositors were having undue difficulty monitoring them, they might have the bank rated by an independent agency whose report would be disseminated in the media. The message coming through to individual depositors would then be fairly simple: either the bank is reasonably safe to leave your money in, or it is not. The depositor's monitoring problem cannot get much easier than that.[6]

The claim that depositors cannot assess individual banks' balance sheets is also empirically falsified, at least under historical circumstances where the absence of deposit insurance or other forms of bailout gave depositors an incentive to be careful where they put their deposits. There is much evidence that depositors did discriminate between banks on the basis of their relative capital strengths. To give but one example, George Kaufman observed that:

> There is . . . evidence that depositors and noteholders in the United States cared about the financial condition of their banks and carefully scrutinized bank balance sheets [in the period before federal deposit insurance was introduced]. Arthur Rolnick and his colleagues at the Federal Reserve Bank of Minneapolis have shown that this clearly happened before the Civil War. Thomas Huertas and his colleagues at Citicorp have demonstrated the importance of [individual] bank capital to depositors by noting that Citibank in its earlier days prospered in periods of general financial distress by maintaining higher than average capital ratios and providing depositors with a relatively safe haven. Lastly, an analysis of balance sheets suggests that banks took . . . less interest rate risk before the establishment of the FDIC.
>
> (Kaufman 1987: 15–16)

The Miles position is also refuted by the empirical evidence on the bank-run contagion issue. If Miles is right and depositors cannot distinguish between banks, then a run on one bank should lead to runs on all the others as well (i.e. we should observe universal contagion): if one bank is in difficulty, and I can't tell the difference between that bank and mine, then mine must be in difficulty too, so I had better get my funds out. Yet the evidence overwhelmingly indicates that bank runs do not spread like wildfire in the way that the Miles hypothesis predicts (see Benston *et al.* 1986: chapter 2). Instead, there occurs a 'flight to quality', with depositors withdrawing funds from weak institutions to re-deposit them in stronger ones. Flights to quality have occurred in every major historical banking crisis, and the fact that they have done so shows that the public have been able to tell the difference between strong and weak banks and demonstrates the very point that Miles denies.

Can regulation improve on the free market outcome?

Finally, there is the issue of whether regulation can improve on the *laissez-faire* outcome: can a regulator formulate a feasible rule to make banks hold socially optimal levels of capital, assuming (but only for the sake of argument) that depositors cannot assess the capital strength of individual banks? I would suggest that they can't. The Miles argument runs into a dilemma: if the information exists (or could exist) for the regulator to formulate a feasible capital adequacy rule, that same information could also be used to convey credible signals to depositors about the capital strength of their banks, and thereby enable them to distinguish one bank's capital strength from another's; but if that information cannot be collected, then the regulator cannot collect it either, and in that case Miles' capital adequacy regulation is not feasible.

To put this point another way, suppose we start by assuming that depositors cannot assess the capital strength of individual banks, but we also follow Miles and assume that a regulator can collect information to make capital adequacy regulation feasible. However, if the regulator can collect the information to make capital adequacy regulation feasible, a private body (e.g. a credit rating agency) should also be able to collect it and publish it in a form that depositors can readily understand.[7] It is also worth emphasizing that the banks would have an incentive to co-operate with the rating agencies (e.g. by providing information and, in many cases, by purchasing the reports to be distributed free to the public) for the same reason that most firms generally co-operate with rating agencies (that is, 'good' firms co-operate because they desire to distinguish themselves from 'bad' firms, and the 'bad' firms generally have to go along with the quality rating exercise if they are not to immediately reveal their true quality). The rating agencies' reports would also be credible because their long-run livelihoods would (and indeed, do) depend on their credibility.[8] It follows that to the extent that the Miles formula gives the regulator sufficient information to regulate banks' capital adequacy, it should also lead to depositors obtaining sufficient information to assess banks' capital adequacy themselves, without the need for regulation. On the other hand, if the information cannot be collected, then no one can use it, including the regulator, and the regulation is not feasible.[9] The regulation is therefore either feasible but unnecessary, or just not feasible.

Conclusions

Bank regulators are deluding themselves if they think that there is any firm economic justification for capital adequacy regulation. No one has yet provided a convincing case for it on market failure grounds, and the standard prudential and paternalistic arguments usually cited to defend such regulation do not meet even basic standards of economic analysis. No one has yet shown that there is anything wrong with banking *laissez-faire* that capital adequacy regulation would put right.

Perhaps the best argument for capital adequacy regulation – and even that is highly problematic – is that it might help to counter the moral hazard created by the regulatory authorities themselves.[10] However this is an argument based on government failure rather than market failure, and it is surely better for regulators to stop creating moral hazard problems in the first place. Regulators should get their own house in order. Government failure does not constitute a good argument for government intervention.

5 Competitive banking, bankers' clubs, and bank regulation

There has been considerable interest recently in what might be called the microfoundations of banking regulation and central banking. Much of this interest is stimulated by the revival of the free banking school which sees government-supported (official) regulation as unnecessary and central banking as the damaging product of state intervention. Yet free banking is still a minority view, and most economists continue to believe that 'official' regulation has a useful role to play. This latter view has been defended and developed in recent years by Gorton and Mullineaux (1987), Mullineaux (1987) and Goodhart (1987, 1988, 1991). In very different ways – Gorton and Mullineaux use a contractual approach and Goodhart the theory of clubs – these writers have argued that information asymmetries in financial markets posed problems that unregulated markets could not handle, and they argue that regulation arose 'spontaneously' to meet these problems. According to this view, banking regulation and central banks should be seen, in part at least, as a 'natural' response to problems inherent in financial markets, and the free bankers' view of them as no more than damaging intrusions should be rejected.

This chapter sets out a contrary view. Information problems do play a large role in financial markets, and these problems might lead free banks to form clubs' or comparable hierarchical structures that restrict (i.e. regulate) the activities of member-banks. However this regulation does not justify the systems of financial regulation or central banking that arose historically because it differs from them in critical ways. Furthermore, since the benefits that regulation can bring are basically economies of scale, arguments for spontaneous regulation would appear to be tantamount to claims that banking is a natural monopoly and the empirical evidence indicates it is not. In any case, arguments for spontaneous regulation are also refuted by the evidence that the historical banking systems that were relatively close to *laissez-faire* developed little or none of it, and there is a plausible argument that the nineteenth-century US cases often cited as examples of 'private' regulation only developed such regulation as a response to branching and other restrictions that prevented a more explicit appropriation of economies of scale. In short, I dispute claims that regulation and central banking were a natural, spontaneous response to inherent market failures, and in doing so I suggest that they are not economically justified as improvements over a free market.

The rationale for banking clubs

Suppose that there is more than one bank in a relatively unregulated equilibrium. It is well understood by now that mutual interest will lead them to co-operate with each other to clear their notes and checks through a clearing-house (White 1984, Selgin and White 1987), but banks will also want to deal with each other for purposes other than clearing (e.g. to lend to each other) and we wish to investigate whether they would co-operate on an explicit 'market' basis (i.e. where each deal was done on a separate commercial basis), or whether they would do so by forming a club to coordinate at least some interbank activity by command.[1] There are three reasons why they might conceivably prefer the latter.

Reducing transactions and monitoring costs for interbank loans

One reason is to minimize the transactions and monitoring costs of banks' lending to each other. Each bank faces a stochastic net demand for reserves from the public that implies its reserves will fluctuate randomly from day to day, and these reserve fluctuations will not be perfectly correlated. Some banks will experience reserve shortages over any given period and will wish to borrow, and others will be flush with reserves and willing to lend. Banks will therefore participate in the market for reserves, and they might even form a special interbank reserve market if the transactions or information costs are lower for interbank transactions than for those involving other parties. It may be that bank co-operation goes no further than participation in the market for reserves – if banks' demands for reserves are relatively small, or if there is only a small number of banks that know each other well and have an informal understanding to help each other out, there might be little scope for a mutually beneficial interbank organization and the unassisted market will suffice without any hierarchy to support it. Nonetheless, it is conceivable that the transactions and monitoring costs of arranging interbank loans might make a bankers' bank an attractive option to the banks for much the same reasons that individual borrowers and lenders often prefer to deal with each other indirectly through an intermediary (e.g. Chant 1992).

In the absence of a bankers' bank, each bank wanting a loan would have to transact with each of its potential creditors, and a bankers' bank can cut down these transactions costs by arranging loans centrally. More importantly, perhaps, a bankers' bank can also eliminate unnecessary monitoring costs where there are multiple lenders. If there is more than one lender and they do not coordinate with each other, then lenders can end up duplicating each other's monitoring or trying to free-ride on each other's (presumed) monitoring efforts, and a bankers' bank can be a good way to coordinate their efforts and ensure that loans are properly monitored. Since it is both difficult and time-consuming to ascertain banks' values, the bankers' bank would not try to assess a bank's value *de novo* each time it applied for a loan. Instead it would monitor borrowers on an ongoing basis to be able to handle loan applications quickly. Since they would hope to be able to obtain loans, its customers would have an interest in keeping it suitably informed, but much of this information would be commercially sensitive information that they might want kept secret from rivals. The banks' sensitivity regarding their accounts implies that an independent outfit would normally be better placed to monitor member-banks than one of their own number.

A bankers' club run by its own independent management is therefore likely to be more effective than a club in which a member-bank takes on the monitoring and management roles. The effectiveness of the club can be further enhanced by officials accepting contracts that give them an incentive to preserve their independence and honour the confidentiality of their work, and which provide for penalties in the event of perceived lapses from duty.[2]

The reserve externality argument

It is sometimes claimed that a banking club (or some other means of assisting bankers) is needed because banks have insufficient private incentive to hold the 'socially optimal' level of reserves (Cothren 1987 or Goodhart 1988: 53–5). According to this argument, each bank holds reserves to equate the marginal private benefits of reserve holdings to their marginal private costs – the former are the expected benefits of not having to go to market or declare bankruptcy in the event a customer demands redemption of bank liabilities, and the latter are the opportunity costs of having to hold redemption media that yield a lower return than some alternative assets – and the bank ignores the 'external' benefits that its reserve holdings confer on other banks.

These external benefits arise because the greater a bank's reserves, the more likely it is to be able and willing to lend to other banks should they desire a loan, and other banks derive the benefit that the reserves-supply curve they face has shifted to the right. The outcome produced by the unassisted market could then be improved upon if all banks could be induced to hold more reserves than they would otherwise choose to hold, because they would all benefit from the external effects of the higher reserves held by the others. Banks could try to appropriate these external benefits by agreeing to hold higher reserves than they would otherwise choose to hold (e.g. by agreeing to minimum reserve ratios), but if such an arrangement is to be viable, it is necessary to find some means of restricting the benefits that go to non-members – if non-members get the same benefits as members, each bank would prefer to free-ride on members' higher reserves and the scheme would never have any members in the first place.

A solution would be for member-banks to pledge a certain proportion of their reserves to be loaned to each other, presumably on more favourable terms than could be obtained on the market, but to be loaned to non-members at a penalty rate of interest, if at all. This discrimination against non-members would give the latter the incentive to join that would otherwise be lacking, and the banks could make these arrangements operational by establishing a club to which they delegated the power to impose reserve requirements and lend member-banks' reserves.

Bank 'contagion'

A third rationale for a banking club, and one that has received considerable emphasis in the literature is the prospect of 'contagious' bank runs, or contagion (e.g. Benston *et al.* 1986; Goodhart 1988). There is a contagion problem when the observation that one bank is facing a run or some other serious difficulty leads those with notes or deposits at other banks to run as well. Since redemption imposes costs on note- and deposit-holders (e.g. it takes time and effort to go to the bank and line up there), an individual will usually demand redemption only if he is sufficiently apprehensive that the bank might default. If the individual were apprehensive, he would demand redemption to avoid the losses that default would inflict on those who continued to hold its debt. Others would think similarly, and the bank would face a run. A shock to one bank could then raise the public's apprehension about other banks to a level where they faced runs as well. Contagion is thus a negative externality that banks impose on each other, and the claim is that banks could reduce these externalities by forming a club.

The most obvious arrangement would be an emergency lending procedure designed to pre-empt any contagion. If a bank got into difficulties, a decision would be made whether to assist it. If the bank qualified for help, the resources of the other banks would be pledged to keep it open, the pledge should restore public confidence, and the run should subside without infecting the other banks. Alternatively, the bank could be refused assistance, and the club would try to prevent contagion by distancing its members from it. Refusal would then send a clear signal to the public that the club regarded the bank as unsound, and this signal would encourage the public to run on it and drive it out of business. The clearinghouse would therefore assist the healthy banks and throw sick ones to the wolves, and either way, ideally, it should ensure that there was no contagion from one bank to the rest.

The regulatory role of clearinghouses

There are thus several reasons – the minimization of the transactions/monitoring costs of lending, 'reserve externalities', and the possibility of contagion – why banks might want to establish a club that would provide a bank in difficulties with loans that would be more expensive or perhaps even unavailable on the unassisted market. However, the existence of the club creates a moral hazard problem for member-banks because they are now effectively co-insuring each other. A typical bank will have an incentive to take more risks on the grounds that it will get all the benefits if the risks pay off but it can offload some of the losses to other banks if they do not. The other banks will do likewise, and the consequence would be socially excessive risk-taking that would leave the typical bank worse off than it would have been if all the banks could somehow have agreed not to take the extra risks in the first place. The solution, if it is feasible, is for the clearinghouse to impose controls on excessive risk-taking by members-banks and ensure that it has the means to monitor compliance. These controls might include minimum capital ratios, restrictions on the quality of assets that member-banks are allowed to hold, and restrictions on deposit rates to prevent the more aggressive banks bidding up deposit rates to obtain the funds with which to take additional risks. In a nutshell, the clearinghouse faces a moral hazard problem that might lead it to acquire extensive regulatory powers over member-banks and establish some form of hierarchy.

It is important to emphasize why an individual member-bank might rationally choose to submit itself to these regulations. Joining a club gives a bank access to emergency loans at rates below what it would otherwise pay, and this superior access to support increases public confidence that the bank's notes and deposits will be honoured. This greater public confidence is not a free good that can be conjured out of thin air, but a rational response to the perceived safety represented by clearinghouse membership, and it depends to a considerable extent on the ability of the clearinghouse to protect the integrity of the banks by controlling the risks they take. If a clearinghouse could not control members' risk-taking at an acceptable cost, the underlying moral hazard could lead the more conservative banks to pull out to avoid liability for the risks being taken by their more aggressive competitors, and the clearinghouse itself could lose public confidence and collapse along with its remaining weak members. The irony is that while banks might not like obeying clearinghouse regulations, those very regulations help make clearinghouse regulation attractive in the first place by increasing public confidence in member-banks.

We need to be clear how this clearinghouse regulation compares with the 'official' regulation we observe historically. Both types of regulation share one key feature – those to whom they apply (usually) perceive them as binding constraints that prevent them doing what they would otherwise prefer to do, and so resources have to be devoted to monitoring to make sure the rules are obeyed – but they differ in four important respects.

First, clearinghouse regulations would be voluntary in a sense that official regulations are normally not. They would be part of the price of membership, but membership itself would be voluntary. While each bank would obviously prefer the benefits of membership and the freedom to do as it wished, the club can only be successful if members are forced to pay the membership price and obey the rules. The choice facing an individual bank is not whether it wants to follow the rules on an 'other things being equal' basis, but whether it wishes to be a member and accept the constraints that go with membership, or whether it wishes to retain its freedom of action and forgo those benefits.[3]

Second, clearinghouse regulations would be imposed by officials whose powers and contract structures would be determined by the banks whom they serve. Since they would not allow their own freedom of action to be restricted for no good reason, the banks would presumably ensure that clearinghouse powers were restricted to areas where a clear case had been established for them, and clearinghouse powers would be constrained as well by the need to get some kind of working majority of member-banks to approve them. The banks would also have an incentive to ensure that clearinghouse officials were effectively monitored and held to account, since they would bear the consequences of clearinghouse actions. By contrast, 'official' regulators have been typically accountable to government-sponsored authorities rather than to commercial bankers, and their regulations have frequently reflected political considerations much more than clearinghouse regulations would have done. In addition, since their powers derived from the political process rather than a mandate from the commercial banks, these regulators have had less incentive to respond to bankers' demands, and have frequently had greater powers and discretion than clearinghouse officials.

Third, following from this last point, official regulation has generally been much more extensive than clearinghouse regulations. To anticipate our later discussion, the historical evidence indicates that under conditions close to *laissez-faire*, clearinghouse powers were usually confined to minor matters such as organizing clearing and dealing with counterfeits. (US banking clubs often had much broader powers, but for reasons explained later, there is reason to believe that they are not typical of *laissez-faire* clubs.) Official regulations were usually much wider ranging, even in the nineteenth century, and included, *inter alia*, restrictions on the issue of notes and deposits, restrictions on asset holdings, amalgamation restrictions, reserve requirements, and subjection to requisitions and 'moral suasion'.

Finally, since the system of regulation imposed by a particular clearing-house would have to prove itself viable without the protection of legal restrictions against entry or exit, those regulations would have to satisfy certain obvious constraints. Member-banks that found clearinghouse rules too irksome could withdraw or set up or join a rival, and this threat of lost business would to some extent limit the degree to which the clearinghouse or its offi-cials could 'abuse' member-banks.[4] In the absence of legal barriers to entry, this threat would also have some impact even if the market for clearinghouse services could only support one clearinghouse in a region.[5] Apart from constraining it, competition would also provide a clearinghouse with infor-mation about the success or failure of alternative product–price mixes as well as an incentive to experiment with new ones to obtain a competitive edge.[6] Official regulations, by contrast, were much more insulated from competition, and gave regulators much less incentive to innovate or adopt successful prac-tices developed elsewhere.

But would there be a regulatory club in the first place?

We have discussed why clubs might arise to regulate member-banks and what such regulations might look like if they did, but it is not obvious that such regulatory clubs would even arise in the first place. Unless there were a large number of banks, the transactions cost savings would be relatively low, and there are other ways around the monitoring problem (e.g. loan syndicates). The historical evidence also suggests that banks did not form clubs for these reasons. Some banks established clubs for clearing purposes, and though some clearinghouses did lend to member-banks, at least on occasion, the fact that banks frequently chose not to set up any multilateral outfit at all suggests that they perceived whatever gains could be obtained from doing so to be outweighed by their set-up and operating costs (Schuler 1992: 17).[7]

Nor is it clear that there would be large benefits from dealing with reserve externalities. Provided they are perceived to be sound, the empirical evidence suggests that free banks can operate safely on relatively low reserve ratios. For example, figures provided by Cameron (1967: 87–8) indicate that Scottish banks of the late eighteenth and early nineteenth centuries usually operated with specie reserves less than 2 per cent, and often less than 1 per cent, of liabilities. The costs of holding reserves would be correspondingly low, and so too would the costs of any 'lost' reserve externalities.[8]

That leaves the contagion argument, and it is not obvious that that would lead to a banking club either. Banks would be aware of the danger of runs, and they would have a clear incentive to invest in confidence-building measures to discourage them. These measures would include the maintenance of an adequate capital ratio and the pursuit of sound lending policies to reassure debt-holders that their holdings were safe. 'Good' banks would also try to prevent contagion by distancing themselves from 'bad' ones. While such measures could not normally provide perfect reassurance – depositors would normally still know less about the state of the bank's financial health relative to management, and so on – the evidence nonetheless indicates that the public did look at factors such as these to discriminate in favour of well-capitalized, prudently managed banks (see e.g. Kaufman 1987: 15–16; 1988: 568–9). When financial crises occurred, the usual result was therefore a 'flight to quality' in which the public would transfer their accounts from weaker to stronger banks, and there is little convincing evidence of contagious runs in which the public ran indiscriminately against all banks regardless of their specific circumstances (see e.g. Benston *et al.* 1986: 53–60, 66; Dowd 1992d).[9] The evidence indicates that sound, reputable banks had little to fear from the difficulties of weaker competitors, and the contagion argument would appear to provide a doubtful basis for a banking club.

We can also think of banking clubs another way. The various factors isolated as possible reasons for forming a club can each be considered as economies of scale external to the firm but internal to the industry, and the point of a club is to internalize them. However one needs to explain why forming a club is the most appropriate way to internalize them when the banks could also have done so by merging into a single firm. Assuming that these economies were sufficiently large to have mattered, there is an argument that forming a single firm was the most natural way to appropriate them, since the unified ownership of a single firm would have avoided the moral hazard that arises where separately owned firms co-insure each other through a club, and the cost of controlling that moral hazard presumably implies that a single firm would have the edge over a club.[10] It would seem to follow that if important economies had existed, we would expect banking to have been a natural monopoly, and the empirical evidence very much indicates it was not. None of the historical experiences of (relatively) free banking showed any tendency toward natural monopoly (Schuler 1992: 16), although there was evidence of some economies of scale. The conclusion that there are economies of scale but no natural monopoly is also supported by the extensive empirical literature on returns to scale in modern banking. Recent surveys by Gilbert (1984), Lewis and Davis (1987: 202–7) and Clark (1988) between them looked at thirty-three separate studies, and not one presented any evidence that banking was a natural monopoly.[11]

The claim that there is little scope for clubs under *laissez-faire* seems to be borne out by the experience of less regulated banking systems in the past. The historical record of such banking systems outside the US – in countries such as Australia, Canada, Ireland, France, Scotland, Sweden, Switzerland, and many others (see the readings in Dowd 1992a) – indicates that (relatively) free banks had little use for banking clubs with extensive regulatory powers. In apparently all such cases, bank cooperation seemed to consist of little more than an arrangement for clearing notes and deposits with occasional ad hoc measures to deal with particular problems as they arose. Apart from clearing itself, clearinghouse policy dealt mainly with minor matters of mutual concern such as procedures to handle 'out of town' cheques and efforts to detect fraud (Schuler 1992: 18). Only rarely did free banks co-operate for more ambitious purposes (e.g. to provide emergency loans), and even then they did so with little formal power other than that to deny loans to applicants who did not co-operate.[12]

In the United States, on the other hand, banks did form private clubs which exercised quite extensive regulatory powers. One of the these was the Suffolk system which arose out of the attempts of the Suffolk Bank of Boston to counter the Boston circulation of the notes of 'out of town' ('country') banks. Branch-banking restrictions had made it difficult to redeem these notes, and they consequently circulated at a discount. In 1819 the Suffolk started buying them at their Boston discount, and gave the issuers the option to redeem them at the price the Suffolk paid for them provided they maintained (non-interest-bearing) deposits at the Suffolk. In 1824 the Suffolk began to allow participating banks the benefit of overdraft facilities, and since it was now extending credit, also started supervising them to ensure they were soundly run. Its position as manager of the system gave it the information to carry out that supervision effectively: any bank that followed a policy of systematic overexpansion would rapidly develop a persistent adverse clearing balance that would reveal what it was doing.

The usual response of the Suffolk to a delinquent bank was moral suasion – lecturing offending banks on the importance of correcting their policies – but it could also limit its overdraft or send back its notes for redemption. In the final analysis, it could also expel it from the system, and the threat of expulsion was a potent sanction because it provided a clear signal to the public that the well-informed Suffolk did not consider the bank to be a good credit risk.

The Suffolk system was thus a banking club in which the Suffolk both set the rules and enforced them. The price of membership was the deposit that members were required to keep and the obligation to obey the club rules. In return, members enjoyed increased public confidence resulting from the widespread par acceptance of their notes and the vetting and support services provided by the Suffolk. Its readiness to lend to member-banks made its vetting of their policies credible to the public, and the credibility of its assessment reduced the pressure on the public to vet a bank themselves. Since non-member banks enjoyed less confidence, banks felt under pressure to join even though they found the Suffolk's conditions irksome.

The other US clubs were the clearinghouse associations in the period from the mid-nineteenth century to 1914. They were first established to facilitate the return of notes to the banks that issued them, but in the 1850s the New York clearinghouse Association began to issue certificates to member-banks which they could use to settle clearing debts, and which economized specie and relaxed legal restrictions against the note issue (Sprague 1910, Timberlake 1984). These benefits were especially useful during panics when notes and coins were scarce and legislative restrictions particularly binding. In later panics, clearinghouses issued certificates that banks could use to meet redemption demands by the public. These certificates were claims against the clearinghouse and enjoyed public confidence because they were free from the default risk attached to individual banks. (In short, they offered banks a way to diversify risks when the most obvious way to do so – explicit merger – was hamstrung by legal restrictions.) They were retired after each crisis and members of the public who accepted them suffered no losses. In the end, clearinghouses were effectively issuing 'hand to hand' emergency currency that the public accepted even though it was issued illegally (Timberlake 1984: 6–7).

clearinghouse associations also developed a formal apparatus to provide banks with last-resort lending, and they developed a regulatory apparatus to accompany it. Banks had to satisfy capital requirements and submit to auditing and the requisitioning of their reserves when required to. Banks that failed to satisfy these conditions were disciplined, and the penalty for extreme violations was expulsion.

To summarize, the claim that there is little useful scope for clubs under *laissez-faire* appears to be broadly consistent with the historical evidence. Historical experiences outside the US suggest that banks had little need for clubs other than to arrange clearing and settle minor issues of mutual concern. The US experience is different, but there is reason to believe that the strong clubs that arose in the US were a response to the unique legislative restrictions under which US banks had to operate. These restrictions – the most significant being those against branch banking – deprived US banks of many scale economies that banks elsewhere appropriated by merging. Forming a strong club was therefore a means to appropriate scale economies where the most straightforward method was prohibited by law, and there is relatively little evidence of strong clubs in permissive legal environments.

Gorton and Mullineaux's analysis of clearinghouse associations

This analysis of banking clubs differs markedly from those found in recent literature. One of these is by Gorton and Mullineaux (1987) and Mullineaux (1987). Their argument goes as follows. The public use two types of bank liability in their everyday exchanges – bank notes, and deposits on which they can write cheques – and these liabilities differ in an important respect. In deciding whether to accept a note, the public need information only on the bank that issues it. To be reasonably confident that they will not suffer any losses, it generally suffices for them to know that the bank that issues the note is in a position to honour it, but with cheques they need to know not only that the bank has the resources to honour the cheque, but also that the agent on whom the cheque is drawn has sufficient funds in his account. Notes therefore require only bank-specific information, but cheques require information on both banks and individual agents. Since all notes issued by a bank are effectively alike, a secondary note market can develop relatively easily, and this secondary market gives the public information about the underlying value of the bank, but a secondary market does not develop in cheques because agents would need information on specific bank accounts as well as on the soundness of the bank on which the cheques are drawn, and these information requirements make the operation of a secondary cheque market (typically) too expensive to be worthwhile to the agents who would be involved.

As the banking system evolved, the public's desired note/deposit ratio gradually declined. Gorton and Mullineaux argue that the secondary note market became less informative about the value of the bank itself, and an information asymmetry developed that made the public more inclined to 'run'. In the past, a shock to a bank's value (e.g. the revelation of a bad loan) would have been reflected in an increase in the discount on banks' notes in the secondary market, and the public would have had a clear signal of the worth of their note holdings. However when deposits supplanted notes there was no longer any secondary cheque market on which the bank's value could be reflected. The public was consequently more inclined to panic and demand redemption because they were deprived of information about the bank's value that they would previously have had, and clearinghouses therefore arose to protect the banks against such panics. The clearinghouses would be delegated various powers over members – among these the powers to set minimum reserve and capital ratios, the rights to monitor their accounts, and the power to requisition member-banks' reserves – and the incentive to submit to these rules was the greater likelihood of clearinghouse support in an emergency. When a run occurred, the clearinghouse would assess whether the banks experiencing the runs were sound or not. If they were deemed to be sound, the clearinghouse would use the resources of other member-banks to guarantee their liabilities, and this measure would usually suffice to reassure the public and dissuade them from continuing to run. If the banks were considered bad risks, on the other hand, the clearinghouse would say so and give the public a clear signal to continue the run and put them out of business.

This analysis fails to explain why banks would prefer to appropriate external benefits by forming a club instead of by merging, but even if this difficulty is set aside, there are also a few others.

First, it ignores the role of the equity market in signalling a bank's net worth and protecting noteholders and depositors. One of the functions of equity holders is to provide a buffer stock to reassure debtholders that they have little reason to fear losses, and the credibility of this buffer-stock signal arises from the stockholders being residual claimants who only get paid after other creditors. If the stock market gives a bank a positive value, it indicates that the bank can pay off all its noteholders and depositors and still have resources left over, and so the latter should have little to fear. Instead of looking at discounts on a secondary note market, liability holders need only check that the bank has a sufficiently positive stock market evaluation to absorb any likely losses that the bank might suffer on its asset portfolio, and we would expect liability holders to run on a bank only if its stock market value had fallen to some danger level where there was some significant likelihood that losses would be passed on to them.

Second, the argument exaggerates the information provided by the secondary note market. White (1984, 1989), Selgin (1988), and Selgin and White (1987) have argued forcefully that banks would agree to accept each other's notes at par, and par acceptance leaves little room for bank note discounts to deviate from zero. It follows, then, that under normal circumstances the only information provided by the secondary note market is that the bank is still considered to be of good standing, and (therefore) that its notes and deposits should continue to be redeemed at par. The corollary is that there should be no obvious difference in the information provided by notes and cheques. Provided the bank keeps its good standing, good cheques (i.e. cheques drawn on accounts with the funds to honour them) will trade at par for the same reasons that notes will trade at par, and the replacement of notes by deposits would make no significant difference to the public's information about the bank.

Third, even if notes and cheques did convey different information about the bank on which they were drawn, the extra information provided by notes would still be publicly available as long as there were some demand for banknotes. It is not the size of the secondary note market that would matter, but the fact that it would still exist. A fall in the public's desired note/deposit ratio would not create an information gap unless that ratio went to zero, and it did not go to zero in the historical banking systems that Gorton and Mullineaux seek to explain.

Finally, the Gorton and Mullineaux analysis makes predictions that are empirically falsified. They deal with how a *laissez-faire* banking system would evolve a system of endogenous regulation to deal with a particular information asymmetry problem reflected in a declining currency/deposit ratio. However, all relatively free historical banking systems apparently experienced falls in the currency/deposit ratio but none evolved endogenous regulation along the lines predicted by Gorton and Mullineaux. The case they emphasized – the late nine-teenth-century United States – was characterized by extensive legislative restrictions anyway. So relatively unregulated banking systems in the past did not experience the banking structures predicted by Gorton and Mullineaux, and the case that they focus on was not characterized by *laissez-faire* or anything reasonably close to it.

Goodhart's analysis of banking clubs

Charles Goodhart (1987, 1988, 1991) presents an alternative treatment of banking clubs. His analysis begins with an information asymmetry between banks and their liability holders. The management of a bank is better informed about the value of the bank than its liability holders, and there is no costless and credible way in which management can pass on their information. A situation can arise, therefore, where the bank is sound but the management cannot easily persuade its customers that they need not fear losses. A simple announcement that the bank is sound will be insufficient because the public would appreciate that the management has an incentive to lie. The management could presumably call in outside monitors (auditors) who could inspect the books and verify that the bank was sound, but such inspections can be expensive and time-consuming, and the public would need reassurance that they could believe the monitor. There can be no guarantee that the monitor can provide the public with the reassurance they want in the time available. The public might choose to play safe and redeem their holdings of bank liabilities, and the bank would face a run.

The problem then is that bank runs cause real damage. When a bank redeems one of its liabilities, it must either reduce its asset holdings or issue more of some other liability. The bank will keep stocks of redemption media on hand to meet demands for redemption, and provided that these demands are relatively few, it will have no great difficulty meeting them. It will also hold other assets that can be converted into redemption media at relatively low cost, and these stocks of marketable assets will provide it with further reassurance that it can meet redemption demands. The difficulty, however, is that the bank will hold many non-marketable assets (e.g. consumer loans) which it cannot liquidate to meet demands for redemption, or can only liquidate at considerable cost. Alternatively, the bank can meet demands for redemption by issuing more liabil-ities, but it must be able to reassure its potential creditors that it is still sound. As it continues to borrow, potential creditors might come to doubt its soundness and the cost of further borrowing would rise. A bank thus faces increasing marginal redemption costs regardless of whether it tries to meet redemptions by running down assets or issuing more debt, and these redemption costs are the reason runs can impose real damage to the banks involved.

Goodhart then suggests that bankers might establish a club to help them handle the problems runs pose. He maintains, nonetheless, that there are a variety of reasons why banks cannot achieve the best outcome on their own and he infers from these that a bankers' club needs help from an outside source (i.e. the state). The reasons he gives fall under three broad headings.

First, he claims that there are certain general problems in the structure of private banking clubs that official regulation could be expected to overcome. One problem is that the rules can be rigged to restrict new entrants or benefit those in charge of key committees (Goodhart 1988: 71). Another is that one cannot always take the independence of club managers for granted, and he cites as an example the refusal of the New York clearinghouse Association to assist the Knickerbocker Trust in 1907 for essentially sectarian reasons (ibid.: 38–9). He also maintains that it 'may well be impossible to check whether club members are obeying the regulations without spot checks, close monitoring, etc.' which he believes would 'be intolerable between competing members' (ibid.: 71). Finally, he suggests that heterogeneity among the members might make it difficult for private clubs to maintain their cohesion, and that government-imposed rules might be required to protect the club's integrity (ibid.: 71)

Second, he suggests that a private club would be unsuited to carry out rescue operations. The 'usual circumstances of a rescue, at very short notice under conditions of severely limited information, make it more difficult for commercial banks to act conclusively than for an independent Central Bank to act swiftly and decisively' (Goodhart 1988: 102). This difficulty in mounting operations is partly due to the influence of commercial rivalry (ibid.: 43–4), partly due to the consideration that crises require 'leadership' that can only be provided by a 'non-competitive, non-profit-maximizing body' that is 'above the competitive battle' (ibid.: 45), and partly due to differences about the appropriate level of support leading to support being watered down to the level of the 'lowest common denominator' (ibid.: 45).

Third, Goodhart argues that only some form of external control can dampen down the cycles to which the banking system is otherwise prone. He cites approvingly an old argument that

> competitive pressures would drive the banks to seek to maintain and expand market shares during normal (noncrisis) periods . . . [and that] during such periods . . . the more conservative banks would lose market share. With the public often being poorly informed, or incapable of discerning whether slower growth was due to conservative policies or lack of managerial effort and efficiency, there was no guarantee that the more conservative banks could recover during panics . . . the market share lost in good times.
>
> (Goodhart 1988: 47–8).

Assuming that these cycles pose a problem that needs to be dealt with, one might ask why a 'private' bankers' club could not deal with them. Goodhart's position seems to be that such a club could not be expected to match the independence and leadership that a central bank could show. He goes on to suggest the LDC debt crisis as an example of the way that profit-maximizing commercial banks can get themselves into this kind of trouble:

> The recent history of the rapid expansion of international bank lending to sovereign LDCs during the 1970s, the resulting crisis, and the subsequent cessation of further voluntary lending would appear to provide an excellent example of this syndrome. Competitive behavior seemed to force all the major banks to take part in an undue expansion of lending . . . the evidence seems incontrovertible that without the intervention of the IMF, and the support of national Central Banks, the crisis in, and after, 1982, arising from these events, would have been contagious, far-reaching, and probably disastrous on a massive scale.
>
> (Goodhart 1988: 48–9)

These arguments need to be considered closely. One point to note, as with Gorton and Mullineaux, is that Goodhart does not show why banks would prefer a club to outright merger, but even if a satisfactory explanation is given to this point, a number of other difficulties remain.

It is true that club rules can be rigged, and that members may use their positions on key committees to pursue their own ends, and it is also true that one cannot take the independence of managers for granted, but the basic answer to these points is that setting up and running a bankers' club, like any other club, is a non-trivial principal-agent problem. All we can really say is that the incentive is there for the principals to deal with these problems in the most appropriate way, so we might presume that they would do so. Club members will generally try to minimize antisocial behaviour on the part of club officials because they would expect to bear the costs of it. They will therefore write contracts with officials that encourage propriety and independence, and they will usually have their activities monitored. The argument about founder-members rigging the rules against later banks is also difficult to substantiate in any depth.[13] And there is in any case the plausible counter-argument that founder-members will be aware that the benefits of a bankers' club tend to rise, and proportionate fixed costs fall, with the number of members, and this reasoning suggests that the club will often find itself trying to attract new members instead of trying to keep them out.[14] In short, while members will never manage to eradicate antisocial behaviour in the club, they have an incentive to minimize the damage it does, and it is not clear why we would expect an outside body with different (i.e. public choice) incentives to produce a superior outcome.

Goodhart suggests that member-banks will find monitoring by fellow-banks intolerable, but that is exactly why they might delegate the task to independent clearinghouse officials. Member-banks might not like being monitored, but they will appreciate that loans would be more difficult and possibly more expensive to obtain if they refused to submit to it. Finally, regarding the argument about the cohesion of clubs, it is not clear why cohesion should be an end in itself. If individual banks perceive their own private interest correctly and choose not to join, then they regard the costs of membership as exceeding the benefits, and it is not clear why we would want to force them to join against their will. We cannot be confident that a club will benefit its members unless they join voluntarily.[15]

Then there is the issue of whether a private club can handle a crisis. It is true that a group of banks might find it difficult to act decisively and in concert in a crisis, and there might be some tendency for the level of support to sink to the level of the lowest common denominator, but it is precisely because of factors like these that we would expect them to delegate crisis-handling to a clearinghouse. We would not normally expect the banks to wait for a crisis to find out the benefits of decisive action and leadership. They would anticipate the way in which a crisis should be handled and delegate appropriate powers. In this they are much like representative systems of government in which it is anticipated that certain types of situation are best handled by delegating emergency powers to the executive. One must also bear in mind that there needs to be some mechanism to restrict the abuse of emergency powers, and the best way to prevent abuse of any powers is for member-banks to make the rules and hold clearinghouse officials responsible. Leadership has its uses, but it needs to be circumscribed to prevent its overuse. This is why parliaments typically hold their executives to account for the way their emergency powers have been used, and the danger with the leadership provided by Goodhart's central bank is that the commercial banks cannot easily restrain it or hold it to account. If clearinghouse leadership corresponds to parliamentary government, the leadership of a central bank is more like a dictatorship which has a tendency to provide too much leadership and be unresponsive to the desires of those whom it is meant to serve.

Lastly, there is the argument that competitive behaviour would lead banks to engage in excessive cycling, but this argument also has its problems. A bank that engages in a policy of aggressive expansion will tend to experience a deterioration in the average quality of its loans, its portfolio may become unbalanced, it may have to bid more for deposits, and so on, and these factors will undermine its longer-run solvency and increase the chances it will face an eventual run. It is not obvious why it would want to pursue such a policy unless it believed that it could pass off some of the costs onto others, and it is doubtful that it could do that under competitive conditions. It would only be able to count on assistance from a private clearinghouse to the extent that it could 'fool' clearinghouse officials into believing that its policies were sound, and the latter would be on their guard against just that eventuality. Nor is there any reason to believe that it could force more conservative banks to go along with a more aggressive policy. It could probably expect to earn some easy profits in the short term, but if they are willing to forgo the lure of quick profits, the more conservative banks could expect to increase their market shares in the longer run when the aggressive bank runs into difficulties.

In the final analysis, the public want stability from their banks, and the banks that provide stability will eventually win out over the cowboys who aim for quick profits.[16] Goodhart might still claim that this is not what happened with the LDC debt crisis, but the debt crisis can hardly be considered an example of what banks will do under *laissez-faire*. Many national monetary authorities were actively encouraging commercial banks to provide loans to the Third World, and the banks could reasonably expect a bailout if their loans turned sour. While no one is disputing that the banks overexpanded their lending, that overexpansion can be plausibly attributed to official policies, and there is no particular reason to believe that a crisis as severe as this one would have occurred had the banks had to rely on their own resources.

Concluding remarks

Two broad conclusions suggest themselves. Recent claims to the contrary notwithstanding, banking regulation and central banking apparently did not evolve to counter inherent deficiencies in (free) financial markets. Real-world banking regulations must therefore have developed for other reasons than market failures, and the most obvious reasons are political ones. The other, complementary, conclusion is that the development of official regulations and central banking were not Pareto improvements over the free market, and cannot therefore be justified on efficiency grounds. The free bankers appear to be right after all – central banking did not evolve to counter market failure, and it presumably cannot be defended by market failure arguments.

6 The invisible hand and the evolution of the monetary system

This chapter re-examines the old question of the desirability of monetary *laissez faire*. However, instead of using standard neo-classical analysis, with its emphasis on formal optimization, it examines monetary *laissez-faire* from the viewpoint of conjectural history: it investigates how the monetary system might plausibly evolve from some initial primitive state, driven primarily by the self-interested behaviour of the parties involved, and without any form of government intervention.

Why a conjectural history approach? Part of the answer is that a conjectural history provides a simple but insightful way of explaining the functions of the various institutions involved in the development of the monetary system. For example, in the story of the goldsmiths, it provides an elegant and powerful explanation for the emergence of paper currency. A conjectural history also provides an effective way of examining a relatively unfamiliar system such as monetary *laissez-faire*. Seeing the conjectural history unfold gives us a feel for how *laissez-faire* might actually work, and also helps to break the conditioning against it that most of us were taught when we first learned our economics. The conjectural history helps us to counter such preconceptions and see the *laissez-faire* system for what it is. Instead of appearing odd because it has no central bank, *laissez-faire* then comes across as very natural, and it is the departures from *laissez-faire* that appear out of place, or at least in need of justification.

A conjectural history provides a benchmark to help assess the world we live in, but it is important to appreciate that it is not meant to provide an accurate historical description of how the world actually evolved. The conjectural history is a useful myth, and it is no criticism of a conjectural history to say that the world failed to evolve in the way that it postulates. Imagine that it could be proved beyond doubt that the Doge of Venice in the sixteenth century had been shrewd enough to recognize that a bank need not maintain a 100 per cent reserve ratio:

> What then of our goldsmiths' story? Does the fact that the Doge beat the invisible-hand [i.e. conjectural history] explanation to it rob the invisible-

hand explanation of its explanatory import? I suggest that the answer is No, and that the argument for this answer goes beyond the mere 'feeling' that we may have that the account of how something could have arisen without anyone devising it is 'interesting' or 'illuminating' in its own right. The argument . . . is that even if the invisible-hand explanation turns out not to be the correct account of how the thing *emerged*, it may still not be devoid of validity with regard to the question of how (and why) it is *maintained*. . . . The availability . . . of a cogent invisible-hand story of how the pattern in question could have arisen . . . may, I believe, contribute to our understanding of the inherently self-reinforcing nature of this pattern and hence of its being successful and lasting.

(Ullman-Margalit 1978: 275; her emphasis)

The conjectural history therefore helps to explain why certain institutions persist – regardless of its historical accuracy – and this in turn helps illustrate the functions they perform.

Apart from wishing to investigate the desirability (or otherwise) of monetary *laissez-faire*, it also makes sense to focus on *laissez-faire* for methodological reasons. One reason is that there is a sense in which the analysis of *laissez-faire* (or anarchy, if one prefers) must logically come before the study of other forms of social order. We cannot assess claims for the necessity of some form of government intervention – the establishment of a central bank, say – without analysing the properties of a social order in which this intervention is absent. For example, to claim that central banking is superior to free banking is to imply the existence of a problem inherent in free banking that central banking puts right, and we cannot justify such a claim without some study of the properties of a free banking system: we must analyse the system without the intervention if we are to be able to assess whether the intervention itself is justified. Dealing with a *laissez-faire* social order also has the advantage that it helps us to focus on the extent to which the solutions to social problems emerge or fail to emerge spontaneously from 'within' the social order, without relying on the *deus ex machina* of state intervention to sort them out. The individuals involved then either solve those problems for themselves or else have to live with them unsolved.

However, if we introduce the government into the picture, we tend to underrate the extent to which the parties involved can solve their problems and we create a corresponding temptation to see state intervention as the solution to whatever problem we are dealing with. All too often, a writer will identify a problem, think of a way in which the government can ameliorate it, and presume that he has found a 'solution'. Assuming the government away provides a mental discipline that helps us avoid the distraction of such spurious 'solutions' and concentrate on the real issue – the extent to which individuals in society can solve their own problems.

The early evolution of the economy

Suppose we begin with an initial 'primitive', anarchic, state of society. Individuals live in groups (e.g. clans), have well-defined preferences, and have endowments consisting of various commodities, chattels, and natural abilities. Individuals can combine these endowments with their own time and effort to produce goods (e.g. they can harvest food) and engage in other economic activity (i.e. exchange and consumption) to improve their well-being. To begin with, most economic activity is organized hierarchically, there is little exchange between groups or between individuals within groups, and concepts of private property are primitive.

However, over time people gradually discover that they can make themselves better off by exchange, and the practice of barter spreads. Trade is initially more or less sporadic (e.g. potential trading partners meet each other randomly as in Jones 1976), but as it spreads a set of social conventions develops spontaneously around it. These relate to good places to find trading partners, the rules of bargaining, and so on. These conventions reduce the costs to individuals of searching for trading partners and carrying out trades with them. The trading process therefore becomes more orderly, and trading fairs and markets gradually evolve at which people meet every so often to exchange their goods. At the same time, trade also alters individuals' relationships to their groups. Individual activity is increasingly directed at people outside their group, and the old group hierarchy slowly breaks down. Individuals form new relationships with each other, and principal among these are firms, organizations in which some individuals agree to take certain kinds of orders from others, in return for agreed compensation. Firms enable certain types of activities to be co-ordinated more efficiently than would otherwise be the case, and thereby enable individuals to reap specialization gains that would otherwise be unobtainable (as explained, e.g., by Coase 1937). As time goes on, an increasing proportion of economic activity is carried on through markets and firms, people become increasingly specialized, and the older groups lose their distinctiveness and gradually merge into a unified economy.

Indirect exchange and the emergence of a dominant medium of exchange

Yet barter has the drawback that trade can only take place if individuals overcome both coincidence of wants and coincidence of timing problems (see e.g. Goodhart 1989: 2). A lot of search – and consequently a lot of (valuable) time – is therefore typically required to carry out a trade, and the outcome of a search is often very uncertain. At some point, individuals therefore start to resort to indirect exchange; instead of accepting only for the good they want to consume, they accept another good with the intention of exchanging that for the good they are really looking for. If the intermediate good is well-chosen, an individual who resorts to indirect exchange ought to be able to obtain the good he wants with less difficulty than he otherwise would and reduce his overall trading costs (e.g. Menger 1892: 247–9).

A good choice of intermediate commodity would be a good that is heavily traded, so that the person who has the commodity one wants will be more likely to accept the commodity one has to offer, but also have a readily recognizable exchange value, be easily portable and non-perishable. Over time, individuals gradually switch to indirect exchange and converge on these kinds of goods to carry out their trades, and this convergence makes these goods even more saleable and therefore further increases their desirability as intermediate goods (ibid.: 250–2). In the end this self-reinforcing process leads to a relatively small number of goods – and perhaps only one – becoming generally accepted as the dominant intermediate good(s). Historically, the preferred intermediary goods have often been precious metals. These were well-suited to be intermediate goods because their quantity and quality were relatively easy to assess, compared to most other goods, and the fact that their value was high relative to their weight meant that storage and transport costs were relatively low (ibid.: 252–5). For the sake of simplicity, we can assume that the process converges on one single good – gold – as the dominant intermediary commodity.

The unit of account

The use of an intermediate commodity considerably simplifies the exchange process. Individuals with goods to sell need look only for individuals with the recognized intermediary good, and trade fairs now become much simpler because of the associated reduction in the number of trading posts. If there are n goods to be traded, there would be $n(n - 1)/2$ separate trading posts under pure barter, one for each pair of goods. However, with a dominant intermediary good, the number of trading posts can be cut to $(n - 1)$: one trading post for every commodity to be exchanged for the intermediate good, and an individual with a particular good to sell need only operate (or look for) a single trading post, instead of the $(n - 1)$ separate posts that previously dealt with his good under barter. Indirect exchange also means that he need keep account of only $(n - 1)$ exchange ratios (or prices) instead of having to keep account of $n(n - 1)/2$ exchange ratios as he did before.

Since the intermediary good, gold, is now handed over in most (if not all) trades, it is natural that prices – the exchange rates of goods – be quoted in terms of gold weights. A trader with a good to sell (buy) will post prices in terms of the weight of gold he is willing to accept (pay):

A seller pursues his self-interest by posting prices in terms of the media of exchange he is routinely prepared to accept. This practice economizes on time spent in negotiation over what commodities are acceptable in payment and at what rate of exchange. More importantly, it economizes on the information necessary for the buyer's and the seller's economic calculation. Posting prices in terms of a numeraire commodity not routinely accepted in payment, by contrast, would force buyer and seller to know and agree upon the numeraire price of the payment media due. This numeraire price of the payment medium would naturally be subject to fluctuation, so that updated information would be necessary. A non-exchange-medium-numeraire would furthermore be subject to greater bid-ask spreads in barter against other commodities, as by hypothesis it is less saleable, than the medium of exchange. It would therefore serve less well as a tool of economic calculation.

(White 1984b: 704)

The economy has now evolved to the point where gold is not only used as the dominant 'medium of exchange', but where agents also use gold units to express the prices of other goods. Gold therefore provides the 'medium of account', and the 'unit of account' – the unit in terms of which prices are expressed – is a specified weight of gold. A good real-world example of this evolutionary process is the famous prisoner of war camp described by Radford:

Starting with simple direct barter, such as a non-smoker giving a smoker friend his cigarette issue in exchange for a chocolate ration, more complex exchanges soon became an accepted custom. . . . Within a week or two, as the volume of trade grew, rough scales of exchange values came into existence. . . . It was realised that a tin of jam was worth 1/2 lb. of margarine plus something else; that a cigarette issue was worth several chocolate issues, and a tin of diced carrots was worth practically nothing. . . . By the end of a month, when we reached our permanent camp, there was a lively trade in all commodities and their relative values were well-known, and expressed not in terms of one another – one didn't quote bully in terms of sugar – but in terms of cigarettes. The cigarette became the standard of value. . . . [Everyone,] including non-smokers, was willing to sell for cigarettes, using them to buy at another time and place. Cigarettes became the normal currency . . .

(Radford 1945: 191)

. . . and so became both medium of exchange and medium (and unit) of account. In our hypothetical economy, gold is both medium of exchange and medium of account, and the unit of account is a particular unit of gold. If we call this unit the dollar, we can then say that prices are expressed in terms of dollars, but the dollar itself is a specific amount of gold.

The evolution of coinage

Although gold might be the most convenient intermediate good to use, it still leaves individuals with the inconvenience of having to assess the weight and purity of heterogeneous lumps of gold. To avoid this inconvenience, traders begin to deal in standardized lumps of gold (e.g. gold rings or bars) and put their own marks on them so that they do not need to reassess their value when they next see them. A trader can then look at the marking and shape of any piece of gold he is offered, and if he recognizes them he can have some confidence that they are of their claimed weight and dispense with the inconvenience of weighing them again.

We thus arrive at the beginning of coinage. There is now a demand for readily authenticated pieces of gold, and mints arise to meet this demand by casting gold into coins and charging a fee for the service. Since the demand for each mint's service depends on the reputation of its coins, each mint has an incentive to maintain its reputation by making it as difficult as possible to tamper with its coins without being detected (e.g. by making coins round, so that tampering is more easily detected), and by issuing coins of full-bodied weight. Market forces will also lead mints to issue coins of standardized weight and fineness, so coins will be issued in standard dollar amounts: any mint that issued non-standardized coins would impose additional inconvenience on its customers and have to charge a lower minting fee to compensate them, and would therefore find it difficult to survive against competitors who issued standardized coins.[1]

The development of banking and the adoption of bank currency

The development of bank currency

A natural further development is the development of bank currency and its gradual displacement of gold coinage as the dominant medium of exchange. One way to think about this process is suggested by the familiar story of the goldsmiths, and this story of course also gives us one account of how banks might evolve. The use of coins still involves considerable costs, particularly those of storing, protecting and moving coins around. To save on some of these costs, some people would be prepared to pay others with the means to do so to store their gold for them. Goldsmiths and some merchants would already have facilities to keep large amounts of gold, and could therefore keep additional quantities of it at a relatively low marginal cost. These people would find it profitable to accept gold for safekeeping for a fee that many current holders of gold would be willing to pay, and depositors would be issued with receipts that gave them the right to demand their gold back. As the practice of making gold deposits spreads, it increasingly happens that when two parties agree to an exchange, one would go and withdraw his gold, and then hand it over to the other who would promptly deposit it again, often with the same goldsmith. Provided that the party accepting payment was satisfied that the goldsmith would still honour his commitment to pay back the gold, it would be more convenient for him simply to accept the goldsmith's receipt and save everyone the trouble of withdrawing the gold and depositing it again. The receipts of goldsmiths therefore begin to circulate as media of exchange in their own right, and the practice of using such receipts as exchange media will gradually replace the older practice of using gold coins. The receipts now become banknotes, and the goldsmiths who issue them become bankers.

The development of fractional-reserve and deposit banking

As time passes, the goldsmith-bankers notice that demands for redemption and new deposits of gold largely tend to cancel each other out over most periods, and so net withdrawals are generally quite low. They then realize that they could lend out much of the gold deposited with them to earn interest on it, and yet still face little danger of being unable to meet depositors' demands for redemption. They therefore start to lend out the gold (i.e. they reduce their reserve ratios below 100 per cent) and then compete for additional gold deposits to lend out. Their competition eliminates the earlier fees charged for accepting deposits, and they are soon offering interest payments to attract deposits. As bank currency is increasingly used as an exchange medium, bank borrowers increasingly accept loans of bank currency instead of loans of gold, and so the banks can make loans simply by issuing more of their own currency. The practice of making gold loans then gradually diminishes, and gold loans have effectively disappeared by the time that gold itself has lost its role as medium of exchange. In the end, the banks only hold gold because they need it to satisfy public demands for redemption.[2]

The convertibility of bank currency and the 'law of reflux'

While bank currency is increasingly used as a medium of exchange, competition still forces the banks to keep their currency – their notes and deposits – convertible into gold. These liabilities are legally binding promises on the part of the bank that issued them to redeem them (i.e. buy them back) under the conditions called for in the contract, and those conditions will normally call for the bank to do so on demand. The holder of a $1 bill – which is legally only a claim to a dollar, not a dollar itself – will therefore have the right to demand redemption for one dollar (i.e. for gold), and a bank that failed to meet such a demand would expose itself to the penalty for defaulting on a contract.

To see why banks would maintain the convertibility of their currency, we have to appreciate that convertibility is a guarantee that their currency will retain its value in terms of gold. A bank cannot simply discontinue convertibility without notice, since it would be bound to honour the contractual promise on outstanding currency to redeem it when required to. A bank could therefore only abandon convertibility by announcing its intention to retire its convertible currency and replace it with inconvertible currency, and any potential currency-holder would interpret such an announcement as an indication that the bank intended to allow the value of its currency to depreciate. If the bank has no such intention, why would it want to dispense with the convertibility guarantee? A currency-holder will therefore refuse to accept the inconvertible currency, and the bank will lose its market share to those competitors who are willing to provide the public with the convertible currency they wanted. To abandon convertibility unilaterally is thus tantamount to surrendering one's market share to rivals. Indeed, even if the banks as a whole organized a concerted abandonment of convertibility, they would still have no way to prevent new banks from undercutting them by offering the public the convertible currency they want. Any concerted abandonment of convertibility would *ipso facto* create profit opportunities for new entrants who were willing to satisfy the public demand for convertible currency, and all the banks that abandon convertibility would lose their market share. Under conditions of free entry, the threat of potential competition prevents even the banks as a whole from being able to abandon the convertibility guarantee. Competition among the banks forces them to maintain convertibility because the public demand it.

The commitment to maintain convertibility then implies that banks can only keep in circulation those issues the public are willing to hold. If a bank issues more currency than the public want to hold, the excess issues will be returned and banks will be legally compelled to redeem them: a 'law of reflux' operates by which unwanted issues are returned to the banks who must redeem them. The circulation of bank currency is then limited by the demand to hold them. Banks cannot issue currency and keep it in circulation, without the public demand to hold them. If a bank wishes to increase its currency circulation, it must therefore increase the public demand for its currency: it must fight more aggressively for market share, open more branches, improve its reputation, advertise more, and so forth.

Bank safety and soundness

Since a bank will normally find it profitable to operate on a fractional reserve, it will not have the gold on hand to redeem all its outstanding notes and deposits if they were all presented for redemption at once. The bank can therefore only continue to operate if it can persuade a major proportion of its creditors not to demand redemption, and it can only do that if it maintains their confidence by persuading them that their investments are safe (i.e. that they can get their money back any time they want it), so that over any given period of time most of them will feel no need to redeem.

In order to provide this reassurance, the bank must persuade its customers that its finances are sound – that is, the bank must be seen as having a sufficiently high net worth (or capitalization) that it can not only pay off current debts, but could still pay them off even in plausible bad-case scenarios where it suffered major losses on its loan portfolio. If a bank has a sufficiently high capitalization that it can withstand any plausible losses and still pay off its creditors without too much difficulty, then those creditors can be reasonably confident that their investments are safe. A bank can also take measures to maintain its soundness by issuing subordinated debt, avoiding excessive risks in its lending, employing qualified and reliable staff, and having its books regularly audited and its credit-worthiness regularly rated.

If it is to retain the confidence of its customers, the bank must also maintain its ability to meet demands for redemption when they should arise (i.e. it should protect its liquidity). At the very minimum, a bank must maintain a certain amount of gold coins, relative to its outstanding demandable liabilities, so that it could meet unforeseen demands for redemption. Given that such reserves are costly to hold, the bank will need to trade off the liquidity benefits of holding them against their holding costs, but experience over time will indicate what an appropriate reserve ratio might be. The bank would also supplement this 'primary' liquid reserve by holding 'secondary' reserves consisting of assets that were less expensive to hold, but could be sold quickly at relatively little cost, if the bank needed to buy more reserves. It could also take out credit lines with other institutions, giving it the right to draw credit if it needed to. Should the bank be faced with unexpected demands for redemption, it would respond in the first instance by drawing down its primary reserve. If the demands continued, it would replenish its gold reserves by drawing down credit lines it had taken out earlier, by taking out new loans, or by selling some of its secondary reserve assets.

Provided the bank maintains its soundness, it should have little difficulty obtaining the loans it needs, and it can be reasonably confident of being able to protect its liquidity and meet redemption demands without defaulting. Indeed, those redeeming a bank's liabilities would have no desire to hold gold as such, but would convert them into other assets instead. Much of the gold would therefore be redeposited in the banking system. Other banks would then be flush with gold and, provided they were satisfied about the soundness of the bank wanting the loan, it would be in their interests to lend to it. A sound bank should therefore have no real difficulty obtaining the gold it needs.

The irony is that a bank that protects its soundness and liquidity would be very unlikely to face large demands for redemption precisely because its creditors would have confidence in it. The very fact that it can persuade its creditors that they could have their funds back whenever they want them is usually enough to ensure that most of them will not want to redeem – in most cases there is no point demanding redemption if one's investment in the bank appears to be safe. The bottom line is that although a safe and liquid bank always faces the theoretical possibility of a run, a run will not actually occur unless something happens that shatters public confidence and gives creditors explicit reason to fear for the safety of their funds. However, if a bank fails to take appropriate measures to maintain its soundness, a point will come when creditors lose confidence and run, and the bank will have difficulty withstanding the run when it occurs. A run thus serves the socially useful purpose of putting a 'bad' bank out of business, and the potential threat of a run keeps the other banks healthy by forcing them to keep their houses in order.[3]

Financial instruments replace gold as redemption media

While banks need to protect themselves against demands for redemption, they also have an incentive to reduce the cost of the reserves they hold to meet such demands. These costs will fall anyway as the banking system develops, because public demands for redemption will fall as their confidence in banks gradually grows, and the lower demands for redemption imply that the banks can operate on lower reserve ratios. However, at some point the banks will reduce these costs further by offering alternative, lower-cost redemption media instead of gold. We must keep in mind that gold is still relatively costly to store and hold, and bears no explicit return, while financial instruments involve lower holding costs and often yield explicit returns for the holder. It is therefore in a bank's interest to offer to redeem its liabilities using less costly redemption media, and it is in the public's interest to prefer such redemption media to gold.

To qualify as a suitable redemption medium, an asset should have a value largely independent of the bank that uses it as a redemption medium (i.e. the bank cannot redeem its own liabilities using more of the same). Obvious examples are the debt or equity of other firms, including the debt or equity of another bank. If a bank uses a financial instrument instead of gold as a redemption medium there may be a possibility that the issuer would default, that the asset would fall in value, and so on, but if members of the public were not satisfied with a particular redemption medium they could always refuse to accept it (e.g. by refusing to accept bank debt that specified that particular redemption medium). If the public accept a particular redemption medium, the very fact that they do so implies that they consider that redemption medium to be at least 'as good as gold' and that they are willing to accept any risks that its use entails.

Banks now redeem their issues, not with a particular *weight* of gold as they did before, but with financial instruments (or other redemption media) of the same *value* as that weight of gold. The earlier directly convertible gold standard in which banks redeemed their liabilities directly with gold has thus given way to an indirectly convertible gold standard in which they redeem their liabilities with something else.[4] The only remaining 'monetary' purpose of gold is now to provide a definition for the dollar.

The development of a mature *laissez-faire* monetary system

The unit of account, the price level and the gold anchor

However, the unit of account, the dollar, is still legally defined as a particular weight of gold and, legally speaking, a banknote with a face value of $1 is still only a claim to a dollar. Nonetheless, by this stage in the economy's evolution gold will have disappeared from circulation, and when he posts a price of one dollar in his shop window the vendor indicates that he is willing to accept a dollar note issued by a reputable bank rather than gold. Indeed, since gold has disappeared from circulation he might be quite unfamiliar with gold coins and even be unwilling to accept them. The dollar note would be more liquid than gold itself, even though the dollar note was legally only a claim to some redemption medium of the same value as the gold dollar. What this means is that even though the dollar is still legally defined in terms of a particular weight of gold, the term 'dollar' as used in everyday trade by now refers to the units in which exchange media are denominated (i.e. to what might be referred to as the 'banknote dollar') and not to units of gold or gold dollars. There is an important distinction between the term 'dollar' in everyday use, which refers to the bank-currency dollar, and the legal definition of the dollar, which refers to the value of a particular amount of gold.

Given this distinction between the bank-currency dollar and the (gold) dollar itself, we can now say that when they issue convertible currency, banks do so according to a rule by which they maintain the price of gold in terms of bank-currency dollars. The fixed bank-currency price of gold then ties down the market price of gold by unleashing arbitrage forces to return the market price of gold to its fixed 'par' value should it ever depart from it. If the price of gold on the market rises significantly above the par value maintained by the banks, arbitragers would make a profit by redeeming currency for redemption media, selling the redemption media for bank currency and ending up with more currency than they started with. In the process, the outstanding quantity of currency would fall, and the falling quantity of currency would put downward pressure on the market price of gold in terms of bank currency. Conversely, if the market price of gold were to fall too low, arbitragers would demand more currency from the banks and use the currency obtained in this way to buy more redemption media, and end up with more redemption media than they started with. The supply of bank currency would rise, and the market price of gold would rise back towards par. Any discrepancy of the market price of gold from the 'par' price maintained by the banks would set in motion arbitrage forces that would return the market price to par.

The price level under this system is then determined by the forces that determine the relative price of gold against goods and services in general. Since the nominal price of gold is effectively fixed by the rules of the indirectly convertible gold standard, the relative price of gold can therefore move if, and only if, there is a corresponding, opposite, change in the price level. The relative price of gold will rise if, and only if, the price level falls, and vice versa. Hence, any factor that causes the relative price of gold to rise will cause the price level to fall, and any factor that causes the relative price of gold to fall will cause the price level to rise. For example, an event such as unexpected discovery of gold ore will lead to a greater gold supply. Given the demand for gold, the gold market will only equilibrate if the price of gold falls relative to goods and services. Since the nominal price of gold is fixed, the relative price of gold can only fall if the price level itself rises. Hence, the gold discovery leads to a higher price level. Conversely, a factor such as a rise in the demand for gold will lead to a rise in the relative price of gold, and the relative price of gold can only rise if the price level falls. A rise in the demand for gold will therefore lead to a fall in the price level.

The replacement of the gold anchor

The price level under the gold standard depends on supply and demand in the gold market, but these factors are unlikely to produce the degree of price-level stability that the individuals living in our economy would prefer. The price-level instability produced by the gold standard would impose various costs on the public, and they would find it harder to distinguish between 'true' price signals and 'irrelevant' price noise, and therefore make 'mistaken' decisions they would otherwise have avoided; they would have less peace of mind about the future; and so forth. A time would therefore come when the banks would decide to reduce price-level instability by changing the gold 'anchor' that ties down the nominal price level.

Given that the price level under the gold standard is only as stable as the relative price of gold, the banks could generate a more stable price level by replacing the gold price-level anchor with an alternative anchor based on a commodity or commodities with a more stable relative price. The most likely candidate would be a basket of goods and services rather than any single alternative commodity. The banks would then announce that from a certain future date onwards they would use the term 'dollar' in new contracts to refer, not to a particular amount of gold as previously, but to a particular amount of a specified basket of goods and services (or something equivalent). This new 'basket dollar' would have the same value as the earlier gold dollar on the day it was first introduced, so as to avoid any jumps in the relative price of the 'anchor' (and, hence, the price level) when the new dollar was brought in, and the public would accept the new basket dollar because they themselves would prefer the greater price-level stability it would produce.[5]

The monetary standard has now evolved into an indirectly convertible system based on a commodity-basket anchor chosen for its desirable price-level properties. Gold no longer has any 'monetary' purposes whatsoever: as medium of exchange, medium of redemption or unit of account. The only vestige of gold in the monetary system is the use of the old term 'dollar' – a term which used to refer to a particular weight of gold – as the name of the unit of account, and even the dollar is now legally defined in terms of a basket of goods and services. Gold no longer has any substantial role to play in the monetary system.

International dimensions

Under *laissez-faire* conditions, we might expect similar monetary systems to develop more or less across the world. We would also expect the various local and regional economies, which were initially separate from each other, to coalesce into one, increasingly integrated, world economy. What kind of international monetary system will result? One possibility is that this world economy will use only one currency unit (e.g. the dollar), whose value would be tied to some particular commodity anchor. However, it is also possible that different currency units might co-exist with each other, each dominant in some particular part of the world (e.g. dollars in the US, pounds in the UK, and so on). If there is more than one currency unit, one or more of these would be primary currency units tied to specific commodity anchors, and those units that were not specifically tied to commodity anchors would be tied at fixed rates of exchange to other currency units that were. All currency units would be tied – directly or indirectly – to commodity anchors.

If there was only one primary currency unit, we would have a situation reminiscent of the post-war Bretton Woods system, under which other currencies were tied to the dollar, and the dollar was tied to a 'basket' of gold. However, the dollar would now be tied to a broader commodity basket rather than gold. All exchange rates would now be fixed, since there would be only one primary currency unit and all others would be tied to it.

It is also possible that there might be more than one primary currency unit, each of which was fixed to its own commodity anchor. The exchange rates between the primary currency units would then fluctuate with changes in the relative prices of the anchor baskets. However, these baskets should have fairly stable relative prices if we assume that each anchor is chosen to stabilize some price index. Exchange rate changes should therefore be relatively small and infrequent. Any other currencies, if there are any, would then be tied to one of these primary currencies. Each of these satellite currencies would therefore have a fixed exchange rate against the primary unit to which it was tethered, and also against any other satellite currencies tied to the same primary unit, and a (slightly) floating exchange rate against all other currencies. This would engender a series of currency blocs, each of which was a fixed-exchange-rate system based on a primary currency, and exchange rates between these various blocs would fluctuate (slightly) against each other.

However, even if there is more than one currency unit in use, there would be no reason for the number of currency units under *laissez-faire* to reflect the number of nation states, as is (just about) the case under the current system. Under *laissez-faire*, there would be no link between a currency unit and a nation state, and so no reason for currency areas to match national territories. Indeed, since there are considerable benefits when people use the same currency unit (e.g. lower accounting costs and no currency-exchange costs), we might expect the *laissez-faire* currency areas to be larger on average than present currency areas, and also better aligned to economic fundamentals such as trading patterns.

In sum, *laissez-faire* would give us one of three possible monetary arrangements: a single currency unit used throughout the world, and tied to a specified commodity anchor; a system of fixed exchange rates, in which all other currencies are tied to one key currency, which is itself anchored to a particular commodity anchor; or a system of fixed-exchange-rate currency blocs fluctuating a little against each other, each of which would be tethered to a particular anchor. If there are multiple currency units, we would also expect them to cover larger areas than present-day units, and to cover areas that made more economic sense.

The evolution of the monetary system under *laissez-faire*: an overview

It perhaps useful at this point to pause and consider the main stages of development of our hypothetical monetary system under *laissez-faire*. These stages are summarized in Table 6.1. The first stage – the Age of Mints – is that in which full-bodied gold coins reign as the dominant medium of exchange (MOE), and these same coins also provide the medium of account (MOA) – the medium in units of which prices are expressed.

This first stage then gives way to the second, in which banks arise and issue currency, and this bank currency displaces coins as the dominant MOE. This second stage is a textbook gold standard, in which bank currency circulates as the main exchange medium, but this currency is denominated in units of gold and banks stand ready to redeem their currency for gold. Gold therefore functions as MOA (or, if one prefers, unit of account (UA)), as the anchor of the system, and as the banks' medium of redemption (MOR). Relative to the previous stage, gold has lost its function as MOE but acquired a new function as MOR.

The third stage arises as banks replace gold with less costly redemption media – financial instruments, and so on – and the gold standard becomes indirectly convertible: instead of being convertible directly into given amounts of gold, bank currency is now convertible into redemption media of the same value as those given amounts of gold. Gold retains its function as MOA/UA and anchor, but has now lost its function as MOR.

The fourth and final stage is where gold is replaced as MOA/UA/anchor by a commodity basket chosen for its more desirable price-level properties. Gold no longer has any substantive monetary role, and the gold standard has been replaced by a commodity-basket standard.

Table 6.1 The stages of development of the monetary system under *laissez-faire*

Stage of Development	Key Features	Comments
Coinage	Gold as MOE Gold as MOA/UA	Use of gold coins as full-bodied money
Directly convertible gold standard	Bank currency as MOE Gold as MOA/UA/anchor Gold as MOR	Textbook gold standard Bank currency displaces coins as MOE
Indirectly convertible gold standard	Bank currency as MOE Gold as MOA/UA/anchor Financial assets as MOR	Financial assets replace gold as MOR
Indirectly convertible commodity-basket standard	Bank currency as MOE Commodity basket as MOA/UA/anchor Financial assets as MOR	Commodity basket replaces gold as MOA/UA/anchor Gold has no monetary role

Note: MOE is medium of exchange; MOA is medium of account; UA is unit of account; and MOR is medium of redemption.

Assessing the *laissez-faire* system

So how does *laissez-faire* actually fare?

Efficiency

One approach is to assess it by its efficiency, and it turns out that the *laissez-faire* system is efficient by virtually any sensible criterion:

- All feasible and mutually beneficial trades take place because there are no barriers to prevent them. The banks provide the public with exactly the exchange media they want, and deposit interest rates, bank charges and the like are all competitively determined. The rents from financial intermediation – from issuing currency, making loans, and so on – are therefore competed away to the public.
- Banks will select appropriate reserve and redemption assets, and optimize their reserve holdings.
- The *laissez-faire* system is also efficient in a dynamic sense: unfettered market forces encourage banks and other parties to innovate and adopt good practices that have been tried elsewhere.
- Competition ensures that banks provide the degree of financial strength their customers want, and are willing to pay for. If the public want stronger (i.e. better capitalized) banks, competition for market share will lead banks to increase their capitalization, and the public will get the stronger banks they want. At the same time, since capital is costly, excessively capitalized banks will not be competitive either, so competition produces banks of optimal strength, bearing in mind the public willingness to pay for it.
- The system is tethered to an anchor chosen to minimize price-level instability, and the costs associated with it.
- The costs of maintaining price-level stability (i.e. the costs of maintaining convertibility, and so on) should be minimal.
- There will either be one currency unit used everywhere, in which case there will be no currency-exchange and other associated costs; or there will be more than one currency in use, in which case currency areas will be aligned to economic fundamentals (i.e. and be optimal, in an appropriate sense).
- Unlike modern central banking systems, this free banking system is also entirely automatic. There is no 'policy problem' as conventionally understood – no need to worry about the incentives faced by the monetary or banking authorities, the time consistency of their policies, and so on – because these authorities do not exist to worry about. Everyone pursues his own self-interest, and all interests are harmonized by the market.

Stability

We can also assess the *laissez-faire* system in terms of its stability, and the *laissez-faire* system is stable in a number of different respects:

- First of all, it is stable in so far as it is self-sustaining: it leaves no group willing and able to overturn some essential feature of it. The *laissez-faire* system is self-sustaining because everyone already pursues their own welfare subject to the various constraints under which they operate. No one therefore has any desire to change their behaviour, given those constraints. In particular, the system does not depend on any 'guardian' who must sacrifice his own welfare and assume an unwanted burden to protect the public good: the safety of the system does not depend on any underpaid night-watchman. Since there is no night-watchman, we do not have to worry about what he might get up to while everyone else is asleep: there is no problem of 'guarding the guardians'.
- *Laissez-faire* also leads to a strong and stable financial system. The public want safe banks, and competition ensures that they get them, by providing financial institutions with incentives to maintain their financial health and cultivate public confidence. A bank that is not regarded as sufficiently strong by the public will lose public confidence, and without public confidence it will lose its market. A bank that wishes to remain in business must satisfy its customers and maintain its financial strength. Such a bank will be able to absorb non-catastrophic loan losses relatively easily and still retain public confidence and, while it will always be subject to the threat of a run, these will not actually occur unless some event shatters public confidence in it. Far from destabilizing banks, as is often supposed, it is the threat of a run that forces banks to maintain their strength in the first place.
- The financial system is also stable in its response to fluctuations in the public demand for bank currency. Banks accommodate changes in the public's demand for currency rapidly and automatically, in much the same way that current banking systems accommodate the public demands to change one form of bank deposit into another, and accommodating these changes does not generally require major disturbances to interest rates, credit markets or economic activity.
- Last, and definitely not least, the *laissez-faire* system is stable in that it delivers price-level stability, and, therefore, among other things, delivers reasonable interest-rate and asset-price stability as well.

The *laissez-faire* system comes out with very high marks, both in terms of its efficiency and in terms of its stability. Indeed, it is hard to see how any system could conceivably fare any better. It is also a vast improvement on our current monetary system, with its excessive proliferation of different currencies; its banking weakness; its chronic instability and often crippling uncertainty; its periodic exchange-rate and other crises; and its near-permanent and, often, catastrophic, inflation. As the lawyers say, *res ipse locitur*; the record of central banking speaks for itself. Which system do you prefer?

7 Are free markets the cause of financial instability?

Most observers would agree that there is something wrong with the world financial system. There is of course far less agreement on what the problems are, but two themes in particular come up repeatedly whenever the subject is raised.

The first is that financial markets are in some sense excessively volatile: that financial prices or rates fluctuate more than is socially desirable because of inherent weaknesses in the ways that markets operate. Different arguments to this effect have been applied to many different financial markets – including the markets for bonds, equities, foreign exchange, commodities, derivatives, and to the financial system generally – by many different writers, including Charles Kindleberger (1978), H. P. Minsky (1982) and, more recently, George Soros (1994, 1998).[1] To quote Soros:

> Instability . . . can give rise to sudden reversals that may take on catastrophic proportions. . . . The prevention of excessive instability is therefore a necessary condition for the smooth functioning of the market mechanism. It is not a condition that the market mechanism can ensure on its own. On the contrary . . . unregulated financial markets tend to become progressively more unstable. . . . Excessive instability can be prevented only by some sort of regulation.
>
> (Soros 1994: 322–3)

A second, related argument is that too many resources are used up in financial activity of one sort or another, again relative to the broader social interest. This claim, too, comes in many different forms: that there is too much financial speculation, that there is too much financial trading activity, that too many resources are used up managing financial risks, that derivatives serve little or no socially useful purpose, and that the financial services sector is too large relative to the real economy.

Both types of financial-market critic believe that they are analysing market failures of one sort or another; in reply, free-market economists often deny that there is any real problem at all. Yet both sides in these debates often share an important, and usually hidden, assumption. The critics tend to assume that they are criticizing *laissez-faire*, and free market economists often assume that they are defending it. To give but one example, Soros (1994: 323) characterizes a world financial system with the regulations he would like to see enacted as 'a nearly free market system', thereby suggesting that what we have now is a totally free one. For their part, free-market economists often respond to this sort of argument by defending a very questionable status quo. One side rushes to attack financial markets, and the other side rushes to defend them, but both sides beg the key issue: the extent to which we can identify the current world financial system as genuine *laissez-faire*.

The world monetary system under *laissez-faire*

To investigate this issue further, we must first clarify what a *laissez-faire* system would probably look like.[2] *Laissez-faire* would mean no central banks, no financial regulatory agencies, and no other government intervention into the financial system, anywhere in the world. There would be no international quasi-governmental financial agencies: no IMF, no World Bank, no Bank for International Settlements, and so forth. Market agents would be free to make whatever financial contracts they wanted, subject only to the general provisions of contract and commercial law (i.e. there would be the usual enforcement of contracts, prohibitions against fraud, and the like).

Under *laissez-faire*, banks would be free to issue whatever currency they wished, but competition for business would force them to make their currencies convertible more or less on demand.[3] The values of different currencies would also be tied to the values of specific baskets of goods and services; these baskets would therefore provide 'anchors' to tie down currency values. The holders of bank currency would then have the right to convert their currency holdings into redemption media of the same value. If a particular bank issued a note or made a deposit denominated in a unit called a dollar, the holder of this note or deposit would have the right to require the bank to convert this holding into some other asset – a lump of gold, or whatever – of the same value. Banks that failed to provide this insurance against depreciation would be driven from the field. Each anchor would likely be chosen to stabilize some target price index (such as the Consumer Price Index in the United States).[4] The anchor would determine the currency's price level and inflation rate, and be a major influence on its exchange rates with other currencies.

The world monetary system might consist of a single world currency or a group of different currencies, each dominant in some particular part of the world (e.g. dollars in the United States). There would be at least one primary currency unit tied to a commodity anchor, and those units that were not specifically tied to such anchors would be tied to currency units that were, at fixed rates of exchange. All currency units would be directly or indirectly tied to commodity anchors. If there were only one primary currency unit, we would have a regime of permanently fixed exchange rates reminiscent of the post-war Bretton Woods system, in which other currencies were tied to the dollar, and the dollar was tied to a fixed quantity of gold.

If there were more than one primary currency unit, each fixed to its own commodity anchor, the exchange rates between the primary currency units would fluctuate with changes in the relative prices of the anchors. However, these anchors should have fairly stable relative prices if we assume that each anchor is chosen to stabilize some consumer price index. Exchange rate changes among anchored or primary currencies should be relatively small and infrequent. Any other currencies, if there were any, would then be tied to one of these primary currencies. Each of these satellite currencies would therefore have a fixed exchange rate against the primary unit to which it was tethered, and also against any other satellite currencies tied to the same primary unit, and a (slightly) floating exchange rate against all other currencies. The result would be a series of currency blocs, each of which was a fixed-exchange-rate system based on a primary currency, and exchange rates between these various blocs would fluctuate (slightly) against each other.

In short, *laissez-faire* would probably give us one of three possible monetary arrangements: a single currency unit used throughout the world, and tied to a specified commodity anchor; a system of fixed exchange rates, in which all other currencies are tied to one key currency, which is itself anchored to a particular commodity; or a system of fixed-exchange-rate currency blocs fluctuating a little against each other, each tethered to a particular anchor. All currencies would also be fairly stable in value, because the anchor(s) would be chosen to minimize price-level instability.

How the status quo differs from *laissez-faire*

The fact that a *laissez-faire* monetary system differs so radically from our own gives the lie to the view that the status quo is a pure free market. The economic instability produced by violent exchange-rate movements can hardly be blamed on capitalism when it is governments that control monetary policy.

Currently there are a large number of different currencies that often fluctuate violently against each other. A small number of these – the dollar, the yen, and the mark (or, more recently, the euro) – are widely used and are, to a certain extent, independent of each other. Remaining currencies tend to be aligned with one of these, with degrees of alignment varying from fully fixed exchange rates to exchange rates that are kept within some target zone. None of the existing currencies is tied to any commodity anchor, so there is nothing to minimize price-level instability. Instead, the price levels of different currencies depend on the monetary policies of the central banks concerned, and the central banks and/or the governments that control them have considerable choice in the monetary policies they pursue.

Under *laissez-faire*, there would be no link between a currency unit and a nation-state, and no reason for currency areas to match national territories. Since there are considerable benefits when people use the same currency unit (e.g. lower accounting costs and no currency-exchange costs), we might expect *laissez-faire* currency areas to be larger on average than present nation-states, and also better aligned to economic fundamentals such as trading patterns. This line of reasoning suggests that there would be fewer separate currencies under *laissez-faire*, larger currency areas, and possibly a single currency area spanning the whole world.

Even if it fell short of this cosmopolitanism, however, a *laissez-faire* regime would tend to produce a high degree of price-level stability because the anchors would be chosen specifically for that purpose. Thus, it would tend to avoid the many (and very significant) costs of both inflation and inflation uncertainty.[5] Interest rates freed of speculation about possible inflation would move only in response to changes in 'real' factors. A *laissez-faire* regime would therefore deliver fairly stable interest rates across the whole term structure, and so lead to fairly stable bond prices. The absence of inflationary shocks and the greater stability of interest rates would make the prices of stocks, shares, real estate and other assets more stable as well.

By contrast, the current regime, cut loose from any anchor, offers no safeguards against inflation. It appears to have a built-in inflationary bias, and has produced erratic interest and inflation rates and very high levels of inflation uncertainty, especially over the long run.[6] Shifts in central bank monetary policy have sometimes led to major (and often unexpected) changes in inflation and interest rates, a case in point being the drastic rise in interest rates in the United States when Federal Reserve policy shifted abruptly in October 1979. Moreover, governments often have incentives to renege on past targets to take advantage of private-sector agents, such as workers locked into wage contracts based on particular inflation expectations (Barro and Gordon 1983a and 1983b). To make matters worse, once private agents anticipate that the central bank might later change its policy, the credibility of policy targets erodes and produces even greater inflation uncertainty.

Inflation also leads to considerable asset price volatility, with longer-term assets particularly unstable due to their greater sensitivity to changes in interest rates. Frequently, inflation also leads people to switch from paper assets such as government debt to real assets such as equity and real estate, fuelling boom–bust cycles in real assets. All these effects have major (and often adverse) effects on investment, the capital structure, employment, and the economy more generally.

The stability of exchange rates under *laissez-faire* contrasts sharply with the exchange rate volatility experienced under current monetary arrangements, especially since the breakdown of the Bretton Woods system in the early 1970s. The adoption of the current fiat monetary system made many exchange rates effectively anchorless. Their value depends on monetary policy and expectations about it, both of which can be very unstable. As a result, exchange rates have often fluctuated very considerably, with adverse – and sometimes disastrous – economic consequences.

Interventionist instability

The excessive instability created by the current monetary regime has many harmful consequences. It exposes almost everyone to risks from price-level volatility (such as the risks of being locked into longer-term contracts at inappropriate prices), interest-rate volatility (e.g. risks of loss on bond and bond-derivative positions, risks associated with the prospect of obtaining future finance at uncertain interest rates), increased exchange-rate volatility (e.g. risks of loss on positions denominated in foreign currencies, risks of shocks to the domestic economy occasioned by exchange-rate changes), and risks associated with excessive asset-price volatility (e.g. more volatile stock and real estate markets). The extra volatility of the current system also leads people to renegotiate contracts more frequently, to make contracts more complex, to shorten contract maturity, to try to avoid longer-term commitments, and to alter their finance and investment strategies to guard against uncertainty. These responses increase negotiation and transactions costs, make it more difficult to plan for the longer term, and preclude otherwise worthwhile investment opportunities. Excess volatility also disrupts cash flows, undermines liquidity, makes planning more difficult, makes counterparties more likely to default, makes longer-term finance harder to obtain, and generally makes everyone less secure about their financial futures.

Inflation-induced uncertainty also undermines 'real' productive activity in other ways. As Peter Howitt observed:

> It is no accident that finance was among the sectors with the most noticeable innovations during the 1970s and 1980s. The need to protect against inflation uncertainty, and the opportunity to take advantage of others' inability to do so, diverted a lot of innovative thinking away from creating new goods and processes and into the invention of new financial contracts, new banking techniques, and new corporate financial strategies. Young people on Wall Street were paid huge salaries, but the cost of those

salaries was paid by the rest of us, who were deprived of the medical services, scientific research, and so on that the financial whiz kids could have been producing.

(Howitt 1990: 93–4)

Critics of financial markets therefore have a good case when they argue that productive resources are being wasted in these activities. However they are mistaken when they attribute this problem to the operation of financial markets as such, rather than to governmental and central bank policies that create unnecessary uncertainty. Private sector parties feel obliged to spend resources to deal with this uncertainty, and critics should focus on why they feel obliged to react this way rather than criticize them for doing so. Of course, there will always be some volatility in financial markets, but one cannot conclude that all of the risks and associated problems we observe in our contemporary world economy are unavoidable products of a *laissez-faire* regime – since such a regime does not currently exist. The real problem is too much state involvement in finance, not (as the critics maintain) too little.

Globalization and instability

Fortunately, increases in capital mobility, lower transactions costs, improving information technology and further developments in financial markets them-selves – most notably, continuing developments in derivatives markets – will make it increasingly difficult for central banks to maintain policies that markets perceive as indefensible.[7] These developments will therefore signifi-cantly reduce central banks' policy options. Markets now have little difficulty undermining crawling peg exchange-rate policies, because these involve predictable exchange-rate changes that speculators can anticipate and so place bets on. Similarly, target-zone policies will become increasingly hard to maintain, particularly when markets perceive monetary policy makers as lacking the will or the resources to make the difficult decisions sometimes needed to keep exchange rates within target ranges. The same applies to 'fixed' exchange-rate regimes, even though they are usually perceived as involving a stronger and more credible exchange-rate commitment.[8] Even fixed-rate regimes are dependent on long-run policy credibility, and their cred-ibility is inevitably limited by the political context within which policy-makers operate. Consequently, these regimes are also likely to be destroyed by speculative attacks once their credibility is undermined.

These factors are likely to drive central banks away from the middle ground between the extremes of zero intervention in foreign-exchange markets, on the one hand, and full currency union, on the other.[9] Each central bank will even-tually need to decide whether to abstain entirely from intervention in foreign exchange markets, or else tie itself increasingly closely to one or more other currencies and eventually join a currency union. Faced with this choice, some of the more important central banks will probably choose the first option, and many of the smaller ones will probably choose the latter and join currency unions with key currencies. The result will be the emergence of a small number of monetary unions, each based on some existing key currency, with relatively freely floating exchange rates between them.

Yet even this arrangement may only be an interim one. As the world economy becomes more integrated and remaining barriers between financial markets dissolve, the remaining currencies should become increasingly close substitutes for each other. However, currency substitution theory then suggests that exchange rates should become more and more volatile.[10] My guess is that the various governments and central banks involved will eventually feel obliged to intervene to counteract this increasing exchange-rate instability. Yet exchange-rate intervention still raises the same old problems – crawling pegs are predictable, target zones are difficult to maintain in the long run, and so on – making this middle ground, too, unsustainable in the long run. Attempts to intervene in foreign exchange markets to harmonize exchange rates are again doomed to eventual failure. However if monetary policy-makers cannot live with freely floating exchange rates, their only logical alternative is to go to the other extreme, full monetary union. We thus arrive at a fairly strong conclusion – the world monetary system appears to be headed for full monetary union – and the only question is how long it will take to get there. Monetary policy-makers might resist it, and in the process create a lot of exchange-rate volatility and associated problems for the private sector (and, of course, a lot of profits for speculators who bet against them), but the outcome itself appears to hard to resist.[11] Exchange-rate volatility should, therefore, eventually disappear. When it does, we might arrive at a financial system that is, in some respects at least, a reasonably close approximation to *laissez-faire*.[12] In the meantime, we will have to live with continued state intervention and the many problems it creates.

Part 2
The monetary regime

8   A proposal to end inflation

This chapter proposes a rule by which the central bank could end inflation and stabilize the price level thereafter. The basic idea is simple. The Bank of England would issue a new kind of financial instrument and be committed to pegging its price at periodic intervals. This new instrument would be similar, though not identical, to price-index forward or futures contracts, and would promise the holder a payment on maturity that was contingent on the 'announced' value of a price index on that date. The expected price level would then be determined by a market equilibrium condition, and arbitrage operations would correct deviations of the expected price level from its equilibrium value. If the expected price level was too high, speculators would buy more financial instruments from the Bank and in the process reduce the supply of base money; expected prices would then fall. If the expected price level was too low, speculators would sell instruments to the Bank, increase the supply of base money, and expected prices would rise. The expected value of the price level should therefore be stable, and there should be relatively little 'slippage' between expected prices and the subsequently realized actual price level. Hence, the actual price level should be reasonably stable as well.

The layout of the chapter is as follows. The first section sets out the core of the proposal and explains the principles behind it. The next section deals with various complications. Among these are the need to synchronize instrument maturity dates with 'announcements' of the chosen price index and the need to ensure that the proposed system would be secure against speculative attack. This section also discusses how a market might arise for the new financial instrument, and explains what the Bank could do to enhance the credibility of its commitment to the new rule in the face of private-sector doubts about that commitment. The third section compares the proposed rule to the most obvious alternatives: a rule to target the money supply, and a rule to target the price level directly. The final section of the chapter discusses practical implementation issues such as what the contract price should be, how frequently the Bank should intervene to set it, and whether the scheme should be legislated or adopted at the Bank's discretion.

The proposal

Suppose one wishes to stabilize the value of a price index that takes the value p_t at time t, p_{t+1} at time $t+1$, and so on. The core of the proposal is that the Bank of England should create a new kind of financial instrument and indefinitely commit itself to buy and sell this instrument every so often at a fixed price. This new financial instrument is related to a price-index futures contract, so I shall refer to it for convenience as a 'quasi-futures contract' (QFC). The QFC is a contract between a purchaser, A, and a seller, B, in which A makes a payment to B at the time t when the contract is made, and B promises in return to make a payment to A the next period that is the product of two terms: a payment indexed to the value of the price index at $t+1$ (i.e. p_{t+1}), and a compounding factor that compensates A for the interest he loses by paying B at t instead of at $t+1$.[1] The reasons for these payment features will become apparent as we proceed. The payment A makes at time t is the price of the contract, and it is this price the Bank would peg.

The equilibrium condition and equilibrating forces

The principles underlying the proposal are relatively straightforward. Let r_t be some reasonably 'representative' market interest rate prevailing between t and $t+1$. If we interpret each period as a quarter, r_t might be the three-month LIBOR rate or something similar. A QFC made at time t might call for B to make an index-linked payment of $£(1+r_t)\,p_{t+1}$ at time $t+1$. (Note that p_t is an index number, but $£(1+rt)\,p_{t+1}$ is a monetary payment and is therefore denominated in pounds sterling. Hence all monetary payments have a '£' prefix, but index-number terms such as p_t on its own do not.) $£p_{t+1}$ is the index-contingent payment mentioned earlier, and $(1+r_t)$ is the compounding factor. In return for the promised future payment, A makes B an immediate payment of $£p_t^c$ (that is, he pays the contract price) and the central bank undertakes to buy or sell contracts as required to keep $£p_t^c$ at a preannounced level. The present value of the expected profit from buying a contract will consequently be:

$$E_t\,£(1+r_t)\,p_{t+1}\,/\,(1+r^*_t) - £p_t^c \tag{1}$$

E_t is the expectations operator taken on information available at t and r^*_t is an appropriate discount rate which we can think of as a 'representative' money market interest rate (e.g. the LIBOR itself, or some closely related interest rate). We can therefore presume that $[(1+r_t)/(1+r^*_t)]$ is equal to unity, or approximately so.[2] The (perhaps approximate) expected profit from buying a contract will then be:

$$E_t\,£p_{t+1} - £p_t^c \tag{2}$$

Ignoring risk premia for simplicity, equilibrium requires that the expected profit from buying or selling contracts is approximately zero.[3] Hence:

$$E_t \text{\pounds} p_{t+1} \approx \text{\pounds} p_t^c \tag{3}$$

(3) gives us an expression for the equilibrium value of the expected future price index. The pegging of $\text{\pounds}p^c{}_t$ by the central bank should then suffice to stabilize the equilibrium value of the expected price index.

As an aside, it should now be apparent from (3) why the contingent payment made by B is compounded to compensate A for his forgone interest. Without that compounding, (3) would be replaced by $E_t \text{\pounds}p_{t+1} \approx \text{\pounds}p_t^c (1+r^*_t)$ and the value of $E_t \text{\pounds}p_{t+1}$ would depend on the nominal discount (or interest) rate r^*_t without the offset from r^*_t that is implicit in (3). The problem then is that the expected price-level would no longer be 'tied down': suppose for example that prices were initially stable, but private sector agents for some reason expected prices to rise by 5 per cent in the next period. Then r^*_t would (under plausible circumstances) jump 5 per cent, and $Et \text{\pounds}p_{t+1}$ would jump by the same amount, and there would be no mechanism to penalize those agents who bet on inflation despite the fact that the central bank was holding $\text{\pounds}p_t^c$ constant. Inflationary expectations could become self-fulfilling, and the system could no longer be relied upon to deliver price stability. To achieve price stability, we need an equilibrium condition in which $E_t \text{\pounds}p_{t+1}$ depends on $\text{\pounds}p_t^c$ alone, and not on r^*_t. The point of having B pay compensatory interest is therefore to ensure that we get such a condition (that is, (3)) because the interest and discount terms effectively cancel out and leave $E_t \text{\pounds}p_{t+1}$ depending only on $\text{\pounds}p_t^c$. In short, the contract with compensatory interest stabilizes the expected future price level, but a contract without compensatory interest does not.

To assess the stability of the equilibrium under the proposed rule, suppose that (3) did not hold and $E_t \text{\pounds}p_{t+1}$ significantly exceeded $\text{\pounds}p_t^c$. Intuitively, the expected future price level is now too high because agents expect an excessive money supply in the future, and the restoration of equilibrium requires that the money supply should fall. Speculators now perceive that QFCs are under-priced relative to the high future payout they expect from them. A speculator who buys a contract pays $\text{\pounds}p_t^c$ but expects to earn a present-value return of about $E_t \text{\pounds}p_{t+1}$: he would therefore expect to make an approximate present-value profit of $E_t \text{\pounds}p_{t+1} - \text{\pounds}p_t^c$. Speculators would then purchase more contracts to reap these profits, and the central bank would have to create the additional contracts they demanded if it was to keep their price constant. However, in order to purchase the additional contracts, speculators would have to hand over base money at the time they make their purchases, and the supply of base money in circulation would fall. The increased speculative demand for contracts would thus translate into a fall in the supply of base money, which would help push expected future prices down.[4] $E_t p_{t+1}$ would therefore fall towards p^c_t. These expected arbitrage profits would continue, and with them the speculative operations and the falling money supply, until $E_t p_{t+1}$ had fallen to about p^c_t and equilibrium been restored. The equilibrating process is illustrated in Table 8.1.

If however $E_t £p_{t+1}$ fell significantly short of $£p^c_t$, the expected future price level would now be too low. A speculator would perceive the contracts as overpriced relative to the low expected future payout, and he could make an expected 'present value' profit of about $£p^c_t - E_t £p_{t+1}$ from selling a contract. Speculators would therefore sell contracts to the central bank, and each such sale would raise the supply of base money and thus the money supply. Expectations of future prices would rise, and equilibrium would be restored. In short, if (3) did not hold for some reason, arbitrage operations would take place that would tend to restore it.[5]

In practice, we might also expect these equilibrating forces to be reinforced by other agents acting on the anticipation that equilibrium would be restored. If the value of the expected price index is too high, a representative supplier will anticipate that the relative price of the commodity he supplies will be high that period. He will plan to increase his supply, and his action and that of others like him will lead expected future prices to fall. High expected future prices will also lead purchasers to reduce their expected future purchases, and these actions will further reinforce the equilibrating process. Similarly, if expected future prices were too low, expected supplies would fall and expected demands would rise, and reinforce the equilibrating process in the other direction.

Though arbitrage forces would push the system towards equilibrium, if it should depart from it, we also need some reassurance that arbitrage forces do not overcompensate – that is, transform a deviation from equilibrium in one direction into a greater deviation from equilibrium in the other direction – and produce an unstable system in which deviations from equilibrium were magnified over time rather than reduced. However a second arbitrage argument

Table 8.1 Equilibration under the QFC rule

Disequilibrium state	Interpretation	Arbitrage	Consequences
$E_t £p_{t+1} > £p^c_t$	Excessive money supply expected in future	Speculators buy QFCs for base money	Money supply falls, expected future prices fall
$E_t £p_{t+1} < £p^c_t$	Insufficient money supply expected in future	Speculators sell QFCs for base money	Money supply rises, expected future prices rise

suggests that this kind of instability should not occur: the equilibrium condition (3) tells us roughly what the price index expected next period should be; by extension, there are longer-term analogues of (3) that tell us roughly what expected prices should be in periods after that; if the kind of instability being discussed here did occur, the price level expected for at least some future times would then be well away from its equilibrium level, and (3) and/or some of its longer-term analogues would be violated; hence, the equilibration arguments that give us (3) and its longer-term analogues would appear to rule out the kind of instability being discussed here. We thus have some reason to believe that arbitrage forces would not only push the system towards equilibrium, but would also produce a reasonably stable expected price level as well.

The stability of the (actual) price index under the proposed rule

However, the critical question is how far the proposed rule would stabilize the actual (as opposed to expected) price level. Assume for the time being that the rule is implemented credibly (i.e. private agents expect the Bank to continue to follow the rule in the relevant future). Given rational expectations, we can decompose the realized price index at $t+1$ into its rational expectation at t plus a shock ε_{t+1} that is orthogonal to information available at t:

$$p_{t+1} = E_t\, p_{t+1} + \varepsilon_{t+1}\,,\ E_t\, \varepsilon_{t+1} = 0 \qquad (4)$$

If we now normalize by dividing throughout by p_t^c, (4) becomes

$$p_{t+1} / p_t^c = (E_t\, p_{t+1} / p_t^c) + (\varepsilon_{t+1} / p_t^c)\ \approx 1 + u_{t+1} \qquad (5)$$

where $u_{t+1} \equiv \varepsilon_{t+1} / p_t^c$ and the approximation comes from (3). (5) tells us that the actual (normalized) price index is (approximately) the sum of an expected component, i.e. unity, and an unexpected price-index forecast error u_{t+1}.

Given that the Bank would peg p_t^c under the QFC regime, (5) tells us that the standard deviation of the actual price index under the QFC regime would be approximately equal to the standard deviation of price-level forecast errors under that regime. While we cannot directly predict the latter standard deviation, we can estimate the standard deviation of price-level forecast errors for historical regimes, and there are good reasons to believe that the historical standard deviation of price-level forecast errors would be higher than the comparable standard deviation under the QFC regime. An estimate of the standard deviation of price-level forecast errors can therefore be regarded as providing an upper bound for such errors under the QFC regime. Perhaps the best estimates for past regimes are those derived from ARCH (Autoregressive Conditional Heteroskedasticity) models, and Engle's (1982) estimates for the

UK over the period 1957:II to 1977:II suggest that (quarterly) price-level forecast errors had standard errors varying from 0.5 per cent in the 1960s to a maximum of 2.2 per cent in the 1970s. These figures are likely to overstate price-level unpredictability under the QFC regime because the price level under previous regimes was subject to various shocks that would not arise under the QFC regime. Under the gold standard, the price level would rise in response to discoveries of gold ore or refinements in the gold extraction process. Under the fiat system, the price level is vulnerable to shifts in government or central bank monetary policy, and there is good reason to believe that at least part of the relatively high price-level forecast errors that Engle estimates for the 1970s were due to the volatile monetary policies of that period. Under the QFC rule, on the other hand, discoveries of gold would have no particular influence on the general price level because there would be no link with gold, and there would be little scope for shifts in monetary policy to affect the price level because a credibly implemented QFC rule would replace monetary policy as it is currently understood.

Further features of the proposed monetary system

The need to avoid the 'interest-free loan problem'

We now consider a number of further issues. Once a contract has been sold by the central bank, there is no reason to prevent agents trading it among themselves before it matures, but it would be unwise for the central bank to maintain the same price for a particular contract throughout the period until it matures. A particular contract might start off with (say) ninety days to mature, and would trade for a particular price when it was first issued, but eighty five days later the same contract would have only a few days to run, and this changing maturity must be acknowledged in the contract price if the central bank is not to expose itself to profitable speculative attack. If the central bank tried to trade contracts of both maturities for the same price, arbitragers could make a riskless profit by selling contracts with a relatively long time to maturity to the central bank, obtaining base money in exchange, investing the base money to earn some interest on it, and then buying the contracts back when they were close to maturity. They would receive the same price for the contracts as they had paid earlier themselves, and they would keep the interest they had earned by investing the money in the interim. Their profit – and the central bank's loss – would then be the interest on the proceeds. The central bank would have effectively committed itself to providing intra-quarter loans at a zero rate of interest. The optimal strategy for arbitragers is then to sell as many contracts as they can when the central bank opens to trade 'new' contracts, invest the proceeds, and buy the contracts back just before they mature. (In other words, the optimal strategy is to maximize the number of interest-free loans one takes out and invest the proceeds.) Private agents could presumably increase their profits to arbitrarily high levels, and the central bank's ability to maintain its pricing policy would be very doubtful.

Perhaps the easiest way to avoid this interest-free loan problem and its consequences would be for the central bank every so often to peg the price of contracts with a specified period to maturity (e.g. ninety days). The central bank would peg the price of contracts with ninety days to mature by offering to buy and sell them on demand at a particular price, and the prices of contracts with less than ninety days to run would be left to the market to determine. Market agents would price contracts with less than ninety days to run as they wished, but they would do so anticipating the central bank's periodic 'interventions' into the QFC market to peg the prices of contracts with exactly ninety days to run. Rational expectations arbitrage would then ensure that the prices of contracts with other than ninety days to run were consistent with the periodically pegged prices of ninety-day contracts, and the central bank would no longer be vulnerable to unlimited demands for interest-free loans.[6]

The market for quasi-futures contracts

At the moment there does not exist any market in QFC contracts or even in 'regular' retail-price-index (RPI) futures contracts. A market for Consumer Price Index (CPI) futures contracts did exist for a short while in the US, operated by the Coffee, Cocoa, and Sugar Exchange in New York (see Horrigan 1987), but trading was so thin that the Exchange eventually closed it down. The question therefore arises: would there be a market for QFC contracts if the rule proposed here were implemented?[7] The answer appears to be that there would be a market, if one were needed. Imagine that the central bank initially offered such contracts but there were no takers. The central bank would nonetheless be committed to buy and sell such contracts at a specified price, and (3) tells us what $E_t \pounds p_{t+1}$ must (approximately) be to equilibrate the market. If there were still no takers for the contract, a time would presumably come when $E_t \pounds p_{t+1}$ would deviate from this equilibrium level. (One would have thought it most unlikely that $E_t \pounds p_{t+1}$ never drifted away from its equilibrium value by a sufficient amount to provoke arbitrage activity in the QFC market, but even in this unlikely event the key point would be that (3) would always be satisfied and we would get the price-level outcome we desired. What really matters is not that trading actually takes place, but that the trading necessary to restore equilibrium (i.e., (3)) would take place if (3) were disturbed.) When that time comes, private agents could expect to make arbitrage profits by buying or selling QFC contracts, and the market would start to come alive. The amount of base money in circulation would alter, expectations of future prices would change, and equilibrium would be restored.

In short, the argument is that given the central bank's offer to buy or sell contracts at a specified price, private agents would have an incentive to trade if their expectations of future prices were not consistent with equilibrium. We can thus rely on private arbitrage activity to ensure that enough trading takes place to restore equilibrium, should equilibrium ever be disturbed.

Enhancing the credibility of the proposed rule

An important advantage of the QFC rule is that it provides a basis from which the central bank, if it needs to, can enhance the credibility of its commitment to the QFC rule in the longer term. It is important for the Bank to have some means of enhancing the credibility of this commitment: if the Bank's commitment were seen as lacking credibility, private agents would attach some significant probability to the rule being altered or abandoned. Their expectations would be altered accordingly (e.g. they might expect inflation in the long term) and these altered expectations might have 'undesirable' consequences such as higher long-term interest rates. Private agents might also speculate against the rule and perhaps even force the central bank to abandon it. Should the Bank adopt the rule, it is therefore important that it do so credibly.

There is a simple and (literally) profitable way for the Bank to establish its credibility. If the Bank adopted the rule but did so lacking credibility, its lack of credibility would be reflected by private-sector expectations of positive rather than (approximately) zero inflation in the long term. If the Bank wished to solve its credibility problem, it must persuade the private sector to expect zero long-term inflation, and it can do so by staking its own wealth on the achievement of zero long-term inflation by offering to bet on it.[8] Suppose the Bank was genuinely committed to indefinite zero inflation, but the private sector doubted its commitment and expected the price level in five years to have risen by, say, 25 per cent. The Bank could then offer to sell instruments promising a pay-off in five years contingent on the realized value of the retail price index in five years' time and private agents would be willing to buy them because they would expect to make a profit from the rising RPI.[9] Since this long-term betting contract provides for Bank payments to be contingent on the RPI in five years' time, it provides for an automatic financial penalty if the Bank creates long-term inflation. The private sector would recognize this financial incentive and consequently revise their own expectations of future inflation downwards. The more of these contracts the Bank sells, the greater that incentive will be and the closer private-sector inflation expectations will be to the Bank's own expectations. In short, if the Bank wishes to bring private-sector expectations of long-run inflation down (e.g. to somewhere 'close' to zero), it can do so by selling enough of these long-term price-level 'bets'.[10]

Selling bets would offer the Bank an ideal way to enhance its credibility if the private sector doubted its commitment to long-term price stability. If it was sincere about its commitment to long-run price stability, the Bank could issue bets to the private sector fully expecting to win them when the period of the bets expired. Private agents who bet against it would lose and the Bank would profit at their expense. In a manner reminiscent of the judo expert who uses his opponent's weight to beat him, the Bank would have turned the weight of private-sector doubt about its commitment into profit for itself. The only cost to the Bank would be that by issuing bets the Bank would be making it more costly for itself to 'renege' on its commitment, but it is precisely because there would be a penalty for 'reneging' that the issue of bets would enhance the Bank's credibility. In any case, a 'sincere' Bank would not want to renege on that commitment and would have no problem exposing itself to a potential financial penalty. A 'sincere' Bank could both enhance its credibility and make a profit, and the only cost of doing so would be to foreclose an option it did not want to exercise anyway.

One may ask why the Bank should bother with QFCs at all when it could always issue price-level bets. Why not have the Bank issue bets of various maturities and forget about the complications arising from QFCs? The answer is simple: a bet (e.g. a 'pure' futures contract) only gives the Bank an incentive to deliver a particular price level, but does not actually deliver it (or tell the Bank how to achieve it). If the Bank dispensed with QFCs and merely issued bets, it would still have to solve the difficult problem of managing monetary policy to ensure that it won its bets, and it would therefore be taking bets without being sure it could win them. The point about the QFC rule is that it would automatically tie down the price level, give or take a 'small' random error, and thus solve the Bank's 'delivery' problem for it. If the Bank adopted the QFC rule and issued price-level bets, it could then be reasonably confident that it would win them. Far from being an alternative to the Bank issuing bets, the QFC rule in fact provides the foundation from which bets can safely be issued.

The proposed rule compared to alternatives

One might wonder how this proposed rule would compare to alternatives. One obvious alternative is to try to achieve price stability by targeting the growth rate of a particular monetary aggregate. However monetary targeting appears to be inferior to the QFC rule in a variety of respects:

1   Unless it targets the monetary base, the central bank cannot directly control the targeted aggregate, and one must either stipulate some supplementary rule for the central bank to follow to ensure that it hits the target accurately, or one must give the central bank discretion over how it should

implement monetary targeting. In the former case, the advocate of monetary targeting must presumably set out the supplementary rule and justify it; in the latter case, one has to live with the consequences of central bank discretion (e.g. greater uncertainty) that can be avoided by adopting the 'automatic' rule proposed here.

2   It is not clear what the most appropriate monetary aggregate would be, and the choice of monetary aggregate has implications for the price level over time because of velocity (and other) differences between the various aggregates.

3   For monetary targeting to be even reasonably successful, the demand for the chosen aggregate must be stable, and it is still not entirely clear how stable the demands for monetary aggregates are. In any case, the demand function for a particular aggregate ought to be identified as stable *ex ante* and not just *ex post* if that aggregate is to be used for monetary targeting. Whatever evidence there might be that the demand for a particular aggregate is stable *ex post* is not sufficient to demonstrate that that aggregate could be targeted to produce the desired price-level outcome.

4   Even if we found a suitable aggregate and had reason to be confident of its *ex ante* stability, we would only get the desired outcome to the extent we estimated the demand function 'correctly' and could predict the future values of relevant variables, and we cannot be particularly confident of being able to do either.

If one wished to implement a monetary target, the alternative would be to target the monetary base. The Bank would then be able to control its target aggregate directly, and problems outlined earlier in (1) and (2) could be avoided. However problems (3) and (4) would still arise, and these latter problems would probably be at least as acute as they were before. The demand for base money appears to be less well understood than the demand for other monetary aggregates: it has been less well researched, monetary economists have less of a 'feel' for the appropriate elasticities, and so on. The demand for base money in the past has also been particularly vulnerable to regulatory and technological changes (e.g. the abolition of reserve requirements, and developments in information technology), and such changes make it difficult to estimate an 'underlying' stable demand function, even assuming one exists. The future demand for base money is therefore difficult to predict even if we could be confident – which we cannot be – that there would be no further regulatory or technological shocks.

Whatever monetary aggregate one might adopt, monetary targeting also involves credibility problems that should not arise with the QFC regime. Leaving aside the point that past experiences with monetary targets might be held to undermine the credibility of a future monetary target, there is also the problem that a central bank that adopted a monetary target as a means to stabilize the price level would have no easy way to enhance its credibility if needed to.

As suggested earlier, the most obvious way for the Bank to try to enhance its credibility would be for it to issue price-level bets, but such bets would be far less helpful to a central bank operating a monetary target than to one operating a QFC rule. Part of the attraction of a price-level bet to a central bank operating a QFC rule is that the bank can be confident of winning the bet because the rule actually delivers stable prices. However, for reasons just explained, a central bank that operates a monetary target cannot be confident about delivering stable prices, and if it then issues bets about the price level, it must do so with a significant danger of losing them. The danger of losing its bets then limits the extent to which it can issue them, and in turn undermines its ability to use bets to enhance its credibility. In effect, a central bank operating a monetary target can do little more than use bets to enhance its credibility at the margin, and even that would involve significant risks.

Another alternative is for the central bank to adopt a price-level target, and be left with the discretion to achieve that target as it saw fit. The question therefore arises: what does the QFC rule achieve that a simple price-level target does not? Part of the answer is that the QFC rule solves the central bank's 'delivery' problem, and a simple price-level target does not. A central bank that adopts a QFC rule has only to buy and sell contracts on demand at the relevant dates, but a central bank that adopts a simple price-level target faces the much more difficult task of designing a policy to achieve the target. As with monetary targets, the need to resolve this delivery problem may also undermine the credibility of the chosen policy and make it more difficult for the central bank to buttress its credibility with price-level bets. Another part of the answer is that there must be some doubt about the ability of the central bank to achieve such a target with the desired degree of accuracy, and to the extent there is such doubt, the QFC rule provides some reassurance about the achievement of price stability. If the central bank can manipulate, say, the supply of base money sufficiently adroitly to maintain price stability, then it could still do so under the QFC rule without calling forth arbitrage forces that would take the supply of base money out of its hands. If the central bank was relatively poor at stabilizing prices, on the other hand, the QFC rule provides for arbitrage forces to take over from the central bank to ensure reasonable price stability. The QFC rule provides virtually free insurance against the event that the central bank itself does not deliver the desired degree of price stability. The QFC rule appears to dominate the alternative of just targeting the price level.

Operational issues

Finally, a few details need to be sorted out over the precise implementation of the QFC rule. We need first to select a target price index, and perhaps the most obvious one would be the RPI. Having chosen our price index, we then need to select the price at which the central bank is to trade QFCs. Given the implications of the QFC price for the price level itself, we would wish to choose a QFC price that would not unduly disturb the price level as the new system was being established. The equilibrium condition (3) suggests that the choice of QFC price is equivalent to the choice of expected price level at the time the contract matures. Given that we wish to establish price stability, we would presumably want that expected price level to be reasonably close to the actual price level at the time the scheme was first implemented. We should therefore choose a QFC price that is roughly consistent with the price index at the time the first contracts are sold.[11]

We then need to select the contract's term to maturity. The longer the term to maturity, the greater the 'slippage' between the expected price index and the actual value the index turns out to take. Since the price-forecast error u_{t+1} picks up influences on the spot-price index that arise between t and $t+1$, but were not predictable at t itself, a longer period between t and $t+1$ should increase the standard deviation of u_{t+1} if only because it leaves less scope for these interim shocks to occur. If we wish u_{t+1} to have a low standard deviation, we should therefore choose a relatively short term to maturity (e.g. a quarter or two, or perhaps a year).

There is also the question of the contract's frequency. Since each contract maturity date must have a price index 'announcement' to go with it, the contract frequency is constrained by the frequency with which the price index is 'announced'. If the price index is announced only once a month, we cannot have more than one contract maturing each month and the maximum contract frequency would be monthly. There is however no need to have the maximum contract frequency, and we may prefer contracts to be somewhat less frequent (e.g. quarterly).

The last issue is whether the QFC rule should be legislated, or whether the Bank should adopt it without explicit legislation. Since current legislation gives the Chancellor of the Exchequer the power to set interest rates, there can be no question of the Bank trying to adopt such a rule in defiance of the wishes of the government. Any attempt to do so could easily be undermined by the government ordering the Bank to set interest rates incompatible with the interest rates required by the QFC rule, and the rule would have to be abandoned. If the rule were to be implemented, it must therefore obtain government approval, and there must in particular be some credible reassurance on the government's part that it would not later undermine the rule by means of its power to set interest rates. The most natural solution would therefore be to pass legislation to protect the Bank by abolishing the government's power to set interest rates or otherwise interfere in monetary policy, and that same legislation could be used to make the Bank's adherence to the rule a legally binding commitment. Such a commitment would give the private sector more confidence that the Bank would continue to adhere to the rule, and thus enhance the credibility of the Bank's commitment to it. Such legislation cannot provide a perfect guarantee of the value of the currency since Parliament cannot completely bind its successors, but having some legislative safeguards must certainly be better than having none, and Parliament can aim to minimize the level of political risk inherent in the monetary system even if it cannot eliminate it entirely. Parliament should therefore legislate, and the legislation should be designed to make it as difficult as possible for future Parliaments to reverse.

If ever the government finally decide that they wish to eliminate inflation, the QFC rule proposed here offers a straightforward and technically feasible way to do it.

9   Reply to Hillier

Brian Hillier makes two substantial points in his 'Comment' on my 'Proposal to End Inflation'.[1] The first is to dispute my argument that fixing the price of quasi-futures contracts (QFCs) would stabilize the price level. I maintain that Hillier is unsound on this issue and that my earlier claim is correct. He argues that a substantial discrepancy could arise between the market interest rate r specified in the QFC and the discount rate r^* applied by the typical private-sector party who buys or sells such contracts, and on whom the underlying arbitrage process depends; such a discrepancy would mean that pegging the price of QFCs would no longer be sufficient to tie down the expected price level, and implies that my scheme could no longer be relied on to stabilize the actual price level.

My response is that there is no reason to believe that a major discrepancy between r and r^* would actually occur. As I noted in my original paper (Dowd (1994b: 830 note 2)), the discount rate applied by our private-sector financial operator is likely to be a short-term market interest rate like r. Now suppose for the sake of argument that we grant Hillier's conceptual experiment about a rise in inflation expectations that leads to a rise in r. My point is simply that the rise in r would lead to a roughly corresponding rise in r^* as well. The interest rate term $[(1+r)/(1+r^*)]$ in my equation (1) would therefore remain close to one, and the expected price level would remain stable by my equation (3).[2] The supposed rise in inflation expectations thus fails to break the link between r and r^*, as Hillier assumes it would. Hillier's mistake is to suppose that r could rise substantially and yet leave r^* unchanged, given that the agent on whom the arbitrage process depends actually uses r (or some similar rate) as his proxy for r^*. It follows that Hillier is also mistaken in his conclusion that the compounding term $[(1+r)/(1+r^*)]$ needs to be tied down: the very forces that pull r^* and r together in fact do just that, and therefore ensure that pegging the price of QFCs would stabilize the price level.

Hillier's second point is essentially an application of unpleasant monetarist arithmetic logic. This argument is perfectly sound on its own terms: if fiscal and monetary policies are fundamentally inconsistent, the demands of the government budget constraint require that one or other must 'give' in the long run; monetary policy (or the appropriate nominal rule) must yield if fiscal policy does not yield; hence, *any* monetary policy or nominal rule, the QFC scheme included, can be undermined by a sufficiently excessive fiscal policy. I accept this logic, but would make two points of my own in reply.

To begin with, I would suggest that the appropriate conclusion to draw is *not* that there is something wrong with my scheme because it could not withstand a sustained fiscal attack; instead, the appropriate conclusion is that something should be done to get the fiscal problem itself under control. Something should also be done to protect the integrity of the monetary system against fiscal demands, or if one prefers, to remove M from the government budget constraint. At the very minimum, I would suggest that this requires genuine independence for the central bank, but my preferred solution would be to abolish the central bank altogether, have the QFC scheme adopted by the commercial banks, and amend the fiscal constitution to limit government borrowing.

However, the key issue is whether my scheme is better or worse than other schemes to achieve a stable price level. Is it better or worse than a gold standard, a monetarist rule, and so on, as a means of stabilizing the price level? I contend that my scheme is at least as good as any other in this regard, and Hillier offers no valid challenge to this claim. Simply pointing out that it cannot withstand a sustained fiscal attack does not tell us whether it is better or worse than any other rules we might choose, bearing in mind that none of them could withstand such an attack either. To use a military analogy, my claim is that I have produced a tank that is at least as good as any other available. This claim may or may not be valid, but Hillier does not challenge it. Instead, he merely points out that it cannot withstand an attack from a tactical nuclear weapon. He is right, of course, but no tank could withstand such an attack, and Hillier gives the tank purchaser no guidance as to which tank to choose. In short, the fiscal issue identified by Hillier *is* a concern, and I readily support measures to limit government deficit spending, but Hillier sheds no light on the merits and demerits of my scheme relative to alternative schemes to stabilize the price level.

10 Using futures prices to control inflation

Reply to Garrison and White

In a recent paper, Garrison and White (1997) offered a thoughtful and sceptical assessment of several recent proposals to use price-index futures contracts to achieve price-level targets. Their main focus is a scheme put forward by Sumner (1995), but they also addressed a scheme that I suggested (Dowd 1994b, 1995a) and made substantial criticisms of price-index futures schemes in general. Sumner (1997) has already replied to those that pertain to his scheme, and this 'Reply' responds to those that pertain to mine.[1]

The objective of my scheme is to achieve price stability while also making the monetary system fully automatic (i.e. so doing away with discretionary monetary policy). This objective would be achieved by the central bank pegging the price of price-index futures contracts, and then relying on private-sector arbitrage to ensure that the money supply is consistent with a stable expected price level. The actual price level would then be equal to this expected price level plus or minus a (hopefully, small) random error.

Futures trading and the feedback mechanism

All price-index futures schemes rely on a feedback mechanism from price-level expectations via money supply to the subsequently realized price level. This mechanism ensures that money is retired from circulation if expected prices are too high, and added to the monetary circulation if expected prices are too low. In the case of my scheme, the changes in money supply would come about as private agents react to arbitrage opportunities in the market for price-index futures contracts and trade such contracts with the central bank for base money (see Chapter 8). These trades would then produce a supply of base money consistent with a zero expected inflation rate. However, Garrison and White (1997: 537) suggest that the feedback process is inadequate, because agents would have no incentive to trade in futures contracts until the latest possible date, and by that time it would be too late for their futures trading (and, hence, the associated changes in base money) to influence the price level on the target date.

There are two problems with this argument as it applies to my scheme. The first is that it presupposes that the central bank would trade a futures contract at the same fixed price throughout the relevant trading period (e.g. that it would trade June CPI futures at a fixed price from the beginning to the end of May). However, the central bank cannot peg the price of a futures contract for any length of time and my scheme does not envisage that it do so (see Chapter 8). If the central bank were committed to maintaining a constant futures price for any length of time, agents could sell long-dated contracts to it, make a riskless investment of the base money they obtain for selling contracts, and then liquidate their short positions later on to make an arbitrage profit. It is to rule out such opportunities that the central bank would peg the price of a futures contract on one particular day only, instead of pegging the price for any significant period of time (see Chapter 8).

There is also another reason why this criticism does not apply to the Dowd scheme. In that scheme, the central bank would peg the price of a given futures contract on one particular day well before it matures. If a contract matures in June, the central bank might trade June contracts on one day in, say, the previous September. If agents wished to trade June contracts against the central bank, they would therefore have to trade on that one day in September or not at all; and the option of waiting until the end of May to trade June futures contracts against the central bank would not arise. If the trading day is placed far enough ahead of the contract expiry date, trading in that particular contract against the central bank would ensure that base money changes have enough time to influence the June CPI – and the feedback mechanism would work.[2]

Nonetheless, Garrison and White (1997: 537 note 6) have a valid point when they say that my earlier scheme does not give members of the public the timely information about the monetary base changes (or about outstanding interest in futures contracts) they would need to be able to judge when to stop speculating further in futures contracts.[3] To meet this objection, the central bank would have to trade contracts simultaneously, rather than sequentially, but the trading would have to be organized so that each individual trader either knows what the rest of the market is doing when his/her own final bid is accepted, or else makes bids conditional on what the rest of the market is doing.

• In the first case, the central bank could invite initial bids, announce the bid total, and then invite revised bids; it would then sum the revised bids, announce the new total, and invite agents to revise their bids again; and it would proceed in this way again and again until no one wished to revise their bids any more. The bids would then be accepted and positions taken accordingly. In effect, the central bank would organize a market reminiscent of Walras' auction with a real *tâtonnement* process, but with the quantity rather than the price of bids as the variable to be determined.[4]

- Alternatively, following Sumner (1997: 543–4), the central bank could invite agents to submit a schedule of conditional bids, with each bid conditional on a suitable variable (such as the total bid or the monetary base). The central bank could then find the equilibrium total bid (i.e. that total bid equal to the total bid on which all individual bids are conditioned), and set individual bids (and, hence, trades) so that they sum to the equilibrium total.

Either way, the information problem should be resolved and the amounts traded by individual traders should be consistent with their individual price-level expectations and the amount traded by the market as a whole.[5]

Does the scheme discipline the central bank?

Another potential problem raised by Garrison and White is that price-index futures schemes might provide relatively weak incentives for the central bank to aim for the target price level (Garrison and White 1997: 539). They suggest that financial losses are a weak discipline on the central bank because it can simply print additional money to pay off its debts. They also raise the possibility that an inflationary process might take hold if the central bank pegs the prices of futures contracts and prices generally turn out to be too high; the central bank then suffers losses when its futures positions mature, prints additional money to meet these losses, and the new money pushes prices even higher; the process is then repeated with each contract cycle, and prices rise indefinitely.

Do these concerns apply to the Dowd scheme? I suggest not, for two reasons. First, the scenario outlined by Garrison and White assumes that the stock of base money can keep rising, and does not allow for the way in which that scheme ensures that the stock of base money is periodically returned to a level consistent with a constant expected price level. Remember that the scheme gives arbitragers an incentive to take long positions in futures if they believe that expected prices are above target. These long positions would imply that private agents return base money back to the central bank. The stock of base money would then fall until the expected price level had fallen back to its 'par' value and zero-arbitrage equilibrium had been restored. Even if the central bank prints base money to pay for its futures losses, private arbitrage would ensure that the stock of base money was subsequently returned to its equilibrium value and the expected price level restored to par. The Dowd scheme therefore prevents a process of inflationary monetary growth, even if the central bank meets futures losses by (temporarily) issuing more money.

There is also another consideration. Part of the motivation behind the Dowd scheme is to automatize the issue of money and so relieve the central bank of its monetary management duties. In such a system, market forces would ensure that the money supply was consistent with the targeted expected price level, automatically, without any need for the central bank to make discretionary money policy decisions. The question of giving the central bank an incentive to achieve the 'correct' money supply or hit any particular price-level target would therefore not arise. The target would be built into the scheme and we would rely on private arbitrage – not central bank monetary policy – to ensure that the target was met. All the central bank would have to do is periodically buy and sell futures contracts as required, at a given price.

Conclusions

I welcome Garrison and White's scepticism about price-index futures schemes. These schemes are still poorly understood and need to be investigated further. Nonetheless, there are also significant differences between the various schemes on offer and I believe that Garrison and White offer no persuasive arguments to suggest that an automatic futures-based monetary system is unsound.

11 The 'compensated dollar' revisited

We have standardized every other unit in commerce except the most important and universal unit of all, the unit of purchasing power. What business man would consent for a moment to make a contract in terms of yards of cloth or tons of coal, and leave the size of the yard or the ton to chance? . . . But the dollar is still left to the chances of gold mining. At first we could not standardize units of electricity because we had no adequate instruments for measuring those elusive magnitudes. But as soon as such measuring devices were invented, these units were standardized. We have hitherto had a similar excuse for not standardizing the dollar as a unit of purchasing power . . . . With the development of index numbers, however . . . we now have at hand all the materials for scientifically standardizing the dollar . . . . In this way it is within the power of society, when it chooses, to create a standard monetary yardstick, a stable dollar.

(Irving Fisher 1913)[1]

It is an old adage that periods of monetary instability always produce renewed interest in stable money and how to obtain it. Much of the recent interest in stable money centres on schemes to make the currency convertible, and it is natural that many should look at the convertible monetary systems of the past. These systems involved pegging the price of one or more precious metals, but had the drawback that they made the price level fluctuate with changes in the relative prices of those metals. This drawback led some writers to believe that the precious-metals standards could be improved upon and the value of the currency stabilized by tying it to a price index, and the most famous scheme to be proposed along these lines was the 'compensated dollar' of Irving Fisher (1911). The idea was for the price of the issuer's medium of redemption, gold, to be lowered (or raised) by a certain amount in proportion to the extent to which a price index exceeds (or falls short of) some target value. The change in the price of gold would counteract the change in the price index and help return the index to par. The compensated dollar scheme should be of obvious interest to modern economists looking for monetary rules to end inflation, but it also should be of interest because it provided the inspiration for a number of recent proposals to stabilize prices and has played a significant part in recent discussions about currency convertibility (see e.g. Yeager and Woolsey 1991, Schnadt and Whittaker 1993, and Dowd 1995b).

Yet despite its importance, there has been relatively little recent interest in the 'compensated dollar' plan as such.[2] This chapter examines the feasibility of the scheme and argues that it has serious problems, some of which have never been adequately recognized. One problem is that the system is not adequately protected against speculative attack, but other problems can arise from the peculiar price-level dynamics stemming from the currency issuer's pricing rule, and these problems are sufficiently serious to suggest that it is very doubtful whether any version of his scheme would in practice deliver the price stability Fisher that promised for it.

The 'compensated dollar'

Fisher first advocated the 'compensated dollar' scheme in *The Purchasing Power of Money* (1911). He then presented papers on the subject to the meeting of the International Congress of Chambers of Commerce in Boston in September 1912 and three months later to that year's meeting of the American Economics Association in Minneapolis. Papers outlining the proposal were subsequently published in the *Economic Journal* in December 1912 and in the *Quarterly Journal of Economics* in February 1913. The *QJE* article was followed later that year by a technical appendix in the same journal, and the presentation and discussion at the AEA meanwhile was published in the *AEA Papers and Proceedings* in March 1913. His proposal attracted a great deal of attention, and he replied to many of the criticisms in an article in the *American Economic Review* in December 1914. The essence of his proposal is

> to make the purchasing power of the dollar constant. It would compensate for any loss of purchasing power of each grain of gold by increasing the number of grains which go to make a dollar. In other words, it aims to standardize the dollar as a unit of purchasing power. We have standardized the yard, the pound, the kilowatt, and every other important commercial unit except the most important of all, the dollar, the unit of purchasing power. We now have a gold dollar of constant weight, but of varying purchasing power. We need a dollar of constant purchasing power and varying weight.
> (Fisher 1913a: 214)

He gave a concrete illustration a little later:

> Today prices are nearly 50 per cent above the level of 1896; that is, a dollar will now buy about two-thirds of what it would buy then. Yet the

dollar has remained the same in weight – 25.8 grains. If the plan here proposed had been in operation since 1896, the weight of the dollar would virtually (but not literally) have increased until today it would have been heavy enough to possess 50 per cent more purchasing power than it actually does possess . . . The level of prices would then be the same today (in terms of this supposed heavier dollar of 38.7 grains) as it was in 1896 (in terms of the actual dollar of 25.8 grains).

(Fisher 1913a: 217–218)[3]

An important question then arises: how would it be possible to know the proper adjustment to be made in the weight of the dollar without putting a dangerous discretionary power in the hands of government officials or anyone else? Fisher suggested that the necessary adjustments could be put on an automatic footing by means of price indices. There are various price indices to choose from, of course,

but they practically all agree remarkably well with one another. When once a system of index numbers is agreed upon, their numerical calculation becomes a purely clerical matter. A statistical bureau . . . would compile and publish these statistics periodically and the actual prices on which they were based. If at any time the official index number showed that the price level had risen 1 per cent above par, this would be the signal for an increase of 1 per cent in the virtual dollar.

(Fisher 1913b: 23)

The plan, in brief, is to 'mark up or down the weight of the dollar (that is, to mark down or up the price of gold bullion) *in exact proportion to the deviations above or below par of the index number of prices*' (ibid.).[4] To indicate how his scheme might have worked, Fisher provided some illustrative simulations that indicated that there would have been a stable price level under any of three slightly different numerical versions of the scheme. 'It is clear', he wrote,

that the proposed system, if not perfect, certainly tends strongly to bring the index number back toward par or to restrain its movements from par, and that if properly planned . . . it could always maintain substantial constancy . . . of the level of prices.

(Fisher 1913c: 394).[5]

Complications from the existence of a gold coinage

There are however some complications. Fisher's system is easiest understood in a world where exchange media are paper or token coins (i.e. ones whose intrinsic value is significantly less than their face value), but complications can arise if there is a full-bodied coinage. Imagine that the weight of the coin dollar is 25.8 grains, as it was when he first wrote, but that the issuer is required to redeem these coins for an amount of gold with a purchasing power equal to that of the dollar at some base year. If that year was 1896, then we would under his scheme have had a 1911 'virtual' dollar with a weight of about 35.8 grains, and the difference of 10 grains can be regarded as the issuer's seignorage. Gold coins, as Fisher explains:

> would simply become what the silver dollar now is, token coins. Or, better, they would be, like the gold certificates, mere warehouse receipts, or, as it were, 'brass checks' for gold bullion on deposit in the Treasury. Otherwise expressed, gold coin would be merely gold certificates printed on gold instead of on paper.
>
> (Fisher 1913b: 24)

But if the weight of the virtual dollar should fall below 25.8 grains, the gold coinage would be worth more as bullion than as its face value in coin, and private agents could melt down gold coins into bullion and make a profit at the Treasury's expense by presenting the bullion at the Treasury for gold coins. If the weight of the virtual dollar were 12.9 grains, for example, a gold coin weighing 25.8 grains could be melted into bullion and then presented to the Treasury to be coined, and an arbitrager would have converted one gold coin into two. He could repeat the operation indefinitely and make arbitrarily large profits at the government's expense (see Fisher 1913a: 226). Some means would therefore need to be found to prevent this 'negative seignorage' outcome, and Fisher suggested that the gold currency could be recoined at a lower weight, much as the Philippine peso had been re-coined when the gold-exchange system had been adopted there, or the gold coinage could be dispensed with altogether, as he actually preferred. As a practical matter, however, he felt that this negative seignorage outcome would be unlikely anyway, since he expected gold to continue to depreciate, but he readily acknowledged that it could not be ruled out and some proviso needed to be made about how to respond should the need arise (Fisher 1913b: 25).

Difficulties from fixing the price of the redemption medium

More serious difficulties for Fisher's scheme arise from the government issuer's fixing of the price of the medium of redemption (MOR), namely, gold. Fisher himself stumbled across the problem in a particular context, but never got to the bottom of it. He understood that the change in the weight of the gold dollar could itself affect the value of gold bullion (see Fisher 1913c: app. 3) and acknowledged that some allowance had to be made for this effect in the government's price-fixing rule. If the weight of the dollar is increased – that is, its price is reduced – domestic gold minting would be discouraged, more gold would be used up in the arts, and so on, and the relative price of gold would fall. If prices were to be stabilized, Fisher concluded that the gold weight of the dollar must increase by *more than* the percentage increase in the price index. The problem is to determine by how much more, and Fisher had no clear answer. He suggested that it might be by twice as much, and felt that any greater increase might be destabilizing because it would 'correct the deviation so much as to produce a deviation greater than the original in the opposite direction' (ibid.: 397), but this suggestion was little more than a guess, and Fisher had nothing further to offer. The point is that the issuer really needs to know what the relative price of gold should be so that it can adjust its nominal price to hit any particular price-level target. This problem is of course virtually intractable. The issuer cannot know the appropriate relative price, and any mistakes it makes will spill over and push the price level away from its target value. Fisher could not give the government the discretionary power to 'do its best' without throwing away the automaticity of his system that was one of its main attractions, and yet he could offer no rule that would give the government issuer an appropriate guide by which to respond.

The problem that Fisher stumbled across is also a more fundamental one than he realized. He came across it whilst exploring the extent to which a change in the nominal price of gold would affect mining, the demand by the arts, and so on, but he appeared to overlook the point that the same basic problem arises whenever any factor changes to influence the relative price of gold. Under Fisher's system, the government has to adopt a rule to change the nominal price of gold in response to changes in the price index, but the effect of that nominal price change on the price index will depend on the factors that determine the relative price of gold, and the government's rule therefore needs to allow properly for what the latter would be. To see what can happen if it failed to make this allowance, suppose the currency issuer follows a Fisher-type rule that changes the nominal price of the medium of redemption, gold, by α times the deviation of the price level from its target value p^*:

$$\Delta p_{g,t} = \alpha(p_{t-1} - p^*) \tag{1}$$

where $p_{g,t}$ is the log of the price of gold in period t, and p_{t-1} is the log of the price-level index in $t-1$. (α is the parameter that Fisher usually took as -1 for illustrative purposes, but actually suggested should be -2 in his discussion in appendix 3 of Fisher (1913c).) If we choose our units such that $p^* = 0$, (1) becomes

$$\Delta p_{g,t} = \alpha \, p_{t-1} \tag{2}$$

Assume that the market for gold clears at all times. We can then write out a relative price equation for gold of the form:

$$p_{g,t} - p_t = \beta_t \tag{3}$$

where β_t can be interpreted as the inverse demand function for gold in period t. (If one prefers, one can also interpret it as the equilibrium relative price of gold.) If we now substitute out the price of gold and rearrange, we derive a first-order difference equation in the (log of) the price level:

$$p_t - (1+\alpha) \, p_{t-1} = - \Delta \beta_t \tag{4}$$

which can be solved in textbook manner. (4) implies that the price level has a 'long-run equilibrium' value given by

$$p_t = - \Delta \beta_t [1-(1+\alpha)L]^{-1} \tag{5}$$

where L is the lag operator, and this 'long-run equilibrium' value is to be interpreted as the value around which actual p_t oscillates, or from which it diverges, or toward which it converges, depending on the dynamics of (4). Given $\Delta\beta t$, the stability or otherwise of the price level depends on the root λ of the auxiliary equation corresponding to (4). A necessary and sufficient condition for p_t to be stable is that

$$-1 < \lambda < 1 \tag{6}$$

(see for example, Goldberg (1958)) and one can easily show that $\lambda = 1+\alpha$.[6] The behaviour of the price level relative to an assumed initial value depends on the value of α, and stability requires that $-2 < \alpha < 0$. The value of α also determines whether p_t oscillates around its initial value or stays on one side of it. If $\alpha < -1$, the root λ is negative, and p_t oscillates around its initial value; and if $\alpha > -1$, the root λ is positive and p_t stays on one side or other of its initial value.[7]

We thus get four principal outcomes, depending on the value of α. First, if $\alpha < -2$, the root λ is negative, and p_t would oscillate with ever greater oscillations around its initial value. The price level would be highly unstable. Second, if $-2 < \alpha < -1$, p_t would oscillate around long-run equilibrium because the root is still negative, but the oscillations would dampen over time. Shocks to the price level would gradually be corrected. Third, if $-1 < \alpha < 0$, the root becomes positive so the price level would stay on one side of its initial value, but would converge toward that value over time. Fourth, if $\alpha > 0$, the price level would move further away from its initial value over time, and would therefore be highly unstable.

In addition to these four cases, we also get three 'knife edge' cases where $\alpha = -2$, -1 and 0 respectively. The first case (i.e. $\alpha = -2$) was the one that Fisher actually preferred. The root λ is then equal to -1, and the price level would fluctuate around its initial value with no tendency ever to settle down. The basic stability requirement that shocks to the price level be corrected would not be satisfied.[8] Fisher's attempt to allow for a changing relative price of gold by choosing $\alpha = -2$ would have proved to be highly counterproductive. The second case is the one Fisher usually quoted for illustrative purposes. The root of the difference equation becomes zero, and (4) implies the price level equation:

$$p_t = - \Delta \beta_t \tag{7}$$

The price level now moves inversely with the rate of change of the relative price of gold. The third case is simply the gold standard in which the price of gold is fixed. (3) then implies that the price level is

$$p_t = - \beta_t \tag{8}$$

The price level now moves inversely with the relative price of gold. If one's objective is to stabilize the price level, the choice between a compensated dollar with $\alpha = -1$ and a gold standard (i.e. $\alpha = 0$) depends on whether one thinks the level of the relative price of gold is more or less stable than its rate of change.

In short, given β_t, any value of α other than -1 or 0 would lead to the price level deviating from its long-run equilibrium value. Any value less than -1 would produce oscillations around the initial value of the price level, and any value less than -2 would produce growing oscillations. A value equal to -1 would produce oscillations with no tendency to increase or decrease over time, any value greater than -1 but less than 0 would produce gradual convergence toward the initial value, and any value greater than 0 would produce gradual divergence away from the initial value. A value of $\alpha = -1$ would make the price level move with the rate of change of the relative price of gold, and an α-value $= 0$ would make the price level move with the level of that relative price.

However, there is no reason to suppose that the long-run equilibrium value of p_t would remain stable even given some initial value p_0. As (5) indicates, any change in the relative price term $\Delta \beta_t$ would alter the long-run equilibrium value of p_t. Ironically, the long-run equilibrium price level under the compensated dollar would therefore be as vulnerable to a change in the relative price of gold as it would have been under the gold standard itself. Even if the price level was (somehow) always maintained at its long-run equilibrium value, the failure of the Fisher rule to allow for changes in the relative price of gold would still prevent it from delivering price-level stability. Fisher was therefore right to worry about changes in the equilibrium relative price of gold, but as we have seen, his attempted solution merely ensured that a fluctuation in the price level away from its target value was never properly corrected.

The difficulty of Fisher's position now becomes clear. He needed a rule that produces stable price-level dynamics around the long-run equilibrium price level and ensures that the long-run equilibrium value itself is not vulnerable to changes in the various factors that determine the relative price of gold. At the same time, Fisher also needed to ensure that the rule he found was not tampered with *ex post* if the system was to retain the automaticity that was one of its key attractions. Fisher's problem is for all practical purposes intractable.[9]

Restrictions to protect the issuer against speculative attack

A third issue with Fisher's proposal relates to his insistence that the Treasury operate a spread between the price at which it would buy bullion and that at which it would sell it, and impose certain restrictions on the rates at which these prices could change. He regarded this spread as an 'essential detail' (Fisher 1913a: 220) and suggested a figure of perhaps 1 per cent. The Mint (or purchase) price would be the lower of the two, and the margin between the two prices he suggested be considered as a 'brassage' charge for minting.[10] The purpose of this spread was not to cover minting charges as such, but to 'avoid speculation in gold [potentially] disastrous to the government' (Fisher 1913b: 25–6). Suppose that agents expected the price of gold to rise from $18 to $18.10 an ounce. Speculators would then buy gold from the government in order to sell it back to the government after its price had risen. They would make a profit at the government's expense of 10¢ an ounce, and in theory could make arbitrarily large profits by demanding arbitrarily large amounts of gold before its price rose. If the price of gold was expected to fall, say, from $18.10 to $18 an ounce, speculators would sell all the gold they could to the government for the present higher price, and then buy it back after its price had fallen, and again make arbitrarily large profits at the government's expense (see also Fisher 1913a: 227; 1913b: 26).

To rule out this sort of speculation, Fisher suggested that the brassage differential should be accompanied by a proviso that any change in the government pair of prices was not to exceed this differential. The profits from speculative purchases or sales of gold within any period would then be outweighed by the brassage charge, and there would be no net profit at the government's expense. Suppose that the government's buy price was $12.28, and its sell price $12.41, representing a brassage charge of 1 per cent, and that price changes were restricted to under 1 per cent as Fisher suggested. If an agent receives interim information that the gold prices next period will rise, the new government buy price would still be less than the present government sell price, there would be no profit to be made by speculating on that information, and the government should be immune to that sort of attack (Fisher 1913b: 26). The only avenue of speculative attack left is that based on expected future prices two or more periods away, when the future government buy price might be more than the current sell price. To rule this sort of attack out, Fisher suggested that it might be 'possible and perhaps desirable' to require that the proportionate rise in the prices of gold should be less than an appropriate rate of interest on short term investments (Fisher 1913a: 227 n.3; 1913c: 386–7). Unlike the previous restriction, this restriction would work only against an expected rise in gold prices – it was designed against a speculative attack in which an agent buys gold and then sells it again later, foregoing the interim interest, and Fisher's suggestion was to make sure that the percentage capital gain is always less than the interest lost – and Fisher argued (incorrectly, as is made clear later) that there is no need for a similar provision against a fall in gold prices. If the brassage charge were 1 per cent and prices were changed monthly, he suggested the upward movement of prices might be restricted to 4 per cent a year, for example, but a downward movement be allowed of up to 12 per cent a year (ibid.).[11]

But these suggestions would still leave the government issuer exposed to damaging speculative attack if the government's gold prices were expected to fall. Let the government's bid-ask spread be $x\%$, the rate of interest over each period $y\%$, and the expected percentage price change (in absolute terms) $z\%$. Fisher's claim that the government is always protected in these circumstances provided $z \leq x$ is wrong. Suppose an agent at the beginning of a period correctly expects that the government's gold prices will fall at the start of the next period, so he sells gold, invests in an interest-bearing asset with the proceeds, and then liquidates the investment and buys gold again when the gold price has fallen. He would obtain a net profit of approximately $z + y + yz - x$ from each operation, and the fact that this profit can clearly be positive even if $z \leq x$ proves that the government is not adequately protected. This example illustrates, indeed, that the government is even more vulnerable to speculative attack when its gold prices are expected to fall than when they are expected to rise. When the prices are expected to fall, arbitragers will sell gold now and invest the proceeds in the interim period before prices fall, and the interest from that investment is therefore to be considered as an additional element in the profit from the arbitrage operation. When gold prices are expected to rise, on the other hand, arbitragers will buy gold and hold it in the interim, and the interest they would have received constitutes a cost of the operation. The arbitrage profit in the one case is $z + y + yz - x$, but in the other is $z - y - yz - x$, which is less. There is an asymmetry, but Fisher got it the wrong way round, and at least one more additional restriction needs to be added to his system to rule these attacks out.[12]

Assessing the 'compensated dollar'

It is difficult to avoid the conclusion that the 'compensated dollar' was ultimately a failure. Leaving aside more minor difficulties, there are three fundamental problems with it. First, the compensated dollar system would lead the price level to follow a difference equation, and my analysis of that equation suggests that under Fisher's preferred version of his scheme the price level would not meet the stability condition that must be satisfied if deviations of the price level from its long-run equilibrium value are to be corrected over time. Second, it is doubtful that the price level's long-run equilibrium value would itself be particularly stable. The long-run equilibrium value appears to be as volatile as the relative price of the MOR (i.e. gold, in Fisher's system). The price level would oscillate around a long-run equilibrium value that itself fluctuated with the relative price of gold. Since the gold standard would at least have dispensed with the oscillations, it is therefore likely that the compensated dollar in practice would have delivered even less price-level stability than the gold standard Fisher intended it to replace. Third, the scheme would be vulnerable to successful speculative attack despite Fisher's attempts to patch it up. Since changes in the price of gold would be predictable, and Fisher's restrictions against gold price movements were not adequate to protect it, the compensated dollar would be open to much the same sort of speculative attack as exchanges rates under a 'crawling-peg' exchange-rate regime.

These weaknesses, it seems to me, all stem from a common feature of the compensated dollar scheme: namely, that it requires the issuer of currency to peg and periodically re-peg the price of the redemption medium it uses. This requirement creates the 'one-way bet' that exposes the issuer to speculative attack, creates the systematic price-level oscillations illustrated earlier, and ensures that the equilibrium price-level in Fisher's system cannot be stable unless the relative price of gold is also stable. In the final analysis, it may be that one may have to choose between keeping the price of the redemption medium constant (e.g. adopting a gold standard) or letting the price of the redemption medium float freely (e.g. adopting a fiat currency, or making the currency indirectly convertible). The problems befalling the compensated dollar suggest that any intermediate position may not be tenable.

12   Money and the market
What role for government?

As communism is at last assigned to its rightful place in the dustbin of history, those who survive it have to come to terms with the task of sorting out the dreadful mess it has left behind. Perhaps the only benefit of having lived through communism is that many of those who have done so have a sound grasp of the dangers of government interference in markets. Such understanding leads naturally to a free-market outlook, and many in the former Soviet empire fully understand that the new order must be a liberal one if they are to have any future worth having. But therein lies an immense problem. We understand that the present situation is a total mess, and we understand that once the transition is made, the new market economy will function smoothly and efficiently, and provide the prosperity and economic security that are so desperately needed. The problem is how to get from here to there, and on that issue we are all to a greater or lesser extent flying by the seats of our pants. We understand reasonably well how healthy free-market economies work, but nursing a chronically sick economy to health is a far more difficult problem that none of us is well equipped to handle, and the problem will not wait until we feel we are ready for it. An immense chasm lies between the present mess here and economic health over there, and we need to think carefully about the transition if the countries of the former Soviet bloc are to avoid falling in it as they attempt to make the leap.

Were we dealing with a particular industry, the bakery industry, say, the solution would be relatively straightforward. We would first change the legal framework to allow private bakers to set up and then grow. They would quickly erode the market share of the state bakery corporation, and at some point we would simply abolish the latter and sell off its assets for whatever we could get. There would be some adjustment difficulties, of course, but on the whole the reform should go through without our losing too much sleep about it. Reforming the monetary system and the banking industry is less straightforward, and we need to tread more carefully. We could – and should – reform the legal framework to allow private bankers to set up and compete, but we cannot simply expect them to produce new brands of money in the same way that private bakers would produce new brands of bread, and then abolish the state bank and forget about it.

Money, or to be precise, the unit of account, is different from bread in a fundamental respect that demands that we acknowledge it.[1] There is no reason to believe that the consumption of bread generates externalities, but we cannot say the same about the use of a particular unit of account. A unit of account is a social convention, like a language, and its utility to a user depends to a considerable extent on how many others use it as well. If one more person decides to use a particular unit of account, his decision generates benefits to those who already use it – benefits that have no obvious analog in our earlier bakery example. A unit of account is like a telephone, the utility of which depends on how many others belong to the same unit of account or telephone network. The problem, from our point of view, is that if the utility of a particular unit of account depends on how many others also use it, then an individual's decision whether to stay with an existing unit or switch to using another will depend on what he thinks the others will do, and each individual faces the same decision. This element of strategic interdependence explains why it has proved so difficult in the past to induce spontaneous shifts away from badly managed units of account to alternatives with demonstrably superior risk and return characteristics. We might all appreciate that the existing unit of account is performing badly, and we might each prefer that we all switched over to use some other, but it may not be rational for any of us to switch unless we can be confident that at least a certain number of others will also switch with us. The optimal strategy for each individual is then to wait for others to take the chance and switch first, and switch himself only when the number of those who have already switched has reached a critical level. Everyone of course adopts much the same strategy, the critical mass is never reached, and the result is that no one ever switches. Everyone then continues to use a unit of account that no one really wants, and that despite the fact that everyone may be perfectly free to switch over to demonstrably superior alternatives. Offering a new unit of account is therefore not as easy as offering a new loaf of bread: producing better bread presumably suffices to win over those who currently obtain theirs from the state, but offering a better unit of account does not. Simply allowing agents to use an alternative unit of account is not enough to get them to adopt it; something more is required than the introduction of new units of account or the abolition of legal restrictions against competing ones.[2] What is needed is a reform package that takes account of these network factors, but that also allows the maximum possible role for the market forces on which a successful monetary and banking system depends.[3]

Stabilizing the value of the currency

The need for immediate monetary stabilization

Perhaps the most urgent need in many countries in the former Soviet empire is to end inflation and stabilize the value of the currency. If the best way to destroy the capitalist system is to 'debauch the currency,' as Lenin reportedly said (Keynes 1919: 77), it is also true that one can never hope to establish a market economy on a sound basis without ensuring that it has a stable currency. Inflation injects 'noise' into the relative price signals that markets give out to guide resource allocation decisions, and distorted price signals lead markets to malfunction and, in some cases, to break down completely.

Damaging as inflation is, both economic theory and experience indicate that it is relatively simple to stop it. It can be stopped by a monetary reform that imposes some discipline on the issue of money and reins in the excessive monetary growth that is at least the proximate cause of inflation. One way to do so would be to impose a monetary growth rule on the central bank, but a better solution is to make the currency convertible.[4] The price of the currency would then be fixed against something else, and with the price fixed, the issuer(s) would have no control over the quantity. The quantity in circulation would be determined by the demand to hold it, and any amounts in excess of that demand would be returned to the issuer(s) for redemption. The price level would then be determined by the relative price of the 'anchor' – the commodity or asset whose nominal price is fixed-against goods and services in general – and the trick is to choose an anchor that would generate a stable nominal price level by having a stable relative price against everything else.

In the past, such monetary reforms usually involved the re-establishment of the gold standard, and were remarkably successful. The historical evidence clearly indicates that credible reforms along these lines can eliminate even hyperinflation, and can eliminate it very rapidly indeed. In the early 1920s, most of Eastern and Central Europe was ravaged by inflation. Germany, Austria, Hungary, and Poland – all countries then suffering from hyperinflation – implemented radical monetary reforms that ended their inflations within a short period of time (Sargent 1986: 115). These reforms re-established the gold standard and reinforced the credibility of the commitment to peg the price of gold by limiting or prohibiting the government's right to borrow from the banking system. In each case the inflation was apparently over well within a month, and in several cases virtually overnight (see Bresciani-Turroni 1937: 334). The same period also saw more moderate inflations cured by similar reforms in Czechoslovakia in 1919 and France in 1926. In both countries inflation stopped very rapidly once a credible monetary reform program was announced, and the key elements in each case were the restoration of the gold standard and the adoption of legal restrictions against government borrowing from the banking system.[5]

A currency board to stabilize the value of the currency

What is required, then, are monetary stabilization programs that can be implemented quickly and easily. An attractive option is to set up a currency board as suggested recently by a number of writers.[6] A currency board is an institution that issues and buys back the domestic currency on demand at a fixed price in terms of some foreign currency, but that also observes a reserve ratio so high that the currency it issues can be considered almost perfectly sound. The board's sole function is to satisfy the public's demand for currency. One can think of the board as providing hand-to-hand currency and, perhaps, redemption media to be used by the commercial banking system, but it would not issue deposits as such.

Currency boards typically hold reasonably safe assets that are dominated in the currency to which the domestic currency is pegged, but that also bear some pecuniary return (such as treasury bills). The reserve ratio is usually over 100 per cent in case the prices of these assets should fall (as when foreign interest rates rise) and inflict losses on their holders. The excess over 100 per cent therefore provides a cushion to keep the board's net worth positive should it suffer any losses on its assets. The board would make profits equal to the difference between the net earnings on those assets and its own operating expenses, and experience suggests the latter should be about 1 per cent of the value of assets (Hanke and Schuler 1991a: 4). Any profits above the level needed to maintain the board's reserve ratio could be remitted to the government as payment for the board's assets, which the government itself would have to provide when it established the board.[7] The board would need to be safeguarded in various ways against the danger of political depredation.[8] It would therefore own the assets it holds for as long as it existed, and most of those assets would be held abroad where they would be safe from plunder. The board would also be legally independent, perhaps with a legal seat in another country, and with its directors serving staggered terms and a number of them being foreign nationals appointed by foreign institutions (e.g. specified commercial banks) that would not be accountable to the domestic government.[9] The currency could be protected further by prohibiting the government from borrowing from the domestic financial system.[10] The appropriate peg for the domestic currency would be a strong Western currency, and perhaps the best one for any country in the former Soviet bloc would be the mark.[11]

Currency boards are ideal for governments that seek a quick and effective means of establishing the stable monetary conditions that are essential for economic recovery. With a currency board, there is virtually no room for discretion, because the monetary system operates more or less automatically. Currency boards are independent of government and are well protected against the danger of political interference. The currency they issue is fully secured by sound foreign assets and is effectively as secure as the foreign currency to which it is anchored. Currency boards are very easy to establish: all that is required is that the legislation be passed to set up the board, the directors be appointed, the right to issue currency be transferred to the board from the existing government bank of issue, and the board be provided with its assets by the government.[12] In sum, currency boards can be established very quickly if there is the political will to do so. They also have a proven track record, and have worked well even under the most unstable political conditions (Hanke and Schuler 1991a: 5).

Competition for the currency board

Unlike historical currency boards, the one proposed here would have no exclusive right to issue currency. There would be complete freedom to issue currency subject only to laws against the unauthorized copying of the currency issues of others and subject to the commercial law that would provide for the enforcement of legally binding promises, such as the promise to redeem currency on demand. New issuers would therefore be allowed to issue their own currency. However given the network problems already mentioned, it is likely that the only ones that would gain any major acceptance would be those denominated in the existing (and now stabilized) unit of account. Like historical free banking systems, there would be one widely accepted unit (or medium) of account.[13] This was a role usually performed by a gold-defined unit of account in the past, but there would in time be multiple issuers of media of exchange of one kind or another whose issues would be clearly distinguishable from each other.[14] To gain acceptance, however, any private currency would have to be able to compete with that issued by the currency board, and perhaps the main requirement to be able to do so is that the private currency be regarded as of comparable soundness. Since no one would normally choose any currency with a significant default risk over the virtually default-free currency provided by the currency board, private currency would gain acceptance only once its prospective issuers had established themselves as sound and reputable financial institutions in the domestic economy.

One would imagine that the first commercial banks to make headway with the issue of private currency would be the large foreign banks that are already setting up branches in Central and Eastern Europe and are increasingly well known there. In the course of time domestic banks would also establish themselves, and they too would issue their own currency to compete with that issued by the currency board and the foreign banks. In time one would also expect the commercial banks – domestic or foreign – to out-compete the currency board in the issue of currency. Commercial banks would eventually establish nationwide branching systems, and each branch would take in the currency of other issuers and hand out its own currency over the counter to the public.[15] These banks would be able to use their conveniently situated branches to keep their own currency in circulation, and though it may operate some branches, the currency board would not be well placed to compete because of its own rigid operating rules.

The eventual need to liquidate the board

The time would therefore come when the currency board's market share would fall to negligible levels and the board itself would have no useful further role. The legislation establishing the currency board ought to anticipate this development by incorporating an explicit 'sunset clause' that would allow for the automatic closing of the board when it ceased to have any further use. The legislation might say, for example, that the board was to be closed three months after its share of the total currency outstanding over the past two months had fallen to 5 per cent. It is important that the board be liquidated and not allowed to continue once it has ceased to serve any useful purpose. The board would not only be redundant, but its rigid institutional structure would generally make it inefficient as an asset manager, and it would be better that it be dissolved so that the resources under its control could be reallocated. Perhaps the best option would be simply to have the board automatically dissolve after its currency share hits the stipulated threshold and have its assets sold off with the proceeds returned to the government.

The main reason for liquidating the currency board is not because it is either useless or inefficient, but because a future government might use it as a platform to establish some form of central banking. The history of currency boards very much bears out this concern. There was (and still is) a tendency to regard currency boards as transitional arrangements between the earlier (relatively) free banking systems that preceded them and the central banking systems that replaced them. A central bank is viewed as necessary to any but the most insignificant of countries, and a central bank, like a national parliament or in many cases a national airline, is regarded almost as a symbol of a country's sovereignty. As a result, virtually all historical currency boards were eventually replaced by central banks, or were transformed into them, and the transition to central banking was considerably eased by the argument that the existence of the currency board already conceded the government's right to go further if it wished and establish a central bank. The money-creation powers of the central bank inevitably invited political interference, and the central bank to a greater or lesser extent always succumbed. Convertibility constraints against the issue of money were gradually relaxed, and eventually abolished altogether, and the central bank was turned into an engine of inflation.

If the new monetary regimes of the old Soviet bloc are to avoid the pitfalls into which their counterparts in the West and elsewhere have fallen, it is important that their currency boards be only transitional arrangements that result in fully private systems of money and banking with no government presence that could be used to undermine the monetary system later on.

The danger of imported monetary instability

The monetary system by this stage would still have one major weakness: the currency would only be as sound as the foreign currency to which it was tied. Should the issuer of that foreign currency inflate, the domestic currency would have to inflate with it because the issuers would still be committed to maintaining its exchange rate with the inflating foreign currency. This danger to domestic monetary stability should not be underrated. Even the Bundesbank – arguably the best of the major Western central banks in terms of its inflation performance – has a good record only in comparison with that of its counterparts, and its record in absolute terms is actually quite poor judged by the more appropriate yardstick of price-level stability. Nor can one assume that the Bundesbank would be able to maintain even this poor inflation record. The limits to its much-vaunted independence from the German government have become much more apparent in the past couple of years, and the German government is in any case now committed by the Maastricht Treaty to replace the mark with a new common currency by 1999. The common currency is supposedly to have a stable value, but one has good reason to be sceptical that this commitment will be honoured. The issuers of most existing currencies are also committed to maintaining their values, but that 'commitment' still does not prevent them from inflating their currencies, and there are good reasons in the Western European context to doubt the value of any 'commitment' to price stability. The fact that much of the drive for a European central bank comes from dissatisfaction with the (relatively) conservative policies of the Bundesbank can only imply that the other European monetary authorities want more inflationary policies, and there is the ever-present danger that the financial problems of the EC will lead to it pressuring the 'independent' European central bank for cheap loans to be financed by printing money (Dowd 1990).

The value of the currency determined on the market

The solution is to look to the market rather than the political authorities to safeguard the value of money. The political authorities should be allowed only a very temporary power to legislate or otherwise control the value the currency – the power needed to clean up the mess that they or their communist predecessors have created – but be denied all powers over the currency once monetary stability has been established. Instead of specifying what the value of the currency should be, except at the beginning, the legal framework should allow the definition of the currency in terms of goods, services, foreign currencies, or whatever to be determined on the market. It might say, for instance, that the value of the rouble is initially so many marks, but private agents would be allowed to use their own 'brands' of the currency if they wished to do so. If the currency is the rouble, equal in value to so many marks, they might issue 'new' roubles or 'superior' roubles, or whatever they choose to call them, equal in value to anything they want.[16] They could issue them with values pegged to pounds, dollars, the CPI, or anything else, subject only to the constraints that they must make their own brands distinguishable from existing ones, and they must not violate existing contracts. Let us now consider each of these requirements in turn and their implications for the behaviour of the banks.

The requirement that private-money producers differentiate their brands effectively prevents banks from issuing an inferior currency. This requirement is important if issuers are to have sufficient incentive to protect their currencies, but is really only the same as requiring that brand names be legally distinguishable. If I can produce autos that look like BMWs, say, but are of inferior quality, and I am also allowed to pass them off as if they were genuine BMWs, then my ability to undercut the genuine BMW producer will obviously make it very difficult for him to maintain his quality, and there is a danger of quality standards falling continuously as the two of us fight it out for market share. The solution is to protect the genuine BMW brand name by penalizing those who use it as a cover to sell a different product. If that is done, car producers can compete on a level playing field and the public will get the quality of product it demands, and there will be no tendency for competition among producers to lead to falling quality standards. So it is with the currency. If I was allowed to pass off an inferior currency as if it were identical to an existing one, competition among producers would lead to the progressive deterioration of the real value of any guarantees, and the value of the currency would fall to its ultimate marginal cost (about zero) in the competitive hyperinflation scenario sometimes described in the literature (see Friedman 1960: 8).

If brand names were protected – if a particular brand of rouble had a particular definition in terms of commodities or something else – then anyone who issued exchange media denominated in that brand of roubles would have a legal obligation to maintain their price at the level implied by the commodity definition of that rouble brand. Any issuer who failed to honour his commitment would be in default of contract and open to the appropriate legal penalties, assuming them to be high enough to discourage default unless the bank was genuinely insolvent. Once this first requirement was satisfied, different banks would be free to compete with different brands of the existing currency. One bank might offer a brand with a convertibility guarantee chosen to stabilize the price level, while another might offer one that would lead to a small amount of inflation. Each brand would have an implied (expected) price-level path attached to it, but brands would otherwise be similar.[17] Competition for market share would consequently lead banks to converge on the brand (or price-level path) most preferred by the public. The path of the price level over time is thus driven by public demand as expressed through the public's willingness to hold different brands of the currency. If people desire zero inflation, as they probably do, then the banks' competition for market share would lead them to offer the public exchange media denominated in a brand of the currency that implies zero inflation.[18] No other brand of the currency would be able to survive in competition with it, and so one would only observe that one brand in equilibrium. It is the threat that inferior banks might lose their market share to banks offering a superior brand that would keep any individual bank or group of banks in line and compel them to provide the brand the public desire. People would always be able to offer alternative brands, but a new brand would only out-compete an old one if it provided a superior price-level path.

The other requirement is that issuers honour any legal commitments they have freely entered into. This constraint has several important implications. One, already mentioned, is that a bank that refused to redeem its exchange media when required to do so would be vulnerable to the penalty for breach of contract. It would therefore have considerable incentive to honour its commitment to buy its issues back, and a law of reflux would operate to ensure that exchange media were roughly compatible with their equilibrium values as implied by the particular brand of the currency.[19] Another implication is that it would severely restrict banks' ability to change the brand of the currency, and this restriction in turn should further help to promote public confidence that the banks would not introduce gratuitous or harmful currency reforms.

Imagine, for the sake of argument, that a bank wished to inflate its currency for some reason, so it announced its intention to replace the existing brand with one that would generate the inflation it desired. It would be immediately constrained by past commitments, of course, and it could not unilaterally change the meaning of the term rouble in pre-existing contracts without exposing itself to lawsuits from creditors who (rightly) considered themselves defrauded. The bank would therefore have to provide its customers with the required advance notice, which could be very long, and to the extent that the latter preferred to stay with the old brand, the bank would either have to offer them business denominated in the old brand, offer them compensation to switch over, or see them go elsewhere. In the first case, the bank would end up having to abandon its plan, or incur the expense of operating on two brands simultaneously; in the second, it would lose out from the cost of compensation; and in the third case it would lose its market share. Any or all of these cases could occur, and the bank would have to pay some penalty in any of them. Even if the bank could maintain its market share by compensating its customers, the very fact that it would have to compensate them because of their preference for the existing brand would put the bank at a competitive disadvantage, and the bank would not be able to maintain the new brand in the longer run. Remember that it is the public's preferences that would be decisive, not those of the bank(s).

In any case, there is no particular reason to suppose that an individual bank or group of banks would actually prefer inflation even if it could keep its market share at a low or negligible cost. Inflation (or, for that matter, deflation) would add to its own accounting costs even if it was fully predictable. Inflation (or deflation) never is predictable, of course, so the bank would also suffer from the noise and related problems created by its own inflation. These costs might be bearable if inflation generated sufficient benefits to offset them, but the benefits of inflation to the issuer, such as they are, come primarily from 'catching out' those who did not anticipate the inflation, and the bank could hardly engineer a 'surprise' inflation precisely because it would be constrained by its own past commitments. Those commitments would force it to announce its intentions well in advance, and its announcement would warn off those it hoped to catch off guard. It turns out, then, that a competitive bank (or group of banks) would almost certainly be unable to engineer any price-level path other than the zero inflation desired by the public, but it is very much doubtful that such a bank would want any other path than zero inflation anyway. The idea of entrusting the value of the currency to the unfettered market might sound unorthodox, but there is no reason to distrust it, and there is certainly no good reason for preferring to give the task of protecting the currency to the politicians instead. One does not put the fox in charge of the chicken house.

Banking and financial reform

The measures outlined earlier are necessary but by no means sufficient to establish the foundations of a sound, free banking system. If they are to succeed, they must be underpinned by other reforms that are essential to any well-functioning market economy. Foremost amongst these is the establishment of clearly defined property rights. The bulk of the property currently belonging to the state or its collectives needs to be privatized, and privatized as soon as possible. Those who obtain it must have a clear and unambiguous title to it, and that title must also include the unrestricted freedom to sell, lease, rent, or use property as collateral to obtain loans. The establishment of solid property rights would also allow individuals the wherewithal to start or expand their own businesses, and to pledge their property as security for bank loans. It would therefore promote an entrepreneurial class from which would come much of the demand for bank credit, but it would also give that class the means to obtain credit. The result would be a growing effective demand for the asset services provided by banks, and profit opportunities for those banks that stepped in to meet that demand.

The banking system itself would need a sound framework of law in which to operate. By and large, banking laws should be governed by the same principles that underscore good commercial law in general. Banks and firms generally need to have well-defined legal identities modelled on Western corporate law, and there need to be clear notions of default and bankruptcy and of the rights and obligations those conditions imply. Entry to the industry should be free and open to all who satisfy certain basic standards. Foreign banks should be free to open and operate on the same terms as domestic banks. Banks should be free to maintain branches wherever they choose. They should be free to engage in any business they want, including insurance, stock underwriting, real estate, and foreign exchange. They should be free of any legal restrictions regarding the reserves they keep, their capital adequacy, the interest they charge or pay, the loans they make, and the deposits they accept. There should be no government-sponsored lender of last resort to protect the banks, and no official deposit insurance scheme. Such schemes only undermine the banks' incentives to maintain their own financial health, and substitute taxpayers' funds for the equity that the banks should maintain themselves. Finally, like most other major institutions, banks

> should be required to publish accurate financial statements frequently. The financial disclosure requirements should be modelled after American and British practice, not after German and Swiss practice that allows banks to keep 'hidden' reserves off balance sheets. Stringent disclosure requirements plus the ordinary penalties on fraud should keep embezzlement at an acceptably low level.
>
> (Schuler, Selgin and Sinkey 1991: 10)

The process of building up the banking system could also be enormously facilitated by foreign banks, and the government should do nothing to discourage them. They would have the advantage of being experienced and already well established in their own countries. They would have their own adjustment problems, but they may still have the initial edge over domestic institutions that would start off with little or no experience, capital, or reputation. A large influx of foreign banks would bring in much-needed bank capital, leading to a more rapid development of the banking system, and a more rapid growth in bank lending. It would also introduce Western banking and financial practices and promote the spread of basic accounting skills, of which all the former Soviet economies are woefully short, and it would give domestic banks clear models from which they could learn good practice more quickly and at less cost than might otherwise be the case.

What applies to banks also applies to foreign firms in general. Foreign direct investment facilitates the rebuilding of the economy's capital structure, promotes the introduction of Western practices, and assists the general shaping up of domestic industry. Domestic firms badly need capital, but there is as yet relatively little of it to be obtained in their own economies and it could take many years before domestic supplies of capital are large enough to meet their demands. Governments should not be afraid to encourage foreigners to invest, and they should resist any xenophobic reactions to foreign 'domination' of the economy. The more foreigners who wish to come in and 'buy up' the country, the better.[20] Foreign investment is an important part of the growth process for countries that need more capital than they can generate themselves, and it implies that investors abroad have confidence in the economy and are willing to invest there because they believe its prospects are good.

Foreign direct investment is desirable not just because Western capital is needed to build factories, introduce Western business practices, restore the infrastructure, and so on. A combination of factors – most industries chronically uncompetitive on world markets, relatively little private property that could be sold off to foreigners, few foreign currency reserves, and a desperate need for Western imports of all kinds – means that these countries have no option but to run up large current account deficits, and financing those deficits requires correspondingly large capital account surpluses (i.e. net investment from abroad). Significant amounts of foreign investment are therefore essential if consumers are not to go short of the food and other goods they need, and if industry is not to be starved of raw materials and other necessary imports. A liberal approach to foreign investment can thus provide a major boost to accelerate the overall recovery process. Without it, consumers could go short of basic goods for years, industry will be crippled for a long time by financial constraints, and economic recovery will be very painful and very slow.

Timing the reforms

It might also be useful to say something about the timing of the various measures discussed here and how they would relate to the overall reform process. Two of the reforms suggested – the establishment of a solid foundation of property law and all that that entails, and a monetary stabilization package – are absolutely basic to the whole reform programme and should be implemented as quickly as possible. Delaying these reforms will only lead to further economic decline, and until they are attended to, any significant economic recovery will be virtually impossible. As mentioned already, the monetary stabilization legislation should ensure adequate protection for the currency board it was setting up, and the same legislation should also authorize the complete removal of any remaining controls on foreign exchange or foreign investment and of any restrictions against the use of alternative units of account. The establishment of a sound foundation of commercial and banking law should follow as soon as possible afterwards, and as with property law, legislators could speed up the process by borrowing large chunks of it from successful legislation in the West.

If these measures are to be fully effective, it is important that they form part of a coherent overall recovery program that would also involve the privatization of the mass of state property inherited from communist days, the deregulation of prices and wages, and the rationalization of the public sector and its finances. The reform of the monetary and banking system is essential, but it is not sufficient on its own, and it is only when all these measures have been attended to that one can be confident of having laid the foundations for a secure and prosperous market economy.

Despite the needs of the moment, it is very important that those responsible for reform in Eastern Europe resist the temptation to become totally preoccupied with short-term solutions and spare no thought for their longer-term consequences. It goes without saying that the short term must be addressed, but it is also important to lay down sound foundations for the future. In the longer run, economic prosperity does not depend on the choice of particular policies by particular governments so much as on the choice of the institutional structure within which everyone has to work. That choice has to be made now, and it is vital to get it right. As many would-be reformers are all too aware, it is much easier to make the right institutional choice in the first place than try to change it once a mistake has been made and then cast into stone.

In trying to make these decisions, it is also important that reforming governments be discriminating in what they copy from the West, and nowhere more so than in money and banking. The West offers many models that could be usefully copied, but it is also the source of many mistakes to be avoided, and the biggest of these is the institution of central banking. Central banking in the West has now produced apparently permanent inflation, and while it might make sense to peg former East bloc currencies to a (relatively) strong Western currency as a short-term crutch, in the long run ex-communist countries should aim to do better and put their currencies on a firm, non-inflationary basis. The former Soviet countries should also avoid the disastrous mistakes that Western countries have made by other interventions in banking (such as the introduction of deposit insurance).

For all its present problems and immediate dangers, the present state of flux offers many opportunities for worthwhile reform that are unlikely to recur for a very long time. If policymakers in the former communist countries are wise enough to embark on market-oriented reforms and to avoid the pitfalls into which the West has fallen – in money and banking especially – then there is every chance that the former East bloc countries could not only reach Western standards of prosperity, but in the long run eventually surpass them.

Part 3
Policy issues

13 Two arguments for the restriction of international capital flows

With K. Alec Chrystal

As the City of London adjusts to the regulatory changes associated with the 'Big Bang' and major countries such as France and Italy liberalize their formerly severe capital controls, several commentators are calling for a halt to the trend towards more integrated international capital markets. In the UK the loudest voices are coming from within the Labour Party. They have argued for many years that capital outflows have been harmful to the UK economy. However, they are not alone in their suspicion of the role of mobile capital. Nobel Laureate economist James Tobin, as long ago as 1978, called for the governments of all major countries 'to throw some sand in the wheels of our excessively efficient international money markets'. This call has recently been backed by Rudiger Dornbusch in a paper presented to the Royal Economic Society in July 1986.[1]

This chapter examines these two arguments for the reintroduction of capital flow restrictions – the first for the UK alone, and the second for the industrial world in general. Before turning to these specific proposals, however, it is helpful to consider some data for the UK and to clarify some points of background.

Fallacies

One of the biggest fallacies which often arises in discussions of capital flows is the belief that there is some connection between outflows and the level of investment in physical plant in the domestic economy. No such connection exists.[2] However, there is a close connection between the capital account and the current account of the balance of payments. In fact, if there were no official reserve changes and no measurement error, the current balance and the capital balance would be identically equal and opposite. This means that a country that has a current account surplus must have a capital account deficit and vice versa. If you spend less than the value of your income (or output), you must necessarily acquire a financial claim on someone else. Those who argue that capital outflows are harmful to employment prospects in Britain

would surely not argue that a current account surplus is harmful, though logically they are equivalent statements. Indeed current account surpluses in
countries like Japan and West Germany have been taken as indicators of
strength, not weakness. Yet such countries are necessarily investing their
surpluses overseas.

The figures for the UK balance of payments from 1975–85 are presented in
Table 13.1. As a general rule, years of current account surplus are years of
capital account deficit and vice versa. Official reserve changes have been
fairly small since 1977 but in one or two years the balancing item is quite
large. As the official financing figures are very accurate and the current
balance figures reasonably reliable, it is safe to conclude that the balancing
item largely reflects unidentified capital flows.

Controversy in the UK relates to the significance of capital outflows since
the abolition of exchange controls in October 1979. The official figures show
a cumulative outflow since 1979 of £27,852 million. This is only a little bigger
than the cumulative current account surplus of £21,847 million over the same
period. Only £1,808 million of this difference is accounted for by reserve
changes. The remainder reflects an unidentified capital inflow of £4,197
million.

Table 13.2 presents a breakdown of the capital account. Notice that the final
column of Table 13.2 is the same as the second column of Table 13.1. Those
who wish to exaggerate the size of capital outflows from the UK usually refer
to column three of Table 13.2. This column shows a cumulative private
investment flow overseas of £77,508 million since 1979. It should be clear,
however, that about £50,000 million of that has been offset by disinvestments
or inflows in other categories. It is therefore an absurdity to argue that this

Table 13.1 UK balance of payments 1975–85 (£ million)

Year	Current balance	Net investment and capital flows	Official financing	Balancing item
1975	-1582	154	1465	-37
1976	-913	-2977	3629	261
1977	-128	4169	-7361	3320
1978	972	-4257	1126	2159
1979	-736	1836	-1905	805
1980	3100	-1547	-1372	-181
1981	6226	-7185	687	272
1982	4033	-3658	1284	-1659
1983	3163	-5071	820	1088
1984	1562	-7184	1316	4306
1985	3763	-3207	-927	371

Source: *Economic Trends*, March 1986, and *Monthly Digest*, June 1986.

Table 13.2 UK capital flows by category (£ million)

Year	Overseas investment in		UK private investment overseas	Official long-term capital	Trade credit	Foreign currency borrowing or lending by UK banks	Sterling reserves		Other external bank and related sterling liabilities	External lending by UK banks	Other	Total investment and other capital transactions
	UK public sector	UK private sector					British govt. stocks	Banking and money market liabilities etc.				
1975	-13	1,527	-1,367	-291	-518	253	7	-622	549	96	533	154
1976	179	1,912	-2,269	-161	-992	-108	12	-1,413	256	-350	-43	-2,977
1977	1,432	2,967	-2,334	-303	-335	367	6	-16	1,481	58	866	4,169
1978	-96	1,973	-4,604	-336	-622	-434	-113	—	293	-504	186	-4,257
1979	901	3,381	-6,802	-401	-789	1,622	247	509	2,580	205	383	1,836
1980	587	4,619	-8,150	-91	-1,123	2,054	945	317	2,558	-2,500	-763	-1,547
1981	195	3,252	-10,393	-336	-836	1,4	207	-1186	2,607	-2,954	-271	-7,185
1982	393	3,094	-10,914	-337	-1,416	4,274	-212	438	4,134	-3,299	187	-3,658
1983	700	4,383	-11,413	-380	-1,540	1,413	227	785	3,167	-1,339	-1,074	-5,071
1984	323	1,270	-14,841	-327	-501	9,075	188	1,089	5,160	-4,718	-3,902	-7,184
1985	1,380	6,279	-21,797	-310	-207	4,453	1,482	95	4,089	-1,663	2,630	-3,207

Source: *Economic Trends*, March 1986 and *Monthly Digest*, June 1986.

£77,508 million somehow represents funds that could have created equivalent real investment in the UK economy or, indeed, that such sums could somehow be 'brought back' in the future. The current balance tells us what the capital balance must be. For a given current balance, any inflows of capital in one category will be exactly offset by outflows in another.

The belief that capital outflows are harmful to domestic investment is based upon a simple misconception: that domestic investment has to be financed out of domestic saving (i.e. that the more domestic savings go overseas, the less is left for domestic investment). The truth, however, is that investment is financed in an open world market, not in the UK alone. There is no effective limit on the finance available for investment projects that are profitable at the going interest rate. Thus the relevant question to ask about the impact of exchange controls is not 'How much money has left the country?' but rather 'What has been the effect on market interest rates?' The answer to the latter question is, almost certainly, none. The reason is that one small country in the world system cannot significantly affect the level of world interest rates.

The Labour Party proposals

In September 1985, the Labour Party outlined a system of exchange controls which it proposes to introduce if it wins the next election.[3] It argues that the abolition of exchange controls in 1979 led to massive outflows of UK capital abroad, and that this capital would have created jobs in the UK had it remained here. It therefore concludes that UK investment abroad should be discouraged. To that end it proposes a new system of exchange controls to penalize UK investment abroad and to encourage 'repatriation' of funds.

The system of exchange controls envisaged by the Labour Party has two main features. The first is a system of fiscal penalties to discourage UK individuals and institutions from investing abroad. In particular, if individuals or firms (especially pension funds) wish to retain their present fiscal privileges their investments must satisfy two criteria:

- Not more than a certain proportion – perhaps 5 per cent – of their total portfolio should be invested abroad.
- They must invest a certain portion of their funds in a National Investment Bank (NIB) to be established by the new government.

The NIB is the second feature of the Labour Party proposals. This establishment will 'invest in Britain' and counter the 'excessive' tendency of UK financial institutions to invest abroad. The NIB would also provide long-term low interest finance in the UK and thereby enable investments to be made that would not otherwise take place. Its funds would come from funds currently invested overseas, and from the government.

The impact of the portfolio restrictions

The purpose of the tax penalty for excessive overseas investment is to encourage more investment in Britain, and most people would probably agree that it would have that effect, even if they disagreed about whether it were desirable or not. After all, it seems reasonable to suppose that if UK residents are encouraged to hold more UK assets, then more UK assets will actually be held.

However, this line of argument involves a *non sequitur*, because it ignores the offsetting effects of outflows of funds by those foreigners who own substantial investments in the UK. There could, for example, be offsetting 'swaps' between UK and foreign institutions. Suppose that a UK firm has a portfolio which does not meet the first criterion required by the new Labour government. If it does nothing it will be penalized by extra taxes on its overseas assets. Suppose, however, that it can find a foreign firm – or a group of them – that holds UK securities in its portfolio. Such a firm will be interested in the risk-return characteristics of its portfolio, and not in the particular assets it holds per se, and it will not, as such, be affected by changes in the new government's tax provisions. In short, the foreign firm will be more or less indifferent at the margin to whether it holds foreign or domestic assets in its portfolio, provided their risk-return characteristics are the same. The British firm could therefore offer to arrange a 'swap' of its foreign assets for the UK assets of the foreign firm. This arrangement would enable it to satisfy the government's portfolio restrictions and avoid the fiscal penalty, and all it would take to induce the foreign firm to agree to the deal would be a small fee or premium.

It follows that although the British firm demands more UK assets, its increase in demand for those assets is matched exactly by the fall in the foreign firm's demand for British assets. The distribution of the assets between the two firms will change, but not overall holdings. Since the total demand for British assets is unchanged, there is no major effect on prices or interest rates and so no effect on real investment. The only 'real' effect of the regulation is to cause the British firm some inconvenience and cost in having to arrange an appropriate swap.

Furthermore, it is not necessary that these swaps should take place directly. They could also happen indirectly through the following simple market mechanism: UK firms sell overseas securities and buy UK securities. This lowers prices and raises yields on foreign securities, and raises prices and lowers yields on UK securities. Foreign firms that were previously indifferent at the margin between UK and foreign securities now see that foreign securities are cheap relative to UK ones. They sell UK securities and buy overseas until the expected yields are equal again. Prices are back where they started and portfolios have been readjusted but there are no other real effects (i.e. no change in the cost of investment funds). The underlying economics is very simple: once efficient financial markets are integrated, a portfolio restriction on one set of institutions will have no effect on equilibrium prices in these markets.[4]

This discussion suggests how institutions would be likely to respond to the first kind of portfolio restriction in the Labour Party proposals (i.e. the restrictions on holdings of foreign assets). The underlying principle at work is straightforward. If a restriction is put on the kind of assets held by one kind of firm, and if there are other firms holding the same kind of assets that are not affected by the restriction, then the first type of firm has an incentive to offer a 'swap' deal to the other. The other will accept because it is indifferent between the underlying assets and will be happy to respond to a small premium on the price. The situation is slightly more complicated with the second kind of portfolio restriction – the requirement that a certain proportion of assets be held in the form of the loan liabilities of the NIB – because there is no one who holds its liabilities at the present time with whom a swap could be made. However, these liabilities are to be guaranteed by the government and will be generally indistinguishable from gilt-edged securities. Institutions already holding gilts will therefore readjust their gilt holdings to offset any required NIB stock holdings. The effect on the market will be identical to that of a new gilt sale of equal size.

There are two possible policy conclusions one can draw from all this. The first and most natural conclusion is that a future government should not impose these regulations if their only 'real' effect is to cause minor inconvenience and cost to UK institutions. However, some might draw the alternative conclusion that the restrictions would only be ineffective because they are not comprehensive enough. According to this line of argument, one might be able to make restrictions work if one could prevent the reverse flows that would otherwise undermine them. Yet this requires restrictions to eliminate all possible channels through which offsetting outflows and swaps could take place. It would, therefore, be necessary to restrict the access of UK residents to all international financial markets, to restrict access of foreigners to all UK markets, and probably to control UK financial markets as well. In short, the only situation in which restrictions might be able to bite would be in a 'siege economy', and the costs of a siege economy are likely to exceed by far any benefits it would produce, if there are any.

The impact of the National Investment Bank

We come now to consider the NIB. Its basic purpose would be to fund investment in the UK. Its capital would come from the assets repatriated to

Britain by the exchange control system and from the government's general revenue. It would be set certain guidelines by Parliament – such as helping to achieve regional and industrial policy targets – but within those guidelines it would be run on a 'strictly commercial basis'. Two immediate problems come to mind. One is that it is not clear how a connection will be established between 'repatriated' funds and investment in the NIB. However, since 'NIB loan stock will carry a market rate of interest and will be guaranteed by the Bank of England', the liabilities of the NIB will be identical to gilts and can be marketed through the usual channels. The talk of 'repatriating' funds for this purpose is thus an irrelevant smokescreen.

The other problem is that the bank's guidelines are inconsistent. Either it is run on a 'strictly commercial basis' or it is not. If it is, then it cannot be used to achieve other policy objectives – like the industrial or regional objectives Roy Hattersley mentions – at the same time. If it is to be used to achieve these other objectives, it will in practice be subject to the whims of ministerial intervention. Projects will be judged on an essentially political basis – how marginal the Parliamentary seat is where the investment is to take place, how bad unemployment is there, and so on. In such circumstances it is impossible for any business to be run on a strictly commercial basis. In any case, if the Bank were run on commercial lines it would simply duplicate the work that many private institutions do at the moment – and then there would be no point in setting it up in the first place.

The truth must be that the NIB would not be run on a strictly commercial basis. After all, it is explicitly intended to subsidize investment. This means that it must lend at lower than market interest rates, and since it would borrow at market rates, it must receive a government subsidy. But if the real intention is to subsidize investment, why not do so directly through the tax system or direct investment grants? Such subsidies do not require the establishment of another large state bureaucracy. If existing investment incentives do not achieve the desired goal, why should a convoluted scheme that is formally identical to such investment incentives be any different?

This takes us to the heart of the problem. What is the justification for setting up a Bank to subsidize investment? The idea is to enable projects to be funded that would otherwise go unfunded, but *why* would they go unfunded? They would go unfunded because private lenders would judge them to be commercially unviable, since if they thought otherwise they would lend to them. So the question then is why the Labour Party would want to fund commercially unviable projects. The answer is that it seems to believe that many commercially unviable projects are nevertheless 'socially worthwhile', and so should be funded anyway. Such political judgments are a famously unreliable method for allocating resources.

What could we expect to happen if the NIB went into business? Since it would offer cheaper loans than anyone else, it would be swamped with applications for loans. It would not be able to satisfy all these requests and it would have to find some way of selecting who should get loans and who should not. It would not be allowed to do that by simply raising its interest rates. If it did, it would end up raising them to market levels, and it would then behave in the same way as a private investment bank. It would therefore have to select some other rule of thumb. Yet, whatever rule it adopted, it would end up investing in many projects that private banks would reject as commercially unviable. Continual injections of government money would then be needed to prevent it going bankrupt, and the main effect of the Bank would be to misallocate investment resources.

The connection between foreign investment and domestic jobs

One of the key ideas underlying the Labour Party proposal is that if investments overseas could be discouraged, they would be channelled into the UK instead and thereby create domestic jobs. There are a number of comments we would make about this kind of argument.

The first is that the total amount of investment is not fixed, but depends in part on the kind of return potential investors can expect to get. If the government passes measures to make any kind of investment less attractive, investment will fall. Thus even if the government could discourage foreign investment, the chances are that overall investment will fall. Not all the discouraged foreign investment will be diverted into the UK economy because some of it will not take place at all.

There is also the question of the relation between the capital and current accounts of the balance of payments. When people refer to capital outflows, they generally refer to capital account deficits – flows of financial capital abroad. However, as we mentioned earlier, with a floating exchange rate regime – and the present regime is approximately that – the states of the capital and current accounts are mirror images of each other: a capital account deficit implies a current account surplus, and vice versa. The current account refers to trade in goods and services. It follows, then, that if the government were successful in reducing a capital account deficit, it would in the very same act also succeed in reducing the current account surplus. That means either an increase in imports or a reduction in exports, or, most likely, some of both. These changes in turn mean a loss of jobs in export and import-competing industries. These losses would then have to be offset against any extra jobs created by the investment diverted into the UK economy. Whether the number of exporting jobs lost would be greater or less than the jobs created by the hoped-for extra investment is hard to say, but it could well be greater.

Finally it is worth pointing out that there may be a strange irony in the

Labour Party's preoccupation with investment. The real intention is obviously to expand output and employment. Yet, while investment subsidies are almost certain to expand output, there is no guarantee at all that they will also expand employment. Whether they would or not would largely depend whether capital (machines) and labour are complements or substitutes; and in the latter case, investment subsidies will encourage firms to buy more labour-saving equipment and cut jobs, rather than create them.

The Tobin-Dornbusch proposal

The Tobin-Dornbusch proposal is to introduce restrictions on the flow of capital at the global level by increasing the cost of transactions. What they are concerned about is the considerable volatility of exchange rates we have seen since the advent of the floating exchange rate regime. This volatility has been associated with fairly large changes in real exchange rates (or competitiveness), which have had serious adverse impacts on a number of countries. A good example is the 1976–81 appreciation of sterling, which devastated UK manufacturing industry.

The original Tobin proposal is for all governments to tax transactions involving a switch of currencies. This tax would supposedly discourage movements into and out of different currencies and have the effect of curbing 'excessive' capital flows. This particular proposal cannot be taken too seriously because it is impossible in practice to distinguish transactions that derive from asset switching and transactions involving trade. However, let us run with the underlying idea and assume that some restriction on capital flows could feasibly be introduced.

Would it be desirable? The answer must be no. The Tobin-Dornbusch view requires capital flows to be an autonomous source of disturbance to the real economy. However, in reality they are an endogenous response to 'news' about real or monetary events. Even in Professor Dornbusch's own model, investors are rational and well informed, and the shocks come from real events (wars, natural disasters, OPEC price rises and so on) or from changes in government policies. The key point is that the foreign exchange markets react to this news quicker than other markets, and it is this faster reaction that can cause exchange rates to overshoot.[5]

Is this a reason for restricting capital flows? Again, no. The impact of shocks on the real economy would be even greater if capital flows were restricted. To make the point, suppose that net capital flows are forced to be zero, which means that the exchange rate would have to move sufficiently to balance the current account on a continuous basis. Now imagine what would have happened in the UK following its rapid transition from an oil importer to an oil exporter, and add in a doubling of the oil price at the same time.[6] In order for the current account to balance, the exchange rate would have had to appreciate far enough to enable the manufacturing trade balance to move in the opposite direction by exactly the same amount (assuming for simplicity that invisibles are very price inelastic). Clearly, this would have required a much larger exchange rate appreciation than actually occurred and would have created even greater devastation than the UK economy experienced.

The point should by now be clear: capital flows ease the adjustment of the real economy to real disturbances. In this respect, the economy is just like an individual who cushions his/her life style to income variation by building up or running down savings. To deliberately remove such a cushion from industrial economies seems like folly in the extreme. As for the UK, it is clear that capital flows in this period helped to cushion the economy and so saved a considerable number of domestic jobs.

There is one other problem with the Tobin-Dornbusch proposal in its 'tax transactions form'. It requires all governments to adopt it, but is not incentive-compatible. Without universal adoption, people would be able to avoid the tax by carrying out their transactions where the tax did not apply. The countries that adopted the tax would see their financial markets move elsewhere, and the only way to stop these 'leaks' would be to make the tax universal. Not only would this require an international agreement, but there is also the more fundamental problem that even if they agreed to the tax in principle, countries would still have an incentive to undermine it. Undermining the tax would allow them to attract more business to their economies, with all the beneficial spin-offs that would provide. Like any other cartel that tries to restrict trade, this one would contain the seeds of its own destruction.

Conclusion

We conclude that neither the Labour Party proposal for portfolio tax incentives nor the Tobin-Dornbusch proposal for 'throwing sand in the wheels of the financial system' would do anything to improve the workings of either the UK or world economies. Indeed it seems strange that both politicians and leading economists should be concerned that an industry has become 'too efficient'. Attention would be far better directed at how to raise the level of efficiency in other sectors of the economy rather than at inventing arbitrary measures to lower the level of efficiency in the financial sector.

14 Monetary policy in the twenty-first century

An impossible task?

One of the most obvious (and I would suggest, welcome) trends over the last two decades or so has been the gradual erosion of central bank power by market forces. Central banks are operating under ever tighter constraints as financial markets integrate further and become more efficient, and as capital itself becomes even more mobile and currencies become better substitutes for each other. More than ever in recent years, central banks need to ensure that they carry the markets with them if their policies are to have any chance of success. If they fail to do so – if they engage in ill-judged attempts to manipulate interest rate or exchanges rates, for example – they leave themselves open to withering speculative attack on a scale that no central bank can resist. As we have seen on a number of occasions, the financial markets impose swift and merciless punishment on those who try to defy them, and central bankers who stick their heads above the parapet must expect to have them blown off. Monetary policy has never been so constrained since the collapse of the Bretton Woods system in the early 1970s.

A new threat to monetary policy: the falling demand for central bank money

As we look into the future, central bankers also face a new and more dangerous threat. Long-run factors – technological ones in particular – will not only further reduce the effectiveness of central bank monetary policy, but are likely to destroy it altogether. The point is that the central bank's leverage over the monetary system – its ability to influence interest rates, exchange rates and the money supply – hinges on the demand for central bank ('base') money, and these new developments threaten to reduce that demand to a level where the central bank's leverage effectively disappears.

One form of base money consists of the deposits held by commercial banks for reserves or clearing purposes. However, the general trend of technological progress is already leading banks to operate with declining reserve ratios. There is also considerable competitive pressure on banks to reduce the costs of their holdings of base money. This pressure is intensified by competition from banks in other jurisdictions which are no longer obliged to satisfy minimum reserve requirements,[1] and also by financial innovations and developments in technology that give banks superior reserve and clearing media to central bank deposits.[2] It is therefore quite likely that bank demand for base money will fall to very low and possibly negligible levels over the foreseeable future.

The other form of base money consists of the cash held by the public for day to day transactions purposes. However, the public demand for cash is also likely to fall as electronic substitutes for cash become more sophisticated and more widely available (see e.g. Browne and Cronin 1997). Indeed, the displacement of cash by electronic alternatives is already a well-established fact (Humphrey, Pulley and Vesala 1996: 936), and there is no doubt that this process of displacement will go much further. The competition has reached the point where a number of central banks are now actively encouraging the use of electronic substitutes for cash to cope with the problems raised by the increasing sophistication of counterfeiters, and many well informed observers also now accept that the virtual disappearance of demand for cash in the next century is, at the least, a very real possibility.

Implications of a declining demand for base money

This declining demand for base money causes major problems for central bankers. First, and most obviously, it means that base money will become increasingly insignificant as a component of the money supply. However, as base money becomes less significant, it will gradually lose its effectiveness as a channel through which the central bank can influence the broader monetary system. The fulcrum on which the monetary policy lever operates will erode away and make monetary policy less and less effective as time goes on.

Second, the central bank must do something to ensure that the supply of base money falls if it is to avoid a major inflation: if the demand for base money falls whilst its supply remains the same, the only way the market for base money can clear is for the value of base money (i.e. the value of the currency) to fall. To avoid this outcome, the central bank must reduce the supply of base money to match the fall in the demand for it. This is a difficult and historically unprecedented task.[3] Such a policy would also create another problem for the central bank: since it would force the central bank to buy its own currency back, the revenue from money creation – seignorage – would become negative, and many (and perhaps all) central banks would need bailing out if they are to avoid bankruptcy.[4]

Finally, the decline in the demand for base money would also make prices and interest rates more vulnerable to external shocks, and in particular, to changes in the technological and other factors that influence the demand for currency.[5] To give but one example, we could all wake up one morning in the not too distant future and find that the latest development in e-money technology was about to make cash redundant. Cash would suddenly become a hot potato to be got rid of as soon as possible. We would all then rush out to get rid of our holdings of it while it still had some value, and in the process its value would plummet (i.e. the price level would rise enormously). This scenario of e-money-induced hyperinflation might sound far-fetched, but is not altogether implausible. The price level would of course also be very vulnerable to other, less dramatic changes in e-money technology as well.

There are also some alarming consequences for the US. If the demand for base money in the US becomes negligible, dollar prices in the US would become entirely dependent on the foreign demand for US currency, and the US price level would become hostage to whatever (largely uncontrollable) factors influence the foreign demand for dollars. Any factors that reduce this demand – the successful re-monetization of the former Soviet Union, which would lead citizens there to switch to local currencies or the legalization of hard drugs, which would undercut much of the need to trade dollars in the black market – could then have devastating consequences for US inflation. There is of course also the irony that the stability of the US monetary system – and, hence, the health of the US economy – would become dependent on the activities of Colombian drug producers, Russian mafia, and other unsavoury elements.

In short, the central bank must come to terms with greater potential price instability just as its leverage (i.e. its ability to do something) gradually dissolves, and it will have to do so whilst 'enjoying' negative seignorage and buying back its own currency to prevent inflation. At some point the central bank's task will clearly become impossible.

What is to be done?

If the central bank can no longer manage the monetary system, it must give up the task and put the monetary system onto an automatic basis, and the only way to do that is to make the currency convertible again (i.e. for the central bank to peg the price of its currency in terms of real goods or services). There are many types of convertibility, ranging from the old gold standard to more modern (albeit as yet untried) systems which aim to achieve price stability by pegging the prices of index-based financial derivatives.[6]

Serious thought would obviously have to be given to the type of system adopted, but convertibility has very definite benefits whatever precise form it takes. It puts the value of the currency on a sure footing, and thereby frees it from its dependence on the demand for base money, on the one hand, or central bank policy, on the other. Provided that private issuers are also free to issue currency of their own, the demand for central bank money can then fall to zero without any serious side-effects.[7] Prices, interest rates, and so forth would no longer be dependent on the vagaries of e-money technology or the foreign demand for currency.

At the same time, the central bank would no longer face the daunting prospect of managing down the currency supply: instead, it would merely need to stand ready (along with other issuers of currency) to buy and sell its currency on demand at a fixed price. The central bank's supply of currency could then fall to zero without any noticeable side-effects. The central bank would also become one currency issuer among many, and it should be manifestly obvious by that stage that there is no justification for giving any one currency issuer – the central bank included – a privileged status over others. Federal Reserve currency could then be retired and the Federal Reserve itself abolished, and the provision of currency can be left to the institution that was always best able to provide it anyway: the market.

15 Reflections on the future of gold

It is a curious fact that a considerable proportion of the world's stock of gold – currently, almost 30 per cent – is held by the world's central banks for no sensible purpose at all. They hold it only because they held it in the past, and yet the reasons they held it in the past no longer apply and, moreover, are unlikely to apply at any forseeable time in the future.

In the past, banks issued currency whose value was pegged to the value of one or other of the two main precious metals, gold and silver, and they maintained this peg by offering to buy back their currency for fixed amounts of a precious metal. Indeed, banks were legally obliged to buy back their currency for precious metals whenever requested to do so. This obligation in the UK ensured that the pound note was as good as gold, and was in fact the central element of the gold standard. However the gold standard was later abolished, in the UK as elsewhere, and no bank anywhere is now obliged to hold stocks of gold with which to buy back its currency. Furthermore, while the gold standard was sometimes temporarily suspended in emergency circumstances – in the UK, it was suspended in 1797, and then again in 1914, both times in response to wartime problems – it was always understood in the past that any suspension would be temporary and that the gold standard would be restored when the emergency was over. However, when the Bretton Woods version of the gold standard was abandoned in the early 1970s, it was made clear that the gold standard was being abandoned for good, without any serious intention of ever restoring it. For the first time in world history, the world's central banks were holding stocks of gold that had no existing significant monetary use and no prospective monetary use in the future.[1] The central banks' stocks of 'monetary' gold had become an anachronism.

The current situation

Nevertheless, twenty-odd years on, central banks continue to hold most of the gold they held then. While they preach commercial rationality to everyone else, central banks still hold massive stocks of a metal that they have not the slightest intention of ever using for any genuine 'monetary' purpose.[2] At the end of 1993, the so-called 'official sector' held 36,300 tonnes of gold (GFMS 1994: 32). If one values gold at its average 1993 price of virtually $360 an ounce, these stocks are worth just over $420 billion. Of this amount, some $94 billion is held by the US and nearly $8.4 billion by the UK.[3] These stocks represent resources tied up for no socially worthwhile purpose.

For central banks to hold stocks of gold currently makes as much sense as their holding stocks of silver, coal, platinum, oil, or any other commodity (i.e. it makes no sense at all). Not only is gold costly to hold – it needs to be stored in expensive vaults, guards need to be employed to guard it, and so on – but, unlike 'paper' assets such as Treasury bills, it also yields no return. A central bank that sold its holdings of gold and bought, say, T-bills, could thus convert a barren asset that currently yields a negative net return into an asset that yielded a positive return instead. If one takes the rate of return on some alternative asset to be, say, 5 per cent, the annual opportunity cost of these holdings (i.e. what the central bank would earn each year if it got rid of them) would be at least 5 per cent of $94 billion for the US, or nearly $5 billion a year, and 5 per cent of $8.4 billion, or $420 million, for the UK. One must bear in mind that this estimate understates the true opportunity cost because it does not take into account the annual cost of storing gold or the prospect (which I develop below) that those who continue to hold gold could suffer serious capital losses from a major fall in the gold price.

One could speculate for a very long time on why central banks have continued to hold these stocks, but the critical question is not so much why they hold them, but whether we can expect them to hold these stocks indefinitely.[4] Whatever their reasons for holding them in the past, it simply beggars belief that they can continue in this way for ever. Commercial rationality is creeping up on central banks in many countries, and they are coming under more and more pressure to justify portfolio decisions by commercial standards.[5] Central bankers will therefore find it increasingly hard to justify why they wish to hold so much of a particular yellow metal that is costly to store and yet yields no return of its own, and a point must surely come where attempts to justify holding gold by stories about the 'historical role' of gold will be seen to be no more than the obfuscation they really are. More importantly, perhaps, the tacit agreement to retain gold will only continue to hold provided no major central bank is seen overtly to undermine it. Yet each central bank is under pressure to get rid of its gold holdings, not only to be able to earn higher returns by holding other assets, but also to avoid losses from being left holding gold if others sell first and the price falls. It must therefore be only a matter of time before the decision of one major central bank to cut and run undermines the cartel and leads the others to follow suit.[6] The central banks will then get rid of their holdings of gold and the price of it will fall, perhaps drastically.

The unstable central-bank cartel

It might help to spell out this scenario in more detail. The point about a cartel is that each individual member agrees to abide by certain rules, but would prefer not to abide by them if he could get away with it. For example, in a conventional producer cartel, the members each agree to restrict their production in order to reduce aggregate supply and thereby increase the price they get for their produce. However, if the cartel is successful in raising the price, each producer would ideally like to produce even more than he produced before the cartel was set up, precisely because the price is higher. If they all do so, however, the supply will rise and the price will fall back again. There is a conflict between the interests of producers acting as a group through the cartel, and the interest of each individual producer given what the others are doing.

A cartel usually tries to address this problem by bringing pressure to bear on any 'deviant' members who might flout the cartel rules and produce more than their allotted amount, but unless this pressure is backed up by explicit legal sanction, a point comes in the history of any cartel when the action of one or more deviants finally undermines the price-fixing agreement and produces a free-for-all in which all restrictions against output collapse and the price falls. A good example is of course illustrated by the history of OPEC. When OPEC raised its prices, many oil producers took advantage by increasing their own output, and OPEC was able to hold up oil prices only for as long as Saudi Arabia was willing to keep cutting back its own supply. A point came, however, when Saudi Arabia could cut back no further and the cartel effectively collapsed. A cartel contains within itself the seeds of its own destruction. A cartel's life expectancy is also reduced further by individual producers' expectations of its demise. If an individual producer expects his cartel to collapse, as he presumably does, he has an even stronger incentive to increase production now and sell at the current high price because he expects to get a lower price later when the cartel has collapsed. The expectation that the cartel will collapse will stimulate additional output that will help to bring that collapse about.

The tacit central bank agreement over gold is not a producer cartel, but it otherwise fits the cartel model very well. In particular, the central banks know that if they do not limit their supply of gold to the market, then the price of gold will fall, perhaps very considerably, and bring about consequences they would prefer to avoid (e.g. in their case, some kind of well-deserved embarrassment). They therefore enter into a tacit understanding not to allow this to happen by agreeing to keep their stocks pretty much as they are. As in many other cartels, this agreement is not openly discussed, but everyone involved nonetheless understands it and is implicitly understood to abide by it. Keeping their stocks off the market then helps to keep the price of gold above its market 'fundamental' value.

However while the central banks might collectively agree to keep their all their monetary gold off the market, each individual central bank is conscious that it would be better off getting rid of its gold – it would earn more by holding other assets, it would not have to pay the costs of holding gold, and so on – while the others were propping up the price. Like an individual producer in a producer cartel, an individual central bank would prefer to increase its own supply to the market, if it could get away with it. It would also be aware that, if a price fall is possible (and there is no offsetting likelihood of a price rise), then there is some benefit to selling earlier, before the majority of the others. The one who sells first gets the highest price, and the one who waits till the others have already sold takes the loss. Hence, there is considerable incentive, not only to sell, but to sell first. The cartelized market is thus highly unstable, rather like a crowd in a burning cinema: once one races for the door, the others will race too. All it really needs to break the cartel is for one or two major central banks to be seen to be overtly breaking the rules, and the others will race to sell to make sure that they do not suffer the losses when the price falls.

The only thing that has stopped this happening already is the 'glue' that holds the cartel together. Yet this 'glue' is very weak. There is no international law that gives the central bank cartel any effective sanctions against any offenders who break its rules. Nor is there any international law that requires a central bank to continue to hold its present stocks of gold. Any threats that a cartel can make to a central bank are usually fairly minimal, and, while there may be some impoverished central banks that might need the goodwill of the more powerful ones (e.g. to get loans), it is hard to see what a relatively powerful central bank such as the Bank of England has to fear. The central bank cartel is extremely weak, and, if the record of other cartels is anything to go by, it must only be a matter of time before this one too succumbs to its own inherent contradictions. The only alternative is to believe that the cartel can go on forever, indefinitely defying as it were the laws of economic gravity. Unless we believe this, we have to conclude that the central banks' selling their gold is not only possible, but inevitable.[7]

The demonetization of silver in the late nineteenth century

Those who still think this scenario is far-fetched might do well to consider the fate of silver in the late nineteenth century. Until the early 1870s, most countries were on a bimetallic standard that meant that both gold and silver could be used to pay debts, with gold being valued at 15½ times the value of gold.[8] In a bimetallic country such as France, an individual could therefore pay a debt with one unit of gold, or 15½ units of silver, and, by and large, coins in both metals circulated side by side as currency. This bimetallic system had existed for centuries, but it always depended for its continued operation on there being not too much of one metal relative to the other.[9] By the late 1860s, there was considerable concern that, with gold production falling off and silver production rising, silver would soon flood the bimetallic countries and drive gold out of circulation. It was feared that, once this happened, the market price ratio between gold and silver would move above its historical value of around 15½ to 1 and silver would depreciate relative to gold. Silver-holders would suffer losses, and the bimetallic countries would find themselves using a depreciated currency. It was also understood that, if such an outcome were to occur, it would be best for any individual bimetallic currency to switch to gold quickly, while silver was still valued relatively highly, than to switch later once silver had depreciated against gold. In the words of Gallarotti:

> Monetary experts of the period described the late 1860s and early 1870s as a period of 'alarm and apprehensions' and even 'panic' over developments in the market for metals that could have grave consequences. . . . Any compelling signs that market conditions were turning against silver, either by a sharp decline in its value or crucial events (like legal changes in monetary practices) that signalled an impending decline, created a sense of urgency to pre-empt others in demonetizing silver, or to follow closely behind the demonetization initiatives of other nations. Any lag was considered with the greatest concern.
>
> (Gallarotti 1993: 37–8)

The result, not surprisingly, was the rapid abandonment of bimetallism in the early 1870s. As soon as governments became convinced of the inevitability of the widespread adoption of the gold standard and the associated demonetization of silver, 'they seemed to be falling over one another's heels as fast as they could to get rid of silver, because the one who sold first would get the best price' (Gallarotti 1993: 38). The prime mover was Germany which adopted the gold standard in 1871. By the end of 1872 the Scandinavian countries had also adopted the gold standard, and France and the rest of the Latin Monetary Union followed soon afterwards. At around the same time, in 1873, the US passed legislation that ensured that when it restored convertibility – the US currency was still inconvertible, convertibility having been abandoned temporarily on the outbreak of the Civil War in 1861 – the US would return to a gold standard and not the bimetallic standard it had been on before the Civil War. By the end of the decade the US currency was again convertible into gold, and all the major trading countries of the world except China and India were on the gold standard.

The demonetization of silver had dramatic effects on the value of silver. As one country after another demonetized silver, the demand for silver for monetary purposes declined, and the price of silver fell. Over the three decades from 1870 to 1900, the market price of silver fell by 53 per cent, and it fell even further in the decade after that.[10] Since prices fell by about a quarter over this period, the fall in the purchasing power of silver – the price of silver relative to the prices of goods and services in general – fell by about 40 per cent from 1870 to 1900, and fell even further in the decade after that. Those in the late 1860s who felt that silver was about to depreciate were proven right.

How much could the price of gold fall?

If the price of gold is going to fall, the critical question, naturally, is by how much. No one can know for sure, but back-of-the-envelope estimates suggest that the price fall could be very considerable. Recall that nearly 30 per cent of stock is held by the official sector. If all of that gold was thrown onto the market, the total stock available for other uses would rise by nearly 1 divided by 0.7, or 43 per cent. To keep the estimate on the conservative side, let us say that it rises by 40 per cent. The price of gold must then fall by enough to ensure that the demand for gold for these other purposes rises by the 40 per cent or so needed to equilibrate the gold market. To estimate the effect on the price of gold, we must then have some idea of the price elasticity of the demand for gold, and no one seems to know what that might be. For want of any better alternative, one way round this problem is to adopt Harry Johnson's dictum and suppose that we take any elasticity to be equal to minus one unless we have any reason to suppose the contrary. If we apply the Johnson rule of thumb, an increase in supply of 40 per cent should therefore produce a price fall of 40 per cent. If we take last year's price of almost $360 as our starting price, the price of gold would then fall to about $216.

This exercise is of course very crude, but it seems to be as good as anything else in the absence of any hard-and-fast evidence about the size of the elasticity of demand for gold, and the reader who has firm views about the elasticity being something else can rework the analysis using his or her own preferred estimate. One may argue that any elasticity estimate is arbitrary, but what is striking is that one must put the elasticity relatively close to zero to produce a small price fall, and the point is that one has no particular reason to presume that the elasticity is in fact in this 'safe' region close to zero. If one took the elasticity to be -½ instead of -1, for example, the price of gold would fall 20 per cent to $288 – still a fairly substantial fall. The appropriate conclusion to draw from this exercise is, therefore, not that it can be dismissed because the elasticity estimate is arbitrary, but, instead, that a substantial price fall is highly plausible; and the very fact that we cannot be confident about the elasticity should concern those whose futures depend on it.

If there are plausible grounds to expect that a price might fall, and no particular offsetting reason to expect it to rise, then the sensible course of action is surely to make plans on the presumption of a price fall. Furthermore, one should also bear in mind that this exercise ignores any changes in private monetary holdings of gold. If the world's central banks get rid of their gold holdings, it is more than likely that many private owners of gold would decide to do likewise. Many of them would decide that there was less prospect of a restoration of a gold standard, and so on. The demand for private holdings of gold for monetary purposes (e.g. storing gold against a rainy day) would then fall along with the demand for gold from the official sector. Since the exercise above makes no allowance for any fall in the private demand for gold, it probably overestimates the likely demand for gold and consequently under-estimates the fall in the gold price. The price of gold might therefore fall by more than 40 per cent.

Consequences and implications

A substantial fall in the gold price would of course inflict considerable losses on those who hold gold. If the price of gold fell 40 per cent, the US official sector would lose 40 per cent of the value of its $94 billion holding, or nearly $38 billion, and its UK counterpart would lose nearly $3.4 billion. These large gold-holders, and indeed, all gold-holders – therefore need to ask themselves why they continue to run the risk. Holding gold not only means forgoing the positive returns to be obtained by holding other assets, but also means exposing oneself to a risk of serious capital loss without any compensating advantage. If any individual central bank is worried about the disapproval of its counterparts or about 'upsetting' the gold market, it can presumably sell gold discreetly, without any formal announcement of any change in policy. Sales would be well under way before other central banks realized what was going on and had much time to respond.

The same goes for private holders of gold as well. Betting against gold by selling it is much like selling a currency that looks as though it will be devalued: they make a profit if the currency is devalued, but they make no loss if it is not. They face, as it were, a one-way bet, and the only sensible option is to take the bet. It is particularly important, I think, for private gold-holders to look dispassionately at gold. One can well understand that they hold gold because they distrust the politicians and central bankers whose inflationary policies have robbed so many people of their assets. They therefore feel that holding 'real' assets is safer, and they have some kind of attachment to gold as the most preferred such asset.

Yet, as already explained, this strategy is potentially very costly. If private agents want to hold 'real' assets, I would suggest that they do not hold any asset with a huge overhang that could come onto the market at any time. They are probably better off holding paper assets rather than real ones (e.g. equity), and the most sensible response to the danger of political risk – expropriation and so on – is probably to hold assets abroad, or at least be on their guard against exchange controls. It would be ironic and sad if the sense of insecurity created by the inflationary policies of the past led the people who had been the main victims of these policies to hold gold and in so doing expose themselves to yet more losses in the future. Being sentimental about gold could turn out to be a very expensive indulgence.

A large fall in the price of gold would also have serious consequences for the gold-mining industry. Suppose that the price of gold did fall by 40 per cent to $218. In that case, any gold that costs more than $218 to extract and bring to market would not be economically feasible. Yet estimates suggest that mining costs are considerably above this amount for all countries for which data are readily available. South African mining costs are $297, Australian mining costs are $277, Canadian costs are $282, Brazilian costs are $263, and so on (GFMS 1994: 26). Even Chinese costs, which are relatively low, are still believed to be around $240 (GFMS 1994: 27). A fall of this magnitude in the gold price would make much of the industry across the world uneconomic, especially bearing in mind that there would be no particular reason to expect the price of gold to recover substantially. What would happen is that output would have to contract to that point where it just became worthwhile again, with all the mines with costs above $218 closing down.

How much the industry would have to contract would depend on how much the cost of gold rises with output (i.e. it depends on the slope of the cost curve). The flatter that curve, the more the industry has to cut back, and, unfortunately for gold producers, this curve appears to be very flat indeed. The estimated cost curves in *Gold 1994* suggest that the industry would have to cut back production to around 10 per cent of current output (GFMS 1994: figure 20). If this estimate is even remotely plausible, the bulk of the world gold-mining industry would have to close down. Even if the price fall were more moderate, say to $250, representing a fall of about 30 per cent, the GFMS cost estimates suggest that production would have to be cut back to around 30 per cent of current production. Seventy per cent of current production would therefore be uneconomic even if the price fell only to $250. The prospects for the gold mining industry thus seem pretty bleak. But then, from a social point of view, what is the point of spending so much to take gold out of the ground when so much of it already lies unused in the vaults of the world's central banks?

16 Too big to fail? Long-Term Capital Management and the Federal Reserve

In September 1998, the Federal Reserve organized a rescue of Long-Term Capital Management (LTCM), a very prominent US hedge fund on the brink of failure. The Fed intervened because it was concerned about the possibility of dire consequences for world financial markets if it had allowed the firm to fail.

Yet there are good grounds to believe that the Federal Reserve's rescue of LTCM was misguided. Federal Reserve intervention was not necessary to prevent the failure of LTCM, because the firm would not have failed anyway. If the Fed intervention achieved anything, it merely helped the shareholders and managers of LTCM to get a better deal for themselves than they would otherwise have obtained: an 'achievement' that hardly justifies a major intervention by the Fed. In any case, even if LTCM had failed, there would not have been the dire consequences that Fed officials feared. Indeed, letting LTCM fail may well have had a salutary effect on financial markets, by sending out a strong and convincing signal that no financial firm – however big – could expect to be bailed out from the consequences of its own mismanagement.

The rescue of LTCM had a number of detrimental consequences. It encourages more calls for the regulation of hedge fund activities, which would be pointless at best and counterproductive at worst. The rescue also implies a massive and very open-ended extension of Federal Reserve responsibilities, without any Congressional mandate. In addition, the rescue implies a return by the Fed to the discredited old doctrine of 'too big to fail' – that the Federal Reserve will rescue big financial firms in difficulties, out of fear of the possible consequences on financial markets of letting them fail. 'Too big to fail' encourages irresponsible risk-taking by financial firms, and so makes them more weak and financial markets more fragile. Finally, the rescue of LTCM does a lot of damage to the credibility and moral authority of Federal Reserve policy-makers in their efforts to encourage their counterparts in other countries to persevere with the necessary but difficult process of economic liberalization.

What are hedge funds?

Hedge funds are private investment funds that aim to make profits for their shareholders by trading securities. In the US, hedge funds with less than 100 shareholders are exempt from regulations under the Securities Act of 1933, the Securities Exchange Act of 1934, and the Investment Company Act of 1940. Most US hedge funds exploit this exemption by restricting the number of their shareholders to less than 100. Overseas hedge funds are also usually subject to little or no regulation, particularly those operating from offshore centres such as the Bahamas and the Cayman Islands. The hedge fund industry is thus largely unregulated.

The industry has grown rapidly in recent years, but despite this growth is still only a very small part of the overall institutional investment sector. Some idea of its relative size can be gauged from figures published in a recent IMF report (IMF 1998). This report estimated that the total amount of capital invested in hedge funds in the third quarter of 1997 was about $100 billion. However, other institutional investors – pension funds, mutual funds, insurance companies, banks, and so on – had a combined capital of well over $20 trillion.[1] Hedge funds therefore account for under 0.5 per cent of the total capital of the institutional investment sector.

Nonetheless, hedge funds have received considerable attention during the last decade, most particularly because of their role in a number of recent exchange rate crises. Perhaps the best-known example is George Soros' 'Quantum Fund', which is reputed to have made over $1 billion at the UK government's expense by betting against sterling in the European exchange rate crisis of September 1992. Hedge funds have also figured prominently in more recent crises, including those in Latin America, the Far East and Russia in the last couple of years. The activities of hedge funds have attracted a lot of criticism, and led to major controversy over their impact on the world financial system and calls from some quarters that hedge funds should be regulated.[2]

Hedge funds vary enormously, but fall into two main classes. The first are macro funds, of which the Quantum Fund is a good example. These funds take speculative (i.e. unhedged) positions in financial markets on the basis of their analyses of financial and macroeconomic conditions: they bet on exchange rate devaluations, changes in macroeconomic policies, interest-rate movements, and so on. Macro funds are thus 'hedge' funds in name only. They make their profits from speculation and their portfolios are often highly risky. Most macro hedge funds are also highly leveraged (i.e. the amounts invested in their portfolios are much greater than their share capital, with investments in excess of capital being financed by borrowing). Leverage increases the potential profits to shareholders, but also increases their risks: the greater the leverage, the bigger the profit to shareholders if investments are successful, but the bigger the loss to shareholders if they are not. A highly leveraged fund can therefore make very high profits, but also runs a relatively high risk of going bankrupt. Macro funds are highly leveraged relative to most other institutional investors, and typically have asset bases five to nine times their capital (IMF 1998).

The other main class of hedge funds are 'relative value' or arbitrage funds. These funds use sophisticated models to detect arbitrage opportunities – differences in the prices of nearly equivalent securities or portfolios – in financial markets. Having detected such opportunities, these funds construct arbitrage trading strategies to profit from them: they buy securities that are underpriced and sell those that are overpriced, whilst simultaneously taking offsetting positions to hedge out any risks involved and lock in their arbitrage profits. Financial-market arbitrage is a relatively low risk activity, so relative value funds often operate with much higher leverage than macro funds.[3]

The story of Long-Term Capital Management

Early history of Long-Term Capital Management

LTCM was founded in March 1994 by John Meriwether, a former Salomon Brothers trading star, along with a small group of associates, most notably the economists Robert Merton and Myron Scholes, who subsequently received the Nobel Prize in economics in 1997. The fund initially specialized in high-volume arbitrage trades in bond and bond-derivatives markets, but gradually became more active in other markets and more willing to speculate. The fund started as an arbitrage fund, but gradually became more like a macro fund as time passed. The fund was very successful: by the end of 1997, it had achieved annual rates of return of around 40 per cent and had nearly tripled its investors' money. This track record and the prestige of its associates made LTCM very popular with investors, and the companies and individuals investing in LTCM 'read like a who's who list of high finance' (Feldman 1998: 2). LTCM was the darling of Wall Street.

By that stage, it appears that the fund's assets had grown to about $120 billion and the fund's capital to about $7.3 billion.[4] However, despite this high leverage – the fund was operating on a leverage (or assets to equity) ratio of over 16 to 1 – the management of LTCM concluded that the capital base was too high to earn the rate of return on capital they were aiming for. They therefore returned $2.7 billion of capital to shareholders, so cutting the fund's capital to $4.8 billion and increasing its leverage ratio to around 25 to 1. In effect, the management of LTCM had taken a major gamble: they made the firm much riskier, in the hope of bolstering the returns to shareholders.

LTCM gets into difficulties

Unfortunately, LTCM's luck ran out not long afterwards. Most markets were edgy during the first part of 1998, but market conditions deteriorated sharply in the summer and led to major losses for LTCM in July. Disaster struck the next month, when the Russian government devalued the rouble and declared a moratorium on future debt repayments. These events led to a major deterioration in the credit-worthiness of many emerging market bonds, and corresponding large increases in the spreads between the prices of western government and emerging market bonds. These developments were very bad for LTCM because the fund had bet massively on these spreads narrowing. To make matters worse, the fund also made major losses on other speculative positions as well. As a result, by the end of August, LTCM's capital was down to $2.3 billion and the fund had lost over half of the equity capital it had had at the start of the year. By this time, its asset base was about $107 billion, so its leverage ratio had climbed to over 45 to 1 – a very high ratio by any standards, but especially in this volatile environment (Lindsey 1998: 4–5).

As its losses mounted, the fund had increasing difficulty in meeting margin calls – calls for more collateral to ensure it could meet its obligations to counterparties. The fund was running short of high quality assets for collateral to maintain its positions, but also had great difficulty liquidating its positions: many of its positions were relatively illiquid (i.e. difficult to sell) even in normal times, and were still more difficult to sell in nervous and declining markets, especially in a hurry.

The fund was now in very serious difficulties, and on 2 September the partners sent a letter to investors acknowledging the fund's problems and seeking an injection of new capital to sustain it. Perhaps not surprisingly, this information soon leaked out and the fund's problems quickly became common knowledge.

LTCM's situation continued to deteriorate in September, and the fund's management spent the next three weeks looking for assistance in an increasingly desperate effort to keep the fund afloat. However, no immediate help was forthcoming and by 19 September the fund's capital was down to only $600m (Lindsey 1998: 5). With an asset base of $80 billion by that point (Sloan 1998: 2), the fund's leverage ratio was now approaching stratospheric levels – a sure sign of impending doom – and no one who knew LTCM's situation really expected the fund to make it through the next week without outside assistance.

The Fed intervenes

Wall Street and the Fed had observed LTCM's deterioration with mounting concern. Many Wall Street firms had large stakes in LTCM themselves, and there was also widespread concern about the potential impact on financial markets if LTCM were to fail. The Fed felt obliged to intervene, and a delegation from the New York Fed and the US Treasury visited the fund on Sunday 20 September to assess the situation.[5] At this meeting, fund partners persuaded the delegation that LTCM's situation was not only bad, but potentially much worse than market participants imagined. The Fed concluded that some form of support operation should be prepared – and prepared very rapidly – to prevent LTCM failing, in order to forestall what it feared might otherwise be disastrous effects on financial markets.

Accordingly, the New York Fed invited a number of the creditor firms most involved to discuss a rescue package, and it was soon agreed that this Fed-led consortium would mount a rescue if no one else took over the fund in the meantime. However, when representatives of this group met on the early morning of Wednesday 23 September, they learned that another group had just made an offer for the fund, and that this offer would expire at lunchtime that day. It was therefore decided to wait and see how LTCM responded to that offer before proceeding any further.

This alternative offer was made by a group consisting of Warren Buffett's firm, Berkshire Hathaway, along with Goldman Sachs and American International Group, a giant insurance holding company. They offered to buy out the shareholders for $250 million and put $3.75 billion into the fund as new capital. This offer would have put the fund on a much firmer financial basis and staved off failure. However, the existing shareholders would have lost everything except for the $250 million takeover payment, and the fund's managers would be fired. The motivation behind this offer was strictly commercial, and had nothing to do with saving world financial markets. As one news report later put it,

> Buffett wasn't offering public charity. He was trying to do what he preaches: buy something for much less than he thinks it's worth. Ditto for Goldman Sachs, which made tons of money dealing in bankruptcies, salvaging financially distressed real estate [etc.] . . . These folks weren't out to save the world's financial markets; they were out to make a buck out of Long-Term Capital's barely breathing body.
>
> (Sloan 1988: 2)

Had it been accepted, this offer would have ended the crisis without any further Federal Reserve involvement – a powerful illustration of the invisible hand, and a textbook example of how private-sector parties can resolve financial crises on their own, without Federal Reserve or other regulatory involvement.

But it was not to be. The management of LTCM rejected the offer, and one can only presume that they did so because they were confident of getting a better deal from the Fed's consortium.[6] The Fed therefore reconvened discussions to hammer out a rescue package, and a package was agreed by the end of the day. The package was promptly accepted by LTCM and immediately made public. Under the terms of this deal, fourteen prominent banks and brokerage houses – including UBS, Goldman Sachs, Merrill Lynch, among others, but not the Fed – agreed to invest $3.65 billion of equity capital in LTCM in exchange for 90 per cent of the firm's equity. Existing shareholders would therefore retain a 10 per cent holding, valued at about $400 million. This offer was clearly better for the existing shareholders than the previous offer. It was also better for the managers of LTCM, who would now retain their jobs for the time being and earn management fees they would have lost under the Buffett takeover. Control of the fund now passed to a new steering committee made up of representatives from the consortium, and the announcement of the rescue ended concerns over LTCM's immediate future. By the end of the year, the fund was making profits again.

Was the Federal Reserve justified?

The immediate reaction of most observers in the financial world was one of relief that the failure of LTCM had been avoided, and the rescue package was generally well received in Wall Street, although some financial observers expressed concerns about its longer-term implications. Elsewhere, reactions were generally less favourable, and there was considerable criticism of the management of LTCM for getting into difficulties and of the Fed for bailing the fund out. Responding to these concerns, the House Committee on Banking and Financial Services called a hearing on the issue, and invited some of the participants to give evidence. Those called included the President of the New York Fed, William McDonough, and the Federal Reserve Chairman, Alan Greenspan, who both testified before it on 1 October. Their testimony focused on three main issues:

- the rescue package itself
- the necessity (or otherwise) of Federal Reserve intervention
- the consequences on financial markets if LTCM had failed.

The rescue: private-sector solution or Fed bailout?

In his evidence, Mr. McDonough defended the rescue package as 'a private-sector solution to a private-sector problem, involving an investment of new equity by Long-Term Capital's creditors and counterparties' (McDonough 1998: 4). He bristled at the claim that the Fed had 'bailed out' LTCM, pointing out that control had passed to the fourteen-member creditor group and that 'the original equity-holders [had] taken a severe hit'. He also stressed that 'no Federal Reserve official pressured anyone, and no promises were made. Not one penny of public money was spent or committed' (ibid.). Dr Greenspan echoed this same argument and claimed that the LTCM episode was one of those 'rare occasions' when financial markets seize up and 'temporary ad hoc responses' are required (Greenspan 1998: 5). He also compared the LTCM rescue with the famous occasion when J. P. Morgan convened the leading bankers of his day to a meeting in his library to discuss how they were going to resolve the financial crisis of 1907 (ibid.).

There is a certain irony in central bankers defending their resolution of the LTCM problem on the grounds that it was much the same as a purely private-sector solution to the same problem. If the central bank merely mimicked the private sector, then why did it need to get involved at all? Why couldn't it have sat back and let Warren Buffett and his associates in the private sector do the job for them? Indeed, what was the point of having a Federal Reserve at all? The arguments put forward by McDonough and Greenspan undermine the very position they were trying to defend.

McDonough's testimony also invites the response that an intervention led by a federal body can hardly be described as a 'private sector solution to a private sector problem'. The Fed did intervene, and pointing out that the Fed did not pressure institutions to participate or spend or commit public money does not alter that fact.

For his part, Greenspan overlooks the point that the 1907 crisis was resolved by private-sector parties operating on their own – as they had to, because there was no central bank at the time – while the LTCM crisis was resolved by a rescue package led by the central bank. The lesson to draw from a comparison of 1907 and LTCM is therefore not that the LTCM rescue was justified because it was like the resolution of 1907. Instead, the appropriate lesson is almost the opposite: namely, that if private-sector parties operating on their own could resolve the crisis of 1907, then there was no need for the Federal Reserve to intervene in 1998. If 1907 tells us anything about the LTCM episode, it suggests that the private sector could have resolved the crisis on its own – a conclusion that is also borne out by the facts of the case itself.

Did the Fed need to intervene to stop the failure of LTCM?

Both officials also argued strongly that the Federal Reserve was obliged to prevent the failure of LTCM out of fear of the adverse circumstances that LTCM's failure might have had on financial markets. As Greenspan put it,

> Financial market participants were already unsettled by recent global events. Had the failure of LTCM triggered the seizing up of markets,

substantial damage could have been inflicted on many market participants, including some not directly involved with the firm, and could have
potentially impaired the economies of many nations, including our own.
... Moreover, our sense was that the consequences of a fire sale triggered
by cross-default clauses, should LTCM fail on some of its obligations,
risked a severe drying up of market liquidity. . . . In that environment, it
was the FRBNY's [Federal Reserve Bank of New York's] judgment that it
was to the advantage of all parties – including the creditors and other
market participants – to engender if at all possible an orderly resolution
rather than let the firm go into disorderly fire-sale liquidation.

(Greenspan 1998: 1, 3)

The Federal Reserve therefore

moved more quickly to provide their good offices to help resolve the
affairs of LTCM than would have been the case in more normal times. In
effect, the threshold of action was lowered by the knowledge that markets
had recently become more fragile.

(Greenspan 1998: 1)

There is no denying that Federal Reserve officials were genuinely concerned
about the impact that LTCM's failure might have had on financial markets.
Nonetheless, Greenspan's argument begs the central question: it presupposes
that LTCM would have failed if the Fed had not intervened, and yet it is manifestly the case that LTCM would not have failed in the absence of Fed
intervention.

If the Federal Reserve had washed its hands of LTCM early on the morning
of 23 September – and made clear to LTCM that it was doing so – the
management of LTCM would have faced a very different set of alternatives
from those they actually faced at the time. Instead of choosing between the
Buffett offer and the likelihood of a better offer later in the day, they would
have had to choose between the Buffett offer and almost certain failure. The
Buffett offer was not a generous one: it would have cost them their remaining
equity, their jobs and any future management fees they might have obtained
from LTCM, but it would at least have left them with a $250 million payment
they could walk away with. The alternative would have been to lose their
equity, their jobs and their management fees, and get nothing in return: in
short, to lose everything. They would therefore have been crazy to turn Buffett
down, and we must suppose they would not have done so. There is thus a very
strong argument that the Fed could have abandoned the rescue as late as the
morning of 23 September without letting LTCM fail. However, if that is the
case, it could also have abandoned its rescue bid earlier without letting LTCM

fail. Indeed, the Fed could have abstained completely from intervention, and LTCM would still not have failed.[7]

What if LTCM *had* failed?

There still remains the hypothetical issue of what might have happened if LTCM *had* failed. Were the Fed's fears plausible? I would suggest not. Central bankers are always worried about the impacts of the failures of large financial firms on market 'confidence', and the argument that they had to intervene to prevent the knock-on effects of such failures has been used to justify every bailout since time immemorial. Nonetheless, no one can deny that financial markets were in a particularly fragile state in September last year. Moreover, LTCM was a big operator which was heavily involved in derivatives trading; it also had large exposures to many different counterparties, and many of its positions were difficult and costly to unwind. One can therefore readily appreciate why the Fed was nervous about the prospect of LTCM failing.

Yet despite these factors, there are a number of reasons to suggest that financial markets could have absorbed the shock of LTCM failing without going into the financial meltdown that Federal Reserve officials feared:

- While many firms would have taken large hits, the amount of capital in the markets is vast – many trillions of dollars. It is therefore difficult to see how the markets as a whole could not have absorbed the shock, given their huge size relative to LTCM. The markets might have sneezed, and perhaps even caught a cold, but they would hardly have caught pneumonia.
- Where firms are forced to liquidate positions in response to a major shock, there are usually other firms willing to buy at the right price. Sellers may have to take a loss to liquidate, but buyers can still usually be found, and competition for good buys usually puts a floor on sellers' losses.
- Market experience suggests that the failure of even a big derivatives player usually has a major impact – if at all – only on the markets in which that player was very active. Worldwide market liquidity has never been threatened by any such failure. It follows, then, though the failure of LTCM might have had a major negative impact on some of the derivatives markets in which LTCM was active, it would not have caused a liquidity crisis on a global scale.
- In any case, even in those rather extreme and unusual markets where liquidity might be paralysed in the immediate aftermath of a major shock, participants have every reason to resume trading as soon as possible. Time and time again in the 1990s, derivatives markets have shown a remarkable

ability to absorb major shocks and quickly return to normality, and there is no reason to suppose that it would have been much different if LTCM had failed.

- Last but by no means least, there have been major developments in derivatives risk management over the last few years.[8] These developments include the widespread adoption of Value at Risk (VaR) systems to measure and manage overall risk exposures, the increasing acceptance of firm-wide risk management guidelines, the rapid growth of methodologies for stress-testing and scenario analysis, and the development of 'credit enhancement' techniques to keep down exposures to counterparties. These techniques include the use of netting agreements, periodic settlement provisions, credit triggers, third-party guarantees, and credit derivatives.[9] As a result, most firms' 'true' exposures are now only a small fraction of what they might otherwise appear to be.

The Fed's nightmare scenario – a mass unwinding of positions, with widespread freezing of markets, and so on – is thus far-fetched, even in the fragile market conditions of the time.

There is also another reason why the Fed was ill-advised to intervene, even if it was right in its assessment that LTCM would otherwise have failed. If the Fed is to promote market stability, it needs to ensure that market participants have strong incentives to promote their own financial health: to avoid excessive risk-taking, keep their leverage down to reasonable levels, maintain their liquidity, and so forth. However, the best incentive of all is the fear of dire consequences if they do not manage themselves properly and as a result default on their obligations. If the Fed wishes to encourage institutions to be strong, it should therefore make an example of those that fail *pour encourager les autres*. In that context, LTCM provided the Fed with an ideal opportunity to make such an example and send out the message that no firm, however prominent, could expect to be rescued from the consequences of its own mistakes. Other firms would have taken note and strengthened themselves accordingly, and financial markets would have been more stable as a result. Throwing LTCM to the wolves would have strengthened financial markets, rather than weakened them.

Consequences of the bailout

Calls for more regulation

One of the most immediate consequences of the LTCM affair was to fuel calls for more regulation of hedge fund activities. Those calling for more regulation included the Treasury Secretary, Robert Rubin, who called for an inter-agency study to look at ways of making the activities of offshore hedge funds more transparent. Many others made similar suggestions. However, as one observer wrote, 'Many of these calls have been pure reflex actions rather than a carefully considered response to the issues – if any – which hedge funds pose for the world financial system' (Weller 1998: 21).

These calls were met with widespread disbelief offshore. Many people familiar with offshore operations pointed out that there was very little that US regulators could actually do about them. Some pointed out that attempts to regulate US hedge funds might also prove counterproductive, by driving more of them offshore where they would be even further out of the reach of US regulators. The sceptics included Greenspan himself:

> It is questionable whether hedge funds can be effectively regulated in the United States alone. While their financial clout may be large, hedge funds' physical presence is small. Given the amazing communication capabilities available virtually around the globe, trades can be initiated from almost any location. Indeed, most hedge funds are only a short step from cyberspace. Any direct US regulations restricting their flexibility will doubtless induce the more aggressive funds to emigrate from under our jurisdiction.
>
> (Greenspan 1998: 5)

It followed, then, that

> The best we can do . . . is what we do today: Regulate them indirectly through the regulation of the sources of their funds. . . . If the funds move abroad, our oversight will diminish.
>
> (ibid.)

He went on to suggest that the primary defence against the problems posed by the failures of hedge funds is for their counterparties to be careful in their dealings with them (so they do not extend too much credit, and so on). Greenspan's assessment is surely correct. Moreover, since it is also in their own interests to be careful, there would appear to be no need (and, indeed, no point) in regulating these dealings. In an efficient economy, parties should be free to make whatever deals they want with hedge funds, and it is in their interests not to over-expose themselves to these or any other risky counterparties.

Massive extension of Federal Reserve responsibilities

The LTCM rescue also implies a very large and problematic extension of the Fed's responsibilities. The LTCM affair indicates that the Fed now accepts responsibility for the safety of US hedge funds, despite the fact that it has no legislative mandate to assume this responsibility. Indeed, the Fed accepts this responsibility even though it has no regulatory authority over hedge funds and even though the chairman of the Fed explicitly argues that it should not have any such authority. The Federal Reserve thus maintains the extraordinary position that it should have responsibility for hedge funds but no power over them. Even if it is legally sound, which is questionable, this position is patently untenable, as it subjects the Fed to a moral-hazard problem over which it has no control. It allows large hedge funds to take risks that the Fed cannot control, with the Fed picking up the tab if they get themselves into difficulties. Heads they win, tails the Fed loses. Responsibility and power cannot be separated indefinitely, however, and at some point the Fed would have to abandon its responsibility for hedge funds or, if its past empire-building is any guide, seek regulatory authority to control them (see e.g. Timberlake 1993).

However there is also a deeper problem. Where does the Fed draw a line between US hedge funds and overseas ones? What is the difference between a US hedge fund based in Greenwich, Connecticut, which also operates in the Cayman Islands, and a Caymans-based hedge fund, which also operates in Greenwich? The two are indistinguishable for all practical purposes, and the Fed cannot realistically support 'American' hedge funds without also supporting other hedge funds as well. If the Fed supports large 'US' hedge funds, it could therefore easily find itself supporting all larger hedge funds, regardless of their 'real' nationality. To make matters even worse, if the Fed becomes responsible for the hedge fund industry, where and how would it draw the line between hedge funds and other investment firms, particularly those that might be similar to hedge funds? Where would the Federal Reserve's responsibility actually stop? Is the logical implication, as one industry commentator asked, that the Fed will 'now try to shore up the Japanese banking system? After all, this is a lot more central to the fate of the world's economy and markets than one particular Greenwich, Connecticut hedge fund manager' (Young 1998:1). The LTCM affair implies a very large and ultimately intolerable increase in Federal Reserve responsibilities, without any legislative mandate whatsoever from Congress.

The return of 'too big to fail'

The LTCM affair also marks a return to the discredited old doctrine of 'too big to fail': the doctrine that the Federal Reserve cannot allow very big institutions to fail, precisely because they are big, for fear of their consequences on the financial system. This doctrine is a direct inducement for large institutions to act irresponsibly, and ever since the bailout of Continental Illinois in 1984,

Federal Reserve officials have been trying to convince larger institutions that they could not count on their support if they got themselves into difficulties. This message seemed to be slowly getting through to financial firms, and then the LTCM rescue wiped out all that progress at a stroke. Not only did the Fed intervene to rescue a large firm, but the reason given for the intervention – the Fed's fears of the effects of LTCM's failure on world financial markets – were nothing less than an emphatic re-statement of the doctrine. 'Too big to fail' was back again, with a vengeance.

The return of 'too big to fail' has serious consequences for longer-term stability. If the financial system is to be stable, individual institutions must be given incentives to make themselves financially strong. Rescuing a firm in difficulties then sends out the worst possible signal, as it leads others to think that they too might get rescued if they get into difficulties. This weakens their incentive to maintain their own financial health and so makes it more likely that they will eventually get into difficulties as well. Bailing out a weak firm may help to calm markets in the very short term, but it undermines financial stability in the long run.

The damage to the moral authority of the Federal Reserve

But perhaps the worst consequence of the LTCM affair was the damage done to the credibility and, more importantly, moral authority of Federal Reserve policy-makers as they encourage their counterparts in other countries to persevere with the necessary but difficult and painful process of economic liberalization. Jim Leach, the chairman of the House Committee on Banking and Financial Services, was absolutely correct when he pointed out that

> The LTCM saga is fraught with ironies related to moral authority as well as moral hazard. The Fed's intervention comes at a time when our government has been preaching to foreign governments, particularly Asian ones, that the way to modernize is to let weak institutions fail and to rely on market mechanisms, rather than insider bailouts.
>
> (Leach 1998: 5–6)

Allan Sloan put the same argument more colourfully in *Newsweek*:

> For 15 months, as financial markets in country after country collapsed like straw huts in a typhoon, the United States lectured the rest of the world about the evils of crony capitalism – of bailing out rich, connected insiders while letting everyone else suffer. US officials and financiers talked about letting market forces allocate capital for maximum efficiency. Thai peasants, Korean steelworkers and Moscow pensioners may

suffer horribly as their local economies and currencies collapse – but we solemnly told them that was a cost they had to pay for the greater good. . . . Cronyism bad. Capitalism good. Then came the imminent collapse of Long-Term Capital . . . the quintessential member of The Club, with rich fat-cat investors and rich hotshot well-connected managers. Faster than you can say 'bailout', crony capitalism US style raised its ugly head . . . John Meriwether and the rest of the guys who ran the fund onto the rocks got to keep their jobs. The fund's investors, whose stakes would have been wiped out in a collapse, salvaged about seven cents on the dollar . . . The rescuers even agreed to pay a management fee on their rescue fund.

(Sloan 1998: 1)

Perhaps the most damaging consequence of the LTCM episode is therefore the harm done by the perception that Federal Reserve policy-makers do not really have the faith to take their own medicine. How can they persuade the Russians or the Japanese to let big institutions fail, if they are afraid to do the same themselves? At the end of the day, economic liberalization is just as necessary as it always was, but in the wake of the LTCM rescue, one can understand why many of those who have to pay the price for it might have their doubts.

17 Paternalism fails again

The sorry story of the Financial Services Act

With Jimmy M. Hinchliffe

> Unless my proposals are implemented . . . further serious scandals undermining public and international confidence are, in my view, inevitable. If they are implemented, scandals will not be wholly prevented but I believe that they would be fewer and that when they occurred less irremediable damage would be suffered.
>
> (The late Professor L. C. B. Gower 1984: 189)

> It's a total disaster.
>
> (Said to be Professor Gower's assessment of the regime
> seven years later)[1]

For over a decade, the retail investment market in the UK has operated under the framework of the Financial Services Act (FSA) of 1986. This Act was passed to give small investors cast-iron protection and ensure that firms in the industry operated with investors' best interests in mind. 'Aunt Agatha' would be able to sleep easily in her bed in the knowledge that an army of regulators was looking after her. The FSA was a textbook case of paternalistic public policy in which issues of economic efficiency and cost effectiveness – and, indeed, even the most basic economics of regulation – were ignored, while policy-makers constructed a very costly and unwieldy regulatory edifice. The result was a catastrophe.

The full story of this fiasco is still not widely known inside the UK, let alone outside it. Here was a case of public policy justified almost entirely by paternalistic considerations, but the result was the biggest financial scandal in British history. Far from strengthening investor protection, the new regime actually had the opposite effect and millions of small investors lost out on a massive scale. The mess has still to be sorted out and many thousands of wronged investors have since died without recompense. All this went on right under the noses of the regulators, who failed to enforce their own rules and repeatedly put industry interests ahead of the interests of the small investors they were supposedly there to protect. Instead, the regulators allowed themselves to be captured by the industry. The story of the FSA regime in the UK is a classic example of public choice theory in action, in which the principal parties involved – the Government, policy-makers and regulators, and the industry – put their own interests first, and did so at huge cost to retail investors despite the watertight protection those investors appeared to enjoy on paper.[2] An ostensibly paternalistic regime became a smokescreen behind which retail investors were blatantly exploited by the industry, with the open connivance of the regulators who were supposed to be there to protect them.

The Gower Report and Financial Services Act

Background

Long-term financial products in the UK – pensions, personal investments, life insurance, and so on – are provided by banks, life and general insurance companies, fund management companies, and similar financial institutions. Some 75 per cent of households in the UK have such bought such products, and the scale of the funds involved is very large indeed. At the end of 1995, for example, the UK personal sector had almost a trillion pounds invested in life and pension funds alone.[3]

Traditionally, the firms involved had been subject to loose prudential supervision by a relevant authority: banks were subject to supervision by the Bank of England, insurance companies were subject to the Department of Trade and Industry, and so forth. This sort of regulatory arrangement was in reality a set of informal cartels, and the regulatory process was one of negotiation and compromise between the supervisory bodies and the firms they supervised. Everyone was reasonable and understood everyone else, and they all paid lip service to the public interest and the dear old consumer while they quietly rigged the market. This sort of arrangement was never particularly efficient, but it was cosy and rolled along tolerably well provided everyone played the game and there were no major scandals to provoke public outcry and possible Government intervention.

However, therein lay its Achilles' heel. Life had been comfortable up to the early 1970s, but since then there had been a series of damaging financial scandals. These created political problems: the media and the opposition parties would blame the Government and ask what they were going to do about it, and the Governments of the day usually felt obliged to respond. They had Sir Humphrey whispering into their ears, 'Yes Minister, you must do something – never mind what – to cover your back'. Some particularly sensitive scandals then occurred in 1981. A minor investment management firm, Norton Warburg, failed in February 1981 with losses of £12m, and this failure provoked a major public outcry.[4] Shortly afterwards, two other minor brokers followed suit and there were further outcries. These scandals led to the predictable criticisms that the regulatory system was not working and there were calls for something to be done to stop people losing out: 'Nanny' should intervene to protect vulnerable old Aunt Agatha, and the like. The Government would have preferred to do nothing, but it was getting a lot of political flak for being soft on its 'friends' in the City, and was certain to get more in the future whenever any other institutions failed. At the same time, the Labour Party and the consumers' lobby wanted a full statutory investor protection scheme and a mega-regulatory agency to prevent further scandals, and the Government's standard response – that such a scheme would create more problems than it solved – did not really cut much political ice.[5]

The Gower Report

The Government felt obliged to do something, and opted for the time-honoured solution of commissioning a report. In July 1981 it commissioned the distinguished company lawyer, Professor L. C. B. ('Jim') Gower, to review the existing framework of statutory protection for small investors in securities and recommend how that protection might be improved. Gower completed his report in October 1983, and his views were to have a decisive (and, alas, unfortunate) effect on the subsequent legislation. Gower was a lawyer's lawyer and saw the problem of investor protection in narrowly legal terms. He had no interest in the economics of regulation, and made no effort to come to grips with the economic issues involved.[6] He therefore ignored the potential role of competition in protecting investors and paid little attention to the compliance or other costs of his recommendations. He also had little to say about the objectives of regulation, and showed no awareness whatever of public choice issues.[7]

Gower therefore proposed a very legalistic, paternalistic, approach to investor protection, with little regard to the costs of what he was suggesting or the danger that his regulatory scheme might be captured by factional interests.

The Financial Services Act

A long, difficult and very confused series of debates then followed. Special interest groups – particularly within the industry – immediately pounced on Gower to argue for all manner of changes, and the Government was anxious to build some sort of consensus around – in other words, to neutralize major opposition to – what it interpreted as the spirit of Gower's proposals. The resulting 'consultation exercise' inevitably involved a vast amount of discussion and behind-the-scenes negotiation to appease key interest groups.[8] The result of all this was the Financial Services Bill, which was presented to

Parliament in late 1985. The Bill then went through a particularly difficult process of Parliamentary scrutiny as the various interest groups continued to fight over it.[9] In the end, over a thousand amendments were tabled to it – a Parliamentary record. Not surprisingly, debates were very wearing and participants often lost all perspective: major questions would remain unanswered while discussions got hung up on trivia and everyone became increasingly confused.[10] The Bill eventually emerged in much-modified form as the Financial Services Act – a kind of financial Frankenstein's monster, and a very overweight one at that – receiving Royal Assent in November 1986.[11]

The FSA regulatory regime

The Act set up a system to regulate financial investments based on the organizing principle of 'self-regulation within a statutory framework': the industry would be regulated by a number of non-governmental regulatory organizations, each of which had its own devolved regulatory powers and responsibilities, and all operating under the statutory framework established by the Act.

The new system of regulation was, to say the least, highly convoluted. At its apex was the Securities and Investments Board (SIB), a non-governmental body with statutory powers, and funded by levies on the industry. The SIB was to oversee a group of so-called Self-Regulatory Organisations (SROs) with a plethora of confusing acronyms: the Life Assurance and Unit Trust Regulatory Organisation (LAUTRO), the Financial Intermediaries, Managers and Brokers Regulatory Association (FIMBRA), the Investment Management Regulatory Organisation (IMRO), the Securities Association (TSA) and the Association of Futures Brokers and Dealers (AFBD). The TSA and AFBD subsequently merged in April 1991 to form the Securities and Futures Authority (SFA), and LAUTRO and FIMBRA were merged in 1994 to produce the Personal Investment Authority (PIA).[12] A further regulator was SIBRO, which was part of the SIB itself and looked after some of the banks and other large institutions. The SIB was also responsible for supervising nine Recognised Professional Bodies and seven Recognised Investment Exchanges. The former were the professional associations for lawyers, accountants and other professions involved in the investment business, and the latter included organized markets such as the London Stock Exchange and the London International Financial Futures and Options Exchange (LIFFE). In theory, the lower bodies were all accountable to the SIB, and the SIB was accountable to the Government and, ultimately, to Parliament.

The overriding justification for the new regime was to protect the small investor, particularly the vulnerable one. The new system sought to protect investors in a number of ways.[13]

First, it introduced a legal requirement for financial advisers to provide 'best advice' to the public (rules 5.02 and 5.03). This meant that advisers must recommend the best (most suitable) product for the clients' needs.[14] The duty to give best advice mirrored common law fiduciary duties, namely of exercising due skill, care and diligence with a view to securing the best bargains for the client and to act at all times in the best interests of the client. Breach of the duty of best advice was a criminal offence under the Act.

Second, the new regulatory system established a strict code of conduct and (in theory) provided for monitoring systems to ensure that rules were complied with. These were intended to promote integrity and best practice. However, unlike regulators in most other countries, the UK regulators prescribed intricate rules of procedure and required detailed documentation to show that procedures had been followed. In particular, sellers were to have detailed knowledge of customers' needs, which required them to conduct lengthy 'Factfinds' often running to twenty pages of detail. These Factfinds were to set out both the circumstances of the customer and the advice given, so the relevant SRO could then determine whether the advice given was 'best' or not. To ensure they got compliance, most – though for some reason, not all – of the SROs also had wide powers to remove licences and fine individuals and institutions that did not comply with these requirements.[15]

Finally, the regime instituted a licensing requirement to ensure that firms conducting investment business passed certain 'fit and proper' criteria.[16]

The ineffectiveness of the FSA regulatory regime

The regulators' failure to enforce compliance

The new regime set up a regulatory structure that was confused, unwieldy, very bureaucratic, and very costly. It also turned out to be very ineffective, and the regulators failed to achieve any reasonable degree of compliance with their own rules. The magnitude of this failure became apparent from evidence presented in a widely cited KPMG report published in December 1993. This report covered the period January 1991 to June 1993 (and therefore did not cover the period when most abuses apparently took place). Nonetheless, it produced a number of disturbing findings:

- In 91 per cent of the cases studied, life assurance salesmen and other financial advisers had collected insufficient information about their clients to justify the advice they had given to transfer to personal pensions. The legal obligation to comply with the 'best advice' requirement was thus apparently ignored in the vast majority of cases. In addition, in a substantial number of these cases the advice given was believed to be suspect, and not merely unsatisfactory.[17]

- Some 89 per cent of cases involving FIMBRA members, 95 per cent of LAUTRO members, and 89 per cent of IMRO members failed to meet compliance standards.
- Even after getting guidance from SROs, the proportion of cases where insufficient information was on file fell from 88 per cent to 69 per cent (i.e. so the regulators managed a 31 per cent success rate in enforcing their own rules on record-keeping!), and the proportion of cases of suspect advice fell from 39 per cent to 33 per cent.

No prosecutions for failure to give 'best advice'

The ineffectiveness of the new regime is also apparent from the way in which regulators have responded to individual wrongdoing. Despite evidence of widespread abuse, much of it criminal, the regulators do not appear to have passed on a single case of mis-selling to the police for prosecution. The best that the regulators have done is to issue a number of very small fines and reveal the names of some of the companies guilty of serious breaches, and they only agreed to those measures reluctantly, under pressure from the media. Individual directors, who are held responsible for the actions of their salesforces under the Act, appear to have escaped any form of punishment whatever.

The industry's capture of the regulatory system

The ineffectiveness of the FSA regime was due, in part, to the reluctance of regulators to stand up against the industry. Time and again, regulators bowed to pressure from the industry and sacrificed the interests of the consumers they were meant to protect.

Disclosure

A good example was the regulators' handling of the disclosure issue – the question of how much information investors should be given (or allowed to get) when they buy financial products. Disclosure is important because it helps consumers make informed choices, and the disclosure of commission charges is particularly important because it forces firms to compete in an environment where consumers have a reasonable idea of what they are paying and getting. Commissions disclosure was long supported by consumers' groups and the Office of Fair Trading (OFT), and was also in the broader social interest because it is a necessary prerequisite for effective price competition among financial firms.

What line then did the consumers' champions, the regulators, take? They argued vociferously *against* it for years. Their arguments were, to be frank, laughable: their main arguments were that investors would be unable to comprehend the information disclosed, and that disclosure would lead to a meltdown in the industry:

- The first argument ignores the points that many consumers are able to understand this sort of information, and that those who do not can always seek advice from people who do. It also ignores the fact that, to the extent that consumers do have difficulty understanding this information, it is to a considerable extent because the sellers of financial products make this information deliberately difficult for consumers – and even their own staff – to understand. If firms really cared about making contracts under-standable to their customers, they would simplify them and provide more straightforward information to their clients. However, the reality was that most firms deliberately sought to confuse their customers so that they could get the better of them.
- The second argument is even less persuasive. The regulators were arguing that consumers should be kept in the dark (and left open to excessive charging) because informed consumers would not stand for it! We should not tell the consumers because they would realize they were being overcharged – a novel argument for regulators whose *raison d'être* was to protect the consumer!

Disclosure was a clear case where the interests of the industry and those of the consumer were opposed, and the regulators sided with the industry. A clearer case of regulatory capture is hard to imagine.

The regulators only accepted disclosure when the Government (of all people!) finally forced it on them in 1995. However, regulators then changed tack and had the nerve to claim that disclosure was one of the main achieve-ments of the regulatory regime:

> From 1986 onwards, the SIB, urged on by the industry, fought a rearguard action against the OFT's recommendation requiring companies and agents to disclose to consumers information on the prices and commission payments they received on policies sold. . . . the SIB was able to hold up the development of price competition in the industry for almost nine years. [Yet] today, the same organisation unblushingly identifies disclosure as one of the principal measures for investor protection.
>
> (Simpson 1996: 45)

The failure to ensure adequate standards of competency

Another instance of regulatory capture was the handling of competency stan-dards in the industry. The functioning of the new system hinged critically on industry staff meeting adequate competency standards. These standards were already an issue before the Act, and became even more of one later due to the volume of detailed regulation involved. If the regime was to function effectively, it was essential that industry staff understood the products they were selling and their obligations to their customers.

However, the industry had little interest in training standards – their main concern was to get sales – and for years the regulators did nothing to ensure that salesforces were adequately trained. The regulators only got round to recommending training and competency standards in 1990, and it took another five years to introduce a requirement for a reasonable level of training and competency in the industry. Even then, when the rules were finally in place, the regulators were often unwilling to force companies to comply with them,[18] and salesmen who failed their exams were often allowed to carry on selling as long as their employers claimed they were supervised.[19]

The mis-selling of financial products

Given that the regulatory system did not enforce its own rules or take consumer interests seriously, it is perhaps hardly surprising that large numbers of consumers were given bad advice and sold inappropriate products in the years after the FSA regime came into operation. One indication of the extent of the mis-selling of financial products is given by the proportion of life and pension products terminated well before they mature. These are designed as long-term investments, and the fact that the commissions are front-loaded makes it very disadvantageous for investors to terminate them early, particularly given the high commission levels involved. Investors who liquidate early see little or no return on their investment, because their investments have gone into commission payments. The extent of early termination therefore gives an indication of mis-selling.

Data on early terminations confirm that there was a considerable increase in mis-selling after the FSA came into force. Lapse rates (as measured by the ratio of annual premiums to new business) fell from 11 per cent in 1985 to 8 per cent in 1988, but then rose dramatically after the FSA came into force to a level of 18 per cent in 1991 (Simpson 1996: 39). Although lapse rates have fallen in more recent times, they still remain above the levels seen in 1985.[20] The latest PIA data (PIA 1997) also indicate lapse rates for life and pensions products have been high in the FSA period and still remain high. For example, approximately a third of policies sold by company representatives in 1993 were terminated within three years. The cost of these early terminations to investors was enormous.

There was also widespread evidence of mortgage mis-selling. There is a large amount of anecdotal evidence to suggest that the mortgage business was riddled with bad practice. For example:

- Investors would sometimes be sold endowment mortgages before they had actually bought their houses.
- It was common for advisers to urge investors to churn their policies: an adviser would suggest to someone moving house that they 'cash in' their existing endowment mortgage, use the lump sum to buy carpets and curtains, and start a new endowment policy bought through the adviser (who of course stood to earn a small fortune in commissions!).[21]

The personal pensions scandal

However the biggest and most serious scandal involved the mis-selling of millions – the exact number is still not clear – of personal pensions in the first five years of the FSA regime. The Government created the personal pension scheme in 1988 and the underlying idea – a very reasonable one in itself – was to give individuals more control over their own pensions. The Government also hoped that the availability of personal pensions would alleviate the growing problem of unfunded pension liabilities and its adverse implications for public finances in the decades ahead. The Government therefore encouraged the adoption of personal pensions by giving them certain tax advantages and funding a heavy advertising programme to encourage individuals to buy them.

A vast new – heavily subsidized – market opened up, and the industry lost little time taking advantage of it. With potentially enormous profits at stake, the industry mounted a huge sales drive and, over the next seven years, persuaded about 8 million people to buy personal pensions. In the process, many firms operated with breathtaking disregard for ethical or legal considerations. For example, it is now known that sales staff in many firms were often told to focus on new sales and not worry about the paperwork.[22] It was often implicitly assumed that audit trails and other regulatory compliance requirements were not particularly important, although few people would actually say so openly, and the regulators themselves did relatively little to discourage such attitudes or ensure that firms' management took their obligations seriously. It was also common for firms to get as many sales staff as they could on a commission basis, make little effort to ensure that they were adequately trained, and then fire the bulk of them when they failed to perform. Not surprisingly, selling practices degenerated, and stories abound of unscrupulous practices.

- One apparently common technique was to hire new sales staff, start them off by encouraging them to target their family and friends, and then fire them when the contracts were in.
- Another common technique was to persuade people in lucrative occupational pension schemes (such as miners, teachers and nurses) to opt out of them and

take out a personal pension, or to transfer their benefits into a personal pension scheme. Many highly unethical sales practices were employed, ranging from omitting to comment on the benefits of the schemes they were in, to undisguised fraud. In addition, many people – miners particularly – were made redundant in the late 1980s and were persuaded to invest their redundancy payments in investments that were obviously inappropriate for them. Many of them ended up paying huge amounts in commission and often made large losses on their investments.

- Another practice was the sale of the so called 'television policy', where salesmen would target the elderly by persuading them to cash in their investment policies (most often policies provided by home service companies) and use the surrender value to buy a new television and video recorder. (During this period, most elderly people in the UK used to rent their television and VCR.) The adviser would then suggest that they should start up a new policy, for which the adviser would earn a substantial commission.

Many – probably most – firms also resorted to clearly illegal practices of one sort or another, and stories abound of salespeople misrepresenting the options put to clients, doctoring paperwork to misrepresent their discussions with clients, and blatantly ignoring the legal requirement to provide 'best advice'.[23] Compliance with regulatory requirements was a joke.[24]

The pressure intensified as the market became saturated and sales became harder. One participant later said that:

> the atmosphere in some sales teams could be best described as Wild West mixed in with eastern bazaar. Although product sales were still strong, the market was beginning to become saturated and the first signs of the early 1990s recession were starting to make selling conditions tougher. Sales people were put under increasing pressure by a range of incentives, some of them fairly obvious, such as bottles of whisky and holidays in the Bahamas. . . . Bizarre punishments were also devised for those who had done badly . . . This culture was made the more frenetic by a rapid ebb and flow of sales people. One authoritative estimate puts the annual turnover of sales representatives in the early 1990s at nearly 60 per cent, compared with 30–40 per cent in more normal times.[25]

Not surprisingly, evidence of mis-selling and other bad practice gradually became public, and the industry was soon facing some well-deserved, very bad, publicity. As the *Economist* ruefully observed in December 1993, 'The British have come to regard life-insurance salesmen with the deepest disdain. They may be too generous'.[26]

At last, the regulators respond . . .

The situation eventually became so bad that even the regulators could ignore it no longer.[27] The SIB therefore stepped in and commissioned KPMG to report. Various other reports also gradually came out, and these reports seemed to confirm suspicions of flagrant abuse on a massive scale:

- Evidence emerged that a very large number – the final figure was to run into millions – of personal pensions had been mis-sold. In many cases, investors had been persuaded to switch out of generous well-funded pension schemes (e.g. in the public sector), and could not possibly have been given 'best advice' to switch despite the 'best advice' legal requirement.[28] It also turned out that many people sold personal pensions had been too old or did not have adequate incomes to benefit from taking them out. Again, it was hard to see how the salespeople involved could not have broken the 'best advice' requirement.
- Evidence also emerged that many firms had been very lax on compliance issues. Many sales people had not taken the trouble to find out their customers' needs or discover the true value of the pensions they were giving up. Similarly, it became clear that many firms had not bothered with the paperwork necessary to back up sales and demonstrate that they had met the 'best advice' requirement. There was thus strong prima facie evidence that many firms – and, of course, many individual salespeople – had broken the law.

If this evidence is accepted, it became very difficult to avoid the conclusion that regulatory supervision and monitoring must also have been very lax. The regulators had signed off millions of personal pensions and other investment products on their compliance visits which it now transpired had been mis-sold!

. . . and the disaster gets worse

The situation now degenerated even further. By this stage it was abundantly clear that the FSA regime had failed to protect consumers, and consumers and their representatives were now clamouring for redress. Given that time is irreversible and that many victims were already at or approaching pensionable age – and, more seriously still, given that thousands of them were dying each year whilst their cases were still outstanding – it was also very important that they received redress as quickly as possible. Did they get it? Not at all. Instead, the system failed them yet again and the parties responsible – the Government, the regulators, and the industry – now closed ranks against them while they argued over what should (or should not) be done, who was to blame, and of course who should pay.

Consumers were therefore denied redress – and the damage done to them increased considerably further – while the guilty parties played pass the parcel at their expense. The most culpable party was clearly the Government, because it was the Government that had sponsored the new regulatory system and the personal pension scheme, and pushed the necessary legislation through Parliament. However, the Government was unwilling to admit its responsibility and, in the modern British Parliamentary system, there was little anyone could do to force it to.[29] At the same time, there was no doubt that the Government was deeply disturbed at the scale of the problem. It was a political time-bomb and a constant source of embarrassing publicity. It also threatened to undermine the Government's attempts to privatize pensions and get to grips with the long-term problems posed by the state pension system. As if that were not bad enough, the scandal also threatened to create panic and destroy public confidence – whatever was left of it – in the UK life and pensions industry. The Government's response was therefore one that any half-decent public choice scholar would readily have predicted: the Government adopted the self-serving line that the regulatory system was well-designed (!) and that it was for regulators and the industry to sort problems out between them. Government ministers then assured the public that all victims of mis-selling would be compensated in full, though who would pay, and how those who died in the meantime would be compensated, were never clear. Meanwhile, ministers sanctimoniously lectured the other parties on the need for them to sort out the mess they had created, and do it quickly, because consumers were being harmed by further delays. Ministers also made occasional dark threats that the Government might have to do something – heaven forbid! – if the other parties did not get their act together. The Government's response was, in short, a combination of hot air and hypocrisy.

The industry was not to be outdone, and their response was to play for time and put up a smokescreen. Again, this response was exactly what public choice theory would have predicted. No firm had any incentive to agree to a speedy resolution of its outstanding mis-selling cases, and every incentive to postpone the issue for as long as possible. To agree to early resolution would have been to admit guilt, with all its attendant consequences (the individuals responsible losing their jobs, facing criminal prosecutions, and so on). On the other hand, delay had many benefits. There was always the chance that the Government might bail them out or reform the system to get them off the hook. Delay was also a useful negotiation tactic with disaffected customers, who might be worn down into accepting inferior offers in their desperation to get their cases resolved. In addition, delay was very much in the interests of the individuals responsible for mis-sales and other dubious forms of behaviour: if they could delay resolution long enough, they might have moved on in the meantime or have retired, and perhaps escape punishment. The individuals responsible could also hope that even if they got caught in the end, they would face smaller penalties the longer it took for justice to catch up with them: after all, many offences look less serious when they took place a long time ago. Finally, there was always the hope that if they all stuck together and refused to do anything, they might collectively get away with it, or at least force the Government or the regulators into some sort of plea bargain and escape with much lower penalties.

While playing for time, firms also fought a hard propaganda war. When evidence of their wrongdoing first emerged, the reaction of most industrial spokespeople was to deny point-blank that they (or their own firms, at least) had done anything wrong. A good example was the response of the Prudential, one of the largest firms in the sector. This firm initially maintained that it had done nothing wrong and had never mis-sold any personal pensions. It continued with the same line even after LAUTRO had investigated it and found evidence of bad practice. Its chief executive, Mick Newmarch, then blatantly defied the regulators and refused to set aside any funds for possible compensation purposes. However, some 41,000-plus cases were subsequently identified as being in need of urgent resolution – not to mention the many thousands of other cases the regulators, though presumably not the clients concerned, regarded as 'non-urgent' – and Mr. Newmarch was eventually forced to resign. Four years later, only ten (or less than 0.025 per cent!) of these 'urgent' cases had been resolved. An inspection visit undertaken by the new Financial Services Authority in 1997 confirmed that the firm had done little to put its house in order. The Authority subsequently reported that the firm 'had failed to implement adequately the requisite corrective action' in respect of earlier breaches of the regulations, and found 'continuing persistent and serious breaches . . . across major areas of its business'. Among other shortcomings, the Authority also reported a 'deep seated and long standing failure in management' which prevented the firm recognizing its own shortcomings, and as well as major compliance problems, most particularly, what the regulators euphemistically described as a 'cultural disposition against compliance' which permeated the whole firm.[30]

Yet as time went on and evidence accumulated, the industry could no longer maintain the pretence of innocence.[31] It therefore reverted to excuses of one sort or another to absolve it of blame and avert prospective punishments. Some of these were perhaps not too unreasonable in themselves (for example, firms claimed they needed time to process such a large number of cases because they lacked sufficient numbers of qualified staff). However, some other arguments were less persuasive:

- Industry representatives argued that they were not really guilty of breaking the 'best advice' rule because the 'best advice' in any situation is always subjective (i.e. in this context, meaningless): the 'You can't prove it was not best advice' ploy. However, this argument does not wash. Even if the 'best advice' is hard to determine (which it is), cases of bad advice can be (and, in many cases are) so glaringly obvious that no reasonable person can dispute them. An individual may never be sure whether he is getting best advice, but he can often be very sure when he is not getting it.

- They blamed their delays on regulatory reviews, claiming that they could not really do anything until the reviews were complete: the 'We do not have to obey the law because the Keystone Kops are still on their coffee-break' ploy.[32]
- They argued that it was wrong to expect the industry to pay, because the penalties would really be paid for out of the profits going to other policy-holders or shareholders. This argument is also highly questionable. After all, corporate governance structures require that residual claimants should be liable for such losses, since otherwise they would have little incentive to hold their management teams to account. In any case, even if one accepts the industry argument, it still fails to explain why the individuals concerned should not be held personally responsible and dealt with accordingly.
- Some firms even blamed delays on their own incompetence, claiming that they had 'lost' their paperwork, and so couldn't process it!

The regulators' response was very weak, to put it politely. The consumers' guard-dog barked, but it did not bite. Instead, they looked after their own interests and did little to advance the interests of the many victims of mis-selling. Alas, Gower spoke truer than he realized when he joked that the FSA structure was based on a confidence trick.[33] Had they been concerned with protecting consumers, regulators would have insisted on cases being rapidly resolved, and used their powers to ensure that they were; they would have imposed large fines on firms found guilty of serious breaches; they would have referred large numbers of cases of alleged individual wrongdoing for prosecution under the Financial Services Act; they would have ruthlessly withdrawn operating licences, and so on. However, the regulators did not have the stomach to fight. They were too close to the industry and probably too sympathetic to its excuses (i.e. they were captured by it). They also had another, very strong, reason not to blow the lid off: they themselves had set up much of the regulatory structure – they had designed the rule books, agreed on reporting and compliance procedures, and so forth – and had been responsible for supervising and monitoring the very firms that were now accused of wrongdoing. To have pushed, when push came to shove, would have dramatically highlighted their own incompetence. The regulators' actions were then a foregone conclusion: they made a few token gestures and tacitly accepted defeat.[34]

It is therefore perhaps not surprising that little has been done to punish the many thousands of salespeople responsible, the managers who failed to control them, or those who routinely ignored legally binding compliance requirements. Meanwhile, investors have continued to face obstruction from the industry and the regulators have not only allowed firms to be obstructive, but have openly abetted them by resisting pressure to publish the names of those delaying their pension review (on the grounds, worthy of 'Yes Minister', that this would not be in the public interest!). They have also abetted this obstruction by failing to publish the deadlines for when the review should be completed (on the grounds that there would be a public outcry if deadlines were not met!).

When firms have failed to meet their deadlines, the regulators responded by pushing the deadlines back, and then back again, and by lecturing firms on the need for them to meet deadlines. A stream of statements has therefore come from the regulatory agencies condemning the industry for dragging its feet and saying that something must be done. However, talk is cheap, and the actions of regulators by contrast suggest a chilling indifference to the plight of the victims. Admittedly, some firms have been fined for one thing or another, but the amounts involved have been derisory and people in the industry have more or less openly laughed at them. The plain fact is that firms still have little reason to take the regulators seriously.[35] The net result, not surprisingly, is that progress on resolving outstanding pensions cases has been very slow. By mid 1998, the vast majority of cases remained unresolved, and there was still no end in sight. The regulators had failed abjectly to protect the consumers in their charge.[36]

Conclusions

There can be little doubt that the regulatory system established by the Financial Services Act has been a dismal failure. It was established to provide very high standards of protection and competence for small investors, and never mind the cost. It was a paternalist's dream that provided immaculate, albeit expensive, guarantees for the people it was meant to protect – on paper. Unfortunately, these guarantees turned out to be worthless in practice, and the result was a nightmare for the many investors whose welfare the system was supposedly set up to safeguard. Cast-iron 'protection' turned out to be a licence for the industry to exploit the public with impunity, while the Government and the regulators stood by and wrung their hands. Poor old Aunt Agatha would have fared much better if the Government had left her to fend for herself.

The Conservative Government's stock response – that the outcome would have been even worse if they had adopted the opposition's recommendations and established an SEC-type system instead – is hardly adequate. Policy-makers cannot justify a disastrous public policy by arguing that it was better than a different disastrous policy put forward by their political opponents. The Government could instead have chosen to continue with the previous, admittedly imperfect, regime. It chose not to, because it took the politically easy attitude of 'something must be done'. So something was done, and millions of innocent people paid the price. Alternatively, the Government could have implemented useful, even limited, reforms to improve the regulatory system (e.g. by promoting disclosure), but no one in the Government was capable of thinking of reform other than in terms of what became the FSA regime. In other words, the Government never seriously considered any other approach to reform.

Yet the outcome should have been fairly predictable. They set up a system that made it almost inevitable that the industry would capture the regulatory agencies, and many people said as much when the proposals were first mooted. The industry's response was also fairly predictable: they would look after themselves and make sure that the regulatory system did not get in their way. The outcome should therefore have come as no surprise to anyone: the Government, the industry and the regulators all looked after their own interest, and a very large number of investors had their pensions and life insurance policies (i.e. their financial futures) wrecked.

Even now, no one in any position of power seems to have learned any lessons. The Government has changed, so the ruling party responsible for the mess has now been replaced by another ruling party whose principal contribution to the FSA debate was to argue for an alternative that would probably have been even worse. The new Labour Government has now established a single new regulatory agency – the Financial Services Authority – whose remit extends across the whole financial services industry. Labour politicians finally got their mega-regulator, and Gordon Brown, the Chancellor, now assures the public that this authority will, unlike its predecessors, 'put the public interest first'. Where have we heard that one before? In the meantime, most of the underlying problems still remain, and the new Government is doing little to sort them out. How long it will take to sort out the mess created by the FSA regime is anyone's guess, and there is no reason to doubt that industry interests will continue to remain the dominant influence on regulatory decision-making. UK policymakers appear to have learned nothing from the whole sorry episode, and we can only hope that those who fail to learn from history do not condemn the rest of us to repeat it.

Notes

2 The case for financial *laissez-faire*

This chapter originally appeared in the May 1996 *Economic Journal* controversy on the theme of 'Should We Regulate the Financial System?', with accompanying papers by George Benston and George Kaufman, and Sheila Dow.

1 There is much evidence of economies of scale in banking, but no evidence that these economies of scale are so large that the industry is a natural monopoly. It follows that one cannot defend the central bank's monopoly privileges over the currency supply on the grounds that free banking would lead to a currency monopoly anyway. Nor should natural monopoly be confused with the use of a single economy-wide unit of account. There will typically be one generally used unit of account (e.g. the pound), but the use of a single unit of account reflects economies of standardization (or economies in use) and not natural monopoly, which necessarily involves economies of production. (See Dowd 1993b: chapter 5.)

2 The alternative is to assume that we have a free banking system based on convertibility into a frozen monetary base (as discussed e.g. by Selgin 1994). It seems to me that a commodity-based system is more natural: all historical free banking systems were of this type, and the assumption of a frozen monetary base presupposes some earlier government intervention, an assumption that can be awkward if one is trying to assess the validity of intervention in the first place.

3 For example, in a gold standard, the rule would require that banks of issue peg the exchange rate between their currency and gold (or if one prefers, peg the nominal price of gold). We can then think of the equilibrium nominal prices of individual commodities as determined by the combination of relative demand factors and the fixed nominal price of gold. Gold can thus be regarded as the 'anchor' commodity that ties down nominal prices throughout the economy.

4 Suppose there is a gold discovery under a gold standard. At initial prices, there is now an excess supply of gold and excess demands for other commodities. The relative price of gold against other commodities must therefore fall, but the nominal price of gold cannot adjust because the rules of the gold standard hold it fixed. Hence, the relative price of gold falls by means of a rise in the nominal prices of other goods. We can therefore think of the price level as determined by the factors that determine the relative price of gold, and hence by demand and supply in the gold market.

5 Proponents of the excessive cycling theory sometimes look to examples such as the excessive bank lending to less developed countries in the late 1970s and early 1980s (e.g. Goodhart 1988: 48–9; Dow 1996: 700, 702). However, episodes like

these are not examples of free banking and can hardly be held up as examples of what would happen under it. Many national authorities were actively encouraging their banks to make loans to less developed countries, and banks could reasonably expect some form of bailout if things went bad. In the circumstances, it was therefore hardly surprising that they over-reached themselves. (See Dowd 1994a: 306.)

6 I also reject her view that the argument for free banking hinges on the ignoring of uncertainty. Uncertainty is intrinsic to economic life, and banks have to live with it as much as anyone else. The critical issue is not whether uncertainty exists, but whether uncertainty makes valuation as difficult as she suggests it does. In my view, she exaggerates these difficulties, and I can only agree with Benston and Kaufman (1996: 691) when they say that banks and the public do in fact find ways of valuing bank assets and liabilities that work reasonably well in practice.

3 Bank capital adequacy versus deposit insurance

This article was first published in the *Journal of Financial Services Research* (17, no. 1, February 2000, pp. 7–15). I would like to thank an anonymous referee for very helpful comments.

1 For some perspectives on the Diamond and Dybvig literature, see, for example, Chant (1992), Selgin (1993) or the survey in Dowd (1992c).

2 The model is a stylized version of the DD model. It is based on theirs to facilitate comparison, but differs in two significant ways: it assumes a more explicit utility function to derive clearer results; and it invokes Wallace's 'isolation' assumption to provide an underpinning for the sequential service constraint on which the existence of financial intermediation depends in this sort of environment. (See also note 4.)

3 This study is not the first to question the DD rationale for deposit insurance, but previous ones are, I believe, less satisfactory. The first of these, Dowd (1988, 1993a) is somewhat informal, and the other, Eichberger and Milne (1990), has a less desirable motivation for the existence of financial intermediaries than the present paper – it motivates them by assuming that small agents do not have access to the investment technology – as well as a less complete treatment of the banker's optimization problem. It also has very little to say about the internal consistency of the DD model or about deposit insurance, both of which are major themes here.

4 This 'isolation assumption' serves two functions. First, it provides a 'friction' in the economic environment that gives an intermediary an advantage over a credit market in period 1 (see e.g. Jacklin 1987, Wallace 1988: 9). Without it, or something similar, the outcome obtainable by an intermediary can also be obtained by the credit market. There would then be no reason for agents to prefer an intermediary, and therefore no reason to suppose that one would arise. Second, the isolation assumption provides a motivation for the sequential service constraint that plays an important role in the DD analysis, but which DD assume rather than derive (Diamond and Dybvig 1983: 408; see also Wallace 1988: 3). This is important because the sequential service constraint turns out to be inconsistent with DD government deposit guarantee.

5 It is also necessary to impose the condition that $\gamma \neq 2$ to ensure that (13) below is determinate.

6 If investors leave deposits with the intermediary, and the type IIs run, the average depositor will get an uncertain return of mean 1: those who get there first get more than one unit each, and those who get there later get nothing. The average investor's implied expected utility is then less than the expected utility under

autarky. If agents expect the type IIs to run, they would be better off investing autarkically, and the intermediary would attract no depositors.

7   An alternative discussed in the DD literature is for the intermediary to suspend payments in certain circumstances (see e.g. Jacklin 1987 or Selgin 1993). The knowledge that the intermediary can or would suspend payments might then reassure depositors that it was not about to run out of resources, and so discourage a run from starting. I prefer to focus only on the way in which equity capital can discourage runs, in order to keep the paper as simple as possible, but exploring the relative merits of suspension clauses and equity capital as reassurance devices would be an interesting extension.

8   The explanation is that as the capital rises, the type III agent becomes less absolutely risk-averse, and therefore more willing to take the risk; consequently, if capital is high enough, the type III agent can always be induced to become a banker at a price (i.e. a premium) that the other agents are willing to pay.

Spreadsheet results also suggest that the amount of capital required can be high, and is usually considerably more than is required to guarantee that the bank can always pay its depositors in full. To give an example, if $R = 2$ and $\gamma = 1.5$, then a premium of $p = 0.01$ is sufficient to make a bank worthwhile for everyone, but only provided the type III agent has around 0.7 units of capital for each depositor (i.e. provided the bank can satisfy a 70 per cent capital-assets ratio).

9   The minimum adequate level of capital varies with the input parameters, but spreadsheet simulations suggest it is usually well under half of the amount the type III agent needs to be induced to become a banker. For example, if $R = 2$ and $\gamma = 1.5$, as in the last note, the minimum adequate capital ratio is 11.5 per cent.

10 There is no room for welfare-improving government intervention in this model. There are three possible cases to consider, depending on the amount of capital the type III agent has. First, if the capital is high enough to induce our type III agent to become a banker and make the bank capital-adequate, then our economic problem is solved and there is nothing the government can do to improve social welfare. Second, if the capital is insufficient to induce the agent to become a banker, but more than enough to meet our capital adequacy condition (14), then the government can set up its own bank and use the type III agent's resources to capitalize it and guarantee deposit repayments. However, this makes the type III agent worse off than under autarky, so this arrangement is not Pareto-superior to autarky. Finally, if the type III agent does not have enough capital to satisfy (14), there is not enough capital for anyone to establish a capital-adequate (i.e safe) bank, and a guarantee – governmental or otherwise – is impossible. Government intervention is redundant in the first case, fails the Pareto efficiency test in the second case, and is not feasible in the third.

4 Does asymmetric information justify bank capital adequacy regulation?

This article first appeared in the *Cato Journal*, vol. 19, no. 1 (Spring/Summer 1999): 39–47. I thank David Maude and David Miles for helpful comments.

1   Traditionally, there are three main arguments for capital adequacy regulation. The first is that capital adequacy regulation is needed for prudential reasons, but most advocates of this position take the argument no further to explain why the prudential 'need' is there in the first place. The second argument is one already alluded to in the text, namely, that capital adequacy regulation is needed to counter moral hazard problems created by the regulators themselves (e.g. Benston and Kaufman 1995).

However, this argument – whatever its merits – gives us no reason to prefer capital adequacy regulation to *laissez-faire*. The final argument, more popular in Europe than in the US, is that capital adequacy regulation is needed to protect small depositors. This argument boils down to pure paternalism, but is also open to other objections (e.g. the objection that protecting depositors undermines the market discipline that would otherwise force banks to be strong). In any case, even if one was sympathetic to paternalistic considerations, it is still unclear why the 'small' depositor should benefit at the expense of the taxpayer, since the typical taxpayer is just as 'small' as the typical depositor.

2 It is important to work within standard neoclassical methodology. Miles sets out to provide a rigorous theoretical justification for capital adequacy regulation, which, in neoclassical terms, requires him to set out a formal model, demonstrate a market failure in the context of this model, and show how capital adequacy regulation corrects for this market failure in the context of this same model. If he is judged to have succeeded, then he can reasonably claim to have established a firm neoclassical justification for capital adequacy regulation. If I am to challenge this claim on its own grounds, I must therefore work within the same neoclassical methodological framework as he does.

3 This point is developed further, for example, in Dowd (1996a: 83–5).

4 He also suggests that evaluation of bank strength is made difficult because it requires information about bank deposits, and obtaining this information is difficult because it 'would require depositors to try to work out the flows of funds in and out of the bank since the last published report' (Miles 1995: 1375). However, there is in fact no need for depositors to 'work out' a bank's flow of funds: all that is required is for the bank to publish (every so often) the total (face) value of its outstanding deposits (and any other relevant information). All that depositors should then need to do to be confident of the safety of their deposits is periodically check that their bank does not face a run.

5 The reasons Miles gives for depositors being unable to assess the capital strengths of individual banks would also apply (if they are valid) to many non-financial firms as well. Many other firms have imperfectly marketable assets whose values may be problematic, for example. The Miles position would therefore appear to be falsified by the abundant evidence that the shareholders of other (i.e. non-bank) firms do in fact manage to assess their firms' capital strengths despite the (real) valuation difficulties Miles points to.

6 There still remain Miles' claims that shareholders face a valuation problem, and that banks might increase their capital values by gearing up. The response to the first claim is that shareholders do indeed face valuation problems, but they choose to take on such problems when they buy shares in the first place. Valuing shares is by no means easy, but shareholders effectively solve it when they decide for themselves the prices at which they are willing to buy and sell their shares. My response to the second point is that there are strong pressures on shareholders to act in ways that maximize the value of shareholder equity and therefore rule out the possibility that firms can increase shareholder value any further, by gearing up or by any other means. This is the case even in Miles' own model. If shareholder wealth is not already maximized in neoclassical equilibrium, it should be.

7 To illustrate: a rating agency might collect this information, and publish reports giving each bank's actual capital relative to its adequate capital (e.g. as given by the Miles formula). It might also supplement this information with a commentary pointing out any implications. It might say, for instance, that bank x's capital is 20

per cent below its adequate level, which makes its deposits unsafe to hold. Depositors would then get a fairly clear signal on which they could act.

8   As Cantor and Packer state in their recent study of US rating agencies, a rating agency's overriding objective must be

> to maintain a reputation for high-quality, accurate ratings. If investors were to lose confidence in an agency's ratings, issuers would no longer believe they could lower their funding costs by obtaining its ratings. As one industry observer has put it, 'every time a rating is assigned, the agency's name, integrity, and credibility are on the line and subject to inspection by the whole investment community' . . . Over the years, the discipline provided by reputational considerations appears to have been effective, with no major scandals in the ratings industry of which we are aware.
>
> (Cantor and Packer 1994: 4)

9   Miles' defence is not too convincing. First, he doubts that banks have the 'right incentives' to provide adequate information, and claims that, given his information asymmetry, banks would have an incentive to play up the size of their capital positions (Miles 1995: 1376–7). Second, he acknowledges the possible role of private rating agencies, but instead of seeing it as restoring the optimality of *laissez-faire*, he dismisses it on the grounds that it 'is much harder to show' how such an equilibrium becomes established (ibid.: 1377). Finally, he suggests that regulation 'cuts through' these problems of 'establishing the right incentive for banks to reveal their true default risks by using the legal system' (ibid.).

In response: first, banks do have strong incentives to signal their individual capital strengths, as explained in the text, and the fact that banks have an incentive to exaggerate their strength if the public cannot tell them apart proves nothing. The relevant issue is not whether banks have an incentive to play up their capital positions, given that the public cannot tell them apart; the real issue is whether an individual bank would wish to signal its true capital position, if it had the means to do so. Second, Miles still fails to explain why a rating agency could not (or would not) provide the information that enables depositors to assess their banks, assuming that they could not otherwise assess them and that the information is technologically attainable as Miles assumes. Third, the incentives to provide information already exist in the free market, since good banks will always want to signal their quality. I therefore deny that regulation 'cuts through' any problems, in a way that could not otherwise be done. In any case, regulation creates a whole new set of problems, since the regulatory process is not costless and we ought not to ignore the regulators' own interests or their record.

10   It is highly questionable whether capital adequacy regulation even does this. Capital adequacy regulation creates a moral hazard of its own, and it is also doubtful whether the particular regulatory system actually used (most particularly, the 'building block' system approved by the Basle regulatory framework) does much to improve banks' capital positions (Dowd 1997: 99–105).

5 Competitive banking, bankers' clubs, and bank regulation

This chapter was first published in the *Journal of Money, Credit, and Banking*, vol. 26, no. 2 (May 1994): 289–308. I thank Charles Goodhart and an anonymous referee for constructive comments that have much improved it.

1   The term 'command' is used as it is in the literature on the theory of the firm.

'Command' is where people are contractually obliged to follow orders, and is what distinguishes firms (and, more generally, hierarchy) from pure markets in which the terms of every service are agreed separately.

2 If bankers are to delegate powers to a club, it would usually make sense to delegate those powers to the clearinghouse that already exists to clear their notes and checks. A clearinghouse can monitor (member) banks at less cost than an alternative club since the clearing process creates a by-product – information on banks' clearing gains and losses over time – that often provides advance warning of future difficulties. The text consequently uses the terms 'club' and 'clearinghouse' interchangeably.

3 This point is not to deny that banks might feel that they have little effective choice in practice but to join the club. Be this as it may, what matters here is that banks cannot expect to enjoy the benefits of club membership without paying the membership 'price'.

4 The historical evidence apparently provides few instances of banks being sufficiently incensed about club rules that they decided to withdraw from the club, perhaps because club powers were so limited, but an important exception occurred with the demise of the Suffolk system in the late 1850s (see next note).

5 There would be costs to entering the market for clearinghouse services, but there is little reason to suppose that they would be so high as to make the market effectively uncontestable. A good example of banks 'voting with their feet' even when the market could only support one clearinghouse is provided by the demise of the Suffolk system. The Suffolk system was a club managed by the Suffolk Bank of Boston, but some members found the club rules too constraining and there were complaints about the Suffolk's high-handed attitude toward members. Discontent led to the founding of a rival, the Bank for Mutual Redemption (BMR), and when the latter opened in 1858 many of the Suffolk's clients defected to it. A brief war followed, but in the end the Suffolk abandoned the market to its rival. The Suffolk system is discussed further by Trivoli (1979), Mullineaux (1987), Selgin and White (1988), and later.

6 The Suffolk experience also provides a useful example of how club competition can provide information about banks' preferences for club services. The Suffolk provided a relatively hierarchical product mix that included loans and monitoring services as well as just note-clearing, but the BMR restricted itself primarily to clearing services, and its victory over the Suffolk suggests that banks preferred its more limited bundle to the Suffolk's.

7 As Schuler notes, since free banking

> often had just a handful of banks, so multilateral clearing had little advantage over bilateral clearing. The author of a handbook for Canadian bankers stated near the turn of the century that there was little gain to be had from establishing clearing-houses in cities with fewer than seven banks. ... Branch banking combined with regular bilateral exchange was often a satisfactory alternative to a clearing-house.
>
> (Schuler 1992: 17)

However, see also note 12.

8 The reserve externality argument also suffers from another drawback, at least insofar as it is used to defend the imposition by banking clubs or central banks of reserve ratios on commercial banks. Reserve ratios can be self-defeating in a crisis because the obligation to hold them effectively freezes reserves and prevents them being used just when they are most needed (as happened, e.g., in US banking

crises during the National Banking era). The logic of the reserve externality argument would appear to suggest that reserve holdings should be subsidized, and it is not clear how we can use it to defend reserve requirements which are effectively a tax on the banks.

9 Most major banking crises exhibited 'flights to quality' rather than indiscriminate runs on all banks. Even in the Australian banking crisis of 1893 – arguably the most severe crisis in any historical free banking system – the two biggest banks in Melbourne experienced deposit inflows so large they were embarrassing (Butlin 1961: 305; Dowd 1992: 62). The banking crisis that most closely resembles the 'run at everything' model is the English crisis of December 1825, but even so, the 'run at everything' interpretation does not fit easily with the fact that the same crisis hardly touched the Scottish free banking system at all – yet another illustration of the superior stability of free banking.

The contagion issue has been most carefully examined in the context of the pre-1914 US. Benston *et al.* found that bank failure rates were generally lower than for other firms, and that less than 1 per cent of US banks actually failed even in the severe crisis of 1907–8 (Benston *et al.* 1986: 58, 60). Rolnick and Weber (1985: 5–8; 1986: 885–7) looked for but found little evidence of contagion in New York, Indiana, Minnesota, and Wisconsin in the antebellum period. They did find that failures were sometimes clustered, but these clusters were associated with shocks common to the banks involved, and there was little tendency for these problems to spread. Their conclusions were challenged by Hasan and Dwyer (1988), but their results are not conclusive. They model the probability of failure as depending on the value of bonds relative to capital, the remoteness of a bank's location, and a dummy variable that takes the value 1 if another bank failed in that county, and zero otherwise, and they interpret the statistical significance of the dummy parameter as evidence of contagion. However, that parameter will also pick up any other factor that the other variables fail to pick up, but which is related to the failure of neighbouring banks (e.g. local conditions), and these alternative factors need to be ruled out first before we can say we have firm evidence of contagion.

10 This is not to deny that there can be substantial control problems within a natural monopoly. However, the argument considered in the text is that having the separated ownership implied by two or more firms adds to whatever agency problems already exist when the firms unite, and if the intraindustry benefits were large enough, it would make sense for the firms to merge. The failure of firms to merge appears to suggest that the external benefits involved, if any, are not important.

11 Nor is there any strong evidence, populist views about banking power notwithstanding, that banks were able to cartelize the market successfully. In a variety of countries, the uniform interest rates that would-be cartels 'set for their members gave way to rate wars as soon as any bank . . . spotted a competitive opportunity, and action to punish renegades was futile' (Schuler 1992: 18). That cartels were unsustainable is also suggested by the evidence that free-banking systems were highly competitive even when there was only a small number of big banks, as in Australia (Dowd 1992b: 58) or Scotland (White (1984: chap. 2).

12 Some writers have maintained that even under conditions of relatively free banking, 'big' banks occasionally made last-resort loans to smaller banks, and their managers sometimes regarded themselves as guardians of the system. The Royal Bank of Scotland made such loans to the Scottish provincial banks, for example, and the Bank of Scotland's Alexander Blair was the Scottish system's self-appointed 'policeman' (Munn 1985: 341). However, I would argue that it is

natural for smaller banks to enter into a client relationship with a larger one in much the same way that a firm would enter into such a relationship with a bank, and to label distress loans as last-resort lending is to exaggerate the similarity between these loans and the last-resort lending of a genuine central bank. However, be this as it may, the lending and supervisory functions of big banks under free banking were still constrained by the primary objective of maximizing profits, and the banks in question had few if any privileges, were heavily exposed to competition, and had no official regulatory status.

13 The evidence in favour is circumstantial and consists of occasional episodes like the victimization of the Knickerbocker Trust in 1907 referred to by Goodhart. The evidence against is stronger. The historical experience of free banking broadly suggests that clubs treated comparable banks, including late entrants, in not-too-unequal ways. Since banking clubs under approximate *laissez-faire* typically had few powers, there seems to have been little to gain by rigging rules anyway, and it is significant that the Knickerbocker case occurred in the US when banks were subject to branch-banking laws and the legal restrictions of the National Banking System.

14 A counter-argument is that a club might engage in anticompetitive behaviour, perhaps on the basis of a cost advantage over rival clubs, but it is not clear what would cause such a cost advantage, and, as discussed already in note 11, the historical evidence indicates that attempts to cartelize banking markets have tended to break down.

15 A possible argument against is that there is some social interest that banks will fail to take properly into account, but Goodhart provides little evidence to support this claim and it is in any case not clear what that social interest might be. Externalities are the most obvious possible source of such an interest, but the existence of externalities is not sufficient to establish that the private outcome would necessarily be suboptimal. As discussed already in the text, the point of establishing the club in the first place is to internalize at least some of the benefits that are external to individual banks, but internal to the group.

16 A good example is provided by the history of Citicorp in the nineteenth-century United States. Citicorp maintained higher-than-average capital ratios and gained market share at rivals' expense in periods of financial distress when depositors were looking for a safe haven (Kaufman 1988: 569).

6 The invisible hand and the evolution of the monetary system

This chapter first appeared in John Smithin (ed.) *What is Money?* London: Routledge, chapter 7: 139–56.

1 In practice, coins of different metals usually coexisted, with the higher value ones (e.g. gold ones) being used for large value transactions and lower value (e.g. copper coins) being used for small transactions. However, nuances like this provide no new insights into our main concerns here, and are therefore best ignored in the present context.

2 To make their deposits even more attractive, banks would also provide depositors with transfer banking facilities, so that they can have deposits transferred to pay their debts (e.g. by writing cheques against them). Banks would also develop note- and cheque-clearing systems to make their currency more attractive and reduce the transactions costs of redeeming and issuing currency. For more on these developments see e.g. Glasner 1989: chap. 1.

3 This aspect of free banking is developed further in Dowd (1996a).

4 The issues involved with indirect convertibility are developed in more detail in Yeager and Woolsey (1991) and Dowd (1995b).

5 The precise mechanics of such a scheme are somewhat involved, and the text deliberately sweeps them under the rug. Any reader who wants to investigate them further is referred to Dowd (1994b; 1996b: chap. 14).

7 Are free markets the cause of financial instability?

This chapter was originally published in the *Critical Review, 2000*. I thank Steve Horwitz for suggesting the theme of this essay, and Dave Campbell and Jeffrey Friedman for many very helpful comments on it.

1 Soros is even more critical of free markets in his later (1998) book, *The Crisis of Global Capitalism*, the main argument of which is that 'market forces, if they are given complete authority even in the purely economic and financial arenas, produce chaos and could ultimately lead to the downfall of the global capitalist system' (Soros 1998: xxvii).

2 Any discussion of what a *laissez-faire* system might look like is inevitably speculative, and there is more than one vision of such a system. The best-known of these is Hayek's vision of competition among floating fiat monies (Hayek 1976), but Hayek's proposal overlooks the likelihood that the public would demand guarantees about both the convertibility of bank currency and the value of the unit of account, so competition would force banks to provide such guarantees. In my view, a genuinely *laissez-faire* system would therefore tend to produce convertible currencies and a commodity 'anchor' for their units of account.

3 Convertibility provides an assurance that bank currency will retain its value, and would arise because the public want this assurance and because competition would force banks to provide it. Any bank that refused to honour its convertibility guarantee (that is, refused to buy back its currency when required to) would be in breach of contract, and could be sued. At the same time, any bank or banks that proposed to get rid of the convertibility guarantee would see its outstanding currency returned to it, and then lose its market share.

4 If the public want price stability, as it evidently does, then competition (or the threat of it) should ensure that banks choose anchors that maximize price-level stability: banks that issue, say dollars, against anchors the public disliked would lose market share to banks that issued dollars against anchors the public preferred. This competitive process would tend to converge on an anchor chosen to maximize the stability of a target price-index, and is discussed in more detail in Dowd 1996b: 286–91.

5 For more on these, see, e.g., Leijonhufvud 1981: ch. 9 and Dowd 1996b: ch. 16.

6 There are several reasons for a built-in inflationary bias. One is that the seignorage revenue from inflation gives the central bank (and/or government) an incentive to inflate; such a bias also arises from work on the time inconsistency of monetary policy, in which the government gains if inflation is higher than expected (e.g. Barro and Gordon 1983a, 1983b). The existence of this bias appears to be confirmed by the historical experience of the past forty years: most countries have experienced inflation almost every year, and there were few years in which prices anywhere actually fell. See also Ball and Cecchetti 1990 and Evans 1991.

7 Indeed, financial markets already have considerable power over central banks and governments. Even the government of the United States is not immune. Thus:

> President Clinton's friends complain that their tax and spend policies were frustrated by the 'bond market vigilantes', who fear the federal government's

multi-trillion dollar debt growing even more gargantuan. James Carville, the talented Clinton spin-doctor remarked: 'I used to think that if there was re-incarnation, I wanted to come back as the President or the Pope . . . but now I want to come back as the bond market. You can intimidate everybody.' The fear of Wall Street's vigilantes is clearly a powerful constraint on Clinton's latent profligacy . . . Clinton is reported to have raged against the constraints imposed by the bond markets on US economic policy.

(Staines 1996: 1)

8 Strictly speaking, so-called 'fixed' exchange rate regimes are really only 'fixed but adjustable' regimes, since central banks retain the power to make changes in exchange rates. It is the potential for exchange rate adjustment that is the main problem here.
9 This argument is developed in much greater detail in Eichengreen 1994.
10 The claim that increasing currency substitution makes freely floating exchange rates more volatile is a well-known theoretical result in the currency substitution literature (e.g. Girton and Roper 1981).
11 There is nonetheless a qualification. A single currency is inevitable if the central bank(s) concerned stick with a fiat monetary regime, but if central banks restore commodity-based anchors, they should be able to prevent any further slide to a single world currency. We would then get a situation reminiscent of the *laissez-faire* arrangement in which there is some, but not much, volatility in exchange rates due to volatility in the relative price(s) of the anchors.
12 There is also the question of whether the underlying monetary regime will continue to be an anchorless fiat system. My own belief is that the fiat system is unsustainable in the longer term, and that some form of commodity-based anchor will eventually be restored. This will happen because the fiat monetary system will become unman-ageable at some point. The problem is that a central bank's leverage over the monetary system – its ability to influence interest rates, exchange rates, and the money supply – hinges on the demand for central bank 'base' money, which is likely to fall very substantially, and perhaps even disappear outright. The declining demand for base money will cause major problems for central banks attempting to manage a fiat monetary system, but perhaps the most serious problem is that it will make prices and interest rates increasingly vulnerable to external shocks, especially changes in the technological and other factors that influence the demand for base money. A fiat system that ties the value of a currency to the demand for base money cannot be expected to deliver nominal-value stability in the face of major falls in the demand for base money, and particularly if this demand disappears altogether. If these con-jectures are correct, fiat monetary systems should produce increasing instability in nominal values, and central banks will find such systems more and more difficult to manage. The only way out would be to end fiat money altogether and tie currencies once again to some commodity anchor.

8 A proposal to end inflation

This chapter first appeared in the *Economic Journal*, vol. 104, no. 425, July 1994: 828–40. The author thanks seminar participants at University College Aberystwyth for helpful dis-cussions, and Anthony Courakis, David Greenaway, Paul Mizen, Wyn Morgan, John Whittaker, Bill Woolsey, Leland Yeager, an anonymous referee and an *Economic Journal* associate editor for constructive comments. The usual disclaimer applies.

1 The difference between this contract and a 'pure' price-index forward contract is in the timing of A's payment: Agent A pays when the contract matures in the

'pure' forward contract, but pays when the contract is agreed in the quasi-futures contract. This difference is important and its significance will be explained presently. To complicate matters somewhat, futures contracts incorporate a margin requirement that obliges the purchaser to make some part of his payment up front. I shall ignore this particular complication, but the interested reader might look at Sumner (1991).

2 One does not have to make this assumption, but if one does not make it, one has to carry the term $[(1+r_t)/(1+r^*_t)]$ through much of the rest of the paper. Dropping the term from the discussion clarifies the argument without loss of generality. In any case, the marginal financial operator on whom our basic equilibration story depends will choose some representative market interest rate as his discount rate, so the assumption that $[(1+r_t)/(1+r^*_t)]$ is approximately unity is not unreasonable.

3 Ignoring any risk premium does not appear to be unduly restrictive. The financial market operators on which the equilibrating process mainly depends would be close to risk-neutral at the margin. In any case, the presence of a risk premium would not essentially alter the story in the text unless agents' attitudes towards risk altered in systematic and significant ways.

4 The reader will now appreciate why it is important that the contract is paid for at the time it is made (i.e. we have a quasi-futures contract), and not on the maturity date (as in a forward contract). If no payment is made when the contract is agreed, the purchase of a contract would make no difference to the supply of base money. If the supply of base money does not fall, the equilibrating process described in the text would be short-circuited, and there is no obvious alternative equilibrating process that could take its place. The point of making purchase payments at the time the contract is made is to ensure appropriate changes in the supply of base money.

5 One may ask whether the equilibration story developed here would be undermined by delays in the effects of changing money supply on prices, or by the effects of 'price stickiness' more generally. These factors complicate but do not undermine the story. If all prices took two periods to adjust, for example, one would have to tell the equilibration story two periods ahead: (3) would become $E_t £p_{t+2} \approx £p_t$, and so on, but the discussion in the text would remain much the same. If one believes that price stickiness is a serious issue in the present context, one might prefer a longer contract term to a shorter one, but the contract length of one year suggested as a possibility in 'Operational Issues' should still be adequate. One must also bear in mind that even though some prices are sticky, the price index itself will still be flexible provided that a significant number of the included goods and services have flexible prices. In any case, what is relevant here is the stickiness of the expected rather than of the actual price index, and arguments about the stickiness of the latter are not sufficient to establish the stickiness of the former.

6 The monetary system proposed here is also immune against the better known form of speculative attack that arises when a central bank periodically changes an asset price, but agents can anticipate the direction and timing of the asset price changes. The usual example is where the central bank tries to operate a policy of crawling-peg exchange rates, but private sector agents anticipate the exchange-rate changes and speculate against them. However a central bank operating a crawling peg type of policy is vulnerable to attack only because it changes an asset price in a predictable way, and a central bank that could credibly commit itself to maintaining an asset price indefinitely would clearly have no such problem. We shall discuss credibility issues shortly, but assuming for the moment it was credibly implemented, the monetary system proposed here would be protected against this form

of speculative attack because there would be no anticipated price changes against which to speculate.

7 It is important to appreciate that asking whether there would be a market for QFCs under the proposed monetary rule is not the same as asking whether QFCs would attract traders if some private institution decided to make a market in them (as happened in the USA). There are good reasons to believe that a British equivalent of the failed US CPI-futures contract would meet much the same fate (see Horrigan 1987), but the text nonetheless argues that the adoption of the proposed rule would still give rise to whatever trading was required despite the failure of the CPI-futures market in the United States. What matters is not that the central bank offers to trade contracts, as such, but that it offers to trade them at a fixed price. Horrigan considers the former, but it is the latter that matters here.

8 The central bank offering to take bets on the price level in the manner to be described in the text is more than simply 'promising to keep its promise' to stabilize the price level by adopting the QFC rule. The QFC rule as such imposes no financial penalty in the event that the Bank fails to deliver price stability (e.g. by subsequently abandoning the rule, as it has done with monetary targets in the past). However the bets described in the text would involve such penalties because they would be legally binding contracts. The only way those penalties could then be avoided would be if Parliament intervened *ex post* to pass legislation to cancel them, but all that is strictly required for these bets to have some impact *ex ante* is that private agents not be certain (i.e. have some doubt) that such retroactive legislation would in fact be passed. Provided that agents are not certain about future retroactive legislation to cancel the Bank's debts, they might expect some profit from betting against the Bank, and so taking such bets helps the Bank to enhance its credibility.

9 The simplest suitable instrument is a 'pure' RPI-futures contract which one can consider as a simple bet on the future RPI (see Horrigan 1987). In its essentials, this contract offers to make an RPI-contingent payment in five years' time, at a price agreed now but paid after five years. Suppose the current RPI has a value of 1 and each contract offers to pay £1 times the realized value of the future RPI. Since the Bank would expect the future RPI to be the same as it is now, the Bank would expect to pay out £1 on each contract it sold, and it would therefore expect to make a profit by selling contracts at any price above £1. Since private agents would expect the RPI to be 1.25, they would expect to receive £1.25 for each contract they bought. They would therefore expect to make a profit from buying contracts at any price less than £1.25. Both the Bank and private agents would consequently expect to make a profit for any contract price between £1 and £1.25. Their different expectations of the future price level thus create scope for a market in RPI-futures.

10 The private sector would of course also want some reassurance that the Bank would not then pursue a policy of deflation to maximize the real value of its winnings against private sector agents. All the Bank needs to do to provide this reassurance is to insert into its betting contracts a clause that implies that the Bank will effectively lose the bet if prices fall, or fall too much. This clause might for example specify that if prices fall, the rate of deflation would be considered as if it were an inflation rate for the purposes of settling the bet. A deflation rate of 1 per cent might be regarded as 'equivalent' for betting purposes to an inflation rate of 1 per cent, a deflation rate of 2 per cent as equivalent to an inflation rate of 2 per cent, and so on. The Bank would then have the same incentive to avoid deflation as it would have to avoid inflation.

11 For example, suppose the first contract is sold at time t and calls for the seller to pay the purchaser $£p_{t+1}(1+r_t)$ at $t+1$, where p_{t+1} and r_t are our specified price index and interest rate. If we want zero inflation from t to $t+1$, then the price of the first QFC at t should be roughly $£p_t$. If one felt there were still positive inflationary expectations in the system when the scheme was first implemented, one may want to allow some 'transitional' inflation to 'soften the landing' to zero inflation, and in that case one might want the QFC price to be higher than suggested in the text. I am sceptical of this 'soft landing' argument, but how hard the landing should be is a separate issue, and what matters here is that the proposed scheme could incorporate a soft landing if one wanted it to.

9 Reply to Hillier

First published in the *Economic Journal*, vol. 106, no. 436, May 1996: 635–6.

1 Hillier also embeds my QFC scheme into a formal model. However, since the driving force behind my scheme is an arbitrage argument, I would expect the scheme to be compatible with any well-specified model, and I fail to see what particular insights Hillier derives from his model that could not otherwise be obtained.
2 The equilibrium expected inflation rate is therefore (about) zero, which tells us that the rise in expected inflation would not in fact occur, at least in equilibrium. Nonetheless, the consideration of a hypothetical rise in inflation expectations helps us to spell out the equilibration process that would bring inflation expectations back to zero in equilibrium: any putative rise in inflation expectations would lead agents to buy QFCs, which lowers the stock of currency and leads to a fall in inflation expectations, and the incentive to buy QFCs and retire currency exists for as long as inflation expectations are positive (see e.g. Dowd 1994b: 830–1).

10 Using futures prices to control inflation

This paper was first published in the *Journal of Money, Credit, and Banking*, vol. 32, no. 1, February 2000. I thank the editor, Peter Howitt, and the two referees, Scott Sumner and Lawrence H. White, for their helpful comments. The usual caveat applies.

1 The two schemes are quite different despite the fact that both depend on the use of price-index futures contracts. The key difference is that Sumner's scheme uses price-index futures targeting as an instrument to improve the precision and credibility of monetary policy; by contrast, mine uses price-index futures targeting as a rule to replace discretionary monetary policy altogether.
2 Naturally, there is the issue of how long the lag must be between the day on which the central bank pegs the price of a given futures contract and the time when the contract matures. I have assumed for expository purposes that a lag of nine months would be adequate, but we could easily choose a longer period if nine months was too short. The period must be long enough to ensure that the induced money-supply changes at the beginning of it can comfortably influence prices by the end of it.
3 A very similar problem also arises in the very different, theoretically more explicit, framework of Bernanke and Woodford (1997: 557). They find that there is a conflict between inflation-forecast targeting and the revelation of private information in rational-expectations equilibrium, and their solution is to have the central bank respond to forecasts of both inflation and their policy instrument (Bernanke and Woodford 1997: 662). However, Sumner and I propose a different

approach to the problem as it arises in our schemes: we propose setting up the market for futures contracts as an auction market, but suggest slightly different ways in which that auction might be organized. There is more on this issue shortly.

4 The auction could be an electronic one, and it ought to be possible to find a suitable algorithm, information feedback process, and set of supplementary trading rules to ensure that the process converged rapidly and easily to a solution. The feedback process would give agents information at each stage in the bidding process to help them revise their bids, and the supplementary rules would discourage traders from disrupting the *tâtonnement* process as it gropes its way to a solution (e.g. they might include ceilings on new bids to prevent traders from waiting until the process was almost complete before 'revealing' their true intentions).

5 It is not clear which of these two suggestions is best. If agents have a fairly good idea of overall market sentiments, then the first suggestion might be expected to lead to a fairly rapid *tâtonnement* to equilibrium. In that case, the first suggestion would probably be better, because it dispenses with the fairly cumbersome schedules of Sumner's suggestion. However, we might prefer Sumner's alternative if we believed that agents were poorly informed of each others' expectations or felt that his approach was more reliable or easier for the central bank to implement.

11 The 'compensated dollar' revisited

This chapter was written in 1994 and has not previously been published. I thank Tom Humphrey, Don Patinkin, and John Whittaker for helpful comments.

1 Fisher (1913b: 27–8).

2 Some notable exceptions are Humphrey (1990, 1992) and Patinkin (1993), but their papers focus on somewhat different issues to those considered here. My paper focuses more on feasibility issues than theirs and is also more critical of the compensated dollar scheme. Furthermore, my three main conclusions – that the price level under Fisher's preferred version of the scheme would not meet the stability condition that must be satisfied if deviations of the price level from its long-run equilibrium value are to be corrected over time; that the 'long-run equilibrium' price level under the compensated dollar would appear to be as volatile as the relative price of the MOR (i.e. gold, in Fisher's system); and that the scheme would be vulnerable to successful speculative attack despite Fisher's attempts to patch it up – are, I believe, substantially new results. A brief discussion of Fisher is also found in Sumner (1990: 111, 115–6).

3 If one prefers, one can translate all statements about the weight of the gold dollar into statements about the price of gold. If each gold dollar consisted of 25.8 grains of gold 9/10 fine and there are 480 grains in the Troy ounce, it required 480 divided by 25.8 – or 18.60 – dollars to weigh one ounce. The price of gold 9/10 fine would therefore be $18.60 an ounce. The greater the weight of the gold dollar, the lower the dollar price of gold. See also Fisher (1913a: 219–20, 223–4).

4 Two important qualifications should be noted. The assumption that the weight of gold in the dollar must change by exactly the same proportion as the increase in the price level is made only for simplicity of exposition, and Fisher did not strictly hold to it. He was well aware that the change in the weight of the gold dollar could itself affect the value of gold bullion in much the same way that prying up a stone infinitesimally moves the earth, and he discussed this problem at length in Fisher (1913c). This issue raises the difficult question of how the central bank is to know what the relative price of gold should be, so that it can allow for it and still hit its

price-level target, and what happens if the central bank should miss. (See also Wicksell 1935: 226.) We shall discuss this issue shortly.

The other qualification is that the Fisher plan requires 'an increase of 1 per cent in the weight of the dollar for every 1 per cent excess of the index number *above par* then outstanding', and it does not require an increase of 1 per cent in the weight of gold for every 1 per cent increase in the index number since the last adjustment (Fisher 1914: 829; see also Fisher 1913d: 50–1). Fisher acknowledged that a number of people interpreted his system in these terms, but he explicitly rejected this interpretation. Imagine the index rose and then stayed at a certain level for several periods. Under the latter, incorrect interpretation of his system, the price of gold would rise to a particular level and stay there until after the index had started to fall again, but under the former, correct interpretation, it would keep rising until after the index had started to fall. The latter system thus provides a much stronger cumulative push to the price index to steer it back in the right direction, but there is a danger, which Fisher underrated, that it could push the price level too much and destabilize it. Yet it would still satisfy Fisher's criterion that it would push the price level in the right direction from wherever it currently was.

5 In view of the fact that his compensated dollar had never been tried in practice, Fisher was keen to stress antecedents that had been tried, and he paid laid particular emphasis on the gold exchange standard. As far as he was concerned, his system was analytically 'almost identical with the gold exchange standard introduced by Great Britain to maintain the Indian currency at par with gold' and would be 'less of an innovation' than that. To 'get rid of the comparatively trifling inconvenience of a fluctuating rate of exchange with India', the British adopted a plan similar, though inferior, to Fisher's, which gave India the

> advantages of a gold standard without changing its coins. This development of the gold exchange standard, afterwards adopted in essence in the Philippines, Panama, the Straits Settlements, Mexico, and Siam, I believe to be one of the greatest steps forward in monetary history. Today it is so recognized, although when first devised it was eyed askance. The present proposal is modeled on the same idea, but applied in such a way as to secure a much more important kind of stability, namely, stability . . . with the general mass of commodities.
>
> (Fisher 1914: 835)

6 The difference equation (4) is easy to solve. Rearranging its homogenous counterpart, $p_t - (1+\alpha) p_{t-1} = 0$, we get $p_t = (1+\alpha) p_{t-1}$. Solving backwards, $p_t = (1+\alpha)^t p_0$, where p_0 is an assumed initial starting value. The root λ is $(1+\alpha)^t$, and the text follows.

7 The argument in the text is not dependent on the assumption that the market for gold 'instantly' clears. Suppose for example we allow for 'disequilibrium' in that market by replacing (3) with a 'partial adjustment' equation $p_{g,t} - p_t = \beta_t + \delta (p_{g,t-1} - p_{t-1})$, where $0 < \delta < 1$. We would then end up with a second-order difference equation with roots $(1+\alpha)$ and δ instead of a first-order difference equation with a single root $(1+\alpha)$, but the basic story would remain the same.

8 There was some contemporary discussion of whether the compensated dollar gave the appropriate degree of 'correction' to movements of the price index from par, but no contemporary writers got to the heart of the problem. Taussig (1913) for example argued that the Fisher rule operated too slowly to correct the price level. Fisher responded that the correction would begin as soon as the price of gold was altered, but it would still take time. Exactly how long it would take 'we have no exact means

of knowing', but he suggested that the recent evidence that Canadian and US price levels under the gold standard 'correspond with each other year by year with extreme precision' gives us some indication of the answer (Fisher 1913: 821). A related objection was that the Fisher plan would be inadequate to check rapid and large changes in the price level owing to the limits Fisher wanted impose on the adjustments in the price of gold. Fisher's response was that half a loaf was better than none, and ultimately, 'after the rapid spurt has abated, the counterpoise, in its relentless pursuit, would overtake the escaped price level and bring it back to par' (1914: 828), a response that neither meets that criticism properly nor ensures that the system does not overcompensate and push the price level too much the other way.

9   Yet, curiously, it is also very avoidable. The problem arises from Fisher's insistence on pegging the price of the redemption medium, gold. Having set up a system in which the government periodically pegs the price of the MOR, the government must know how the relative price of the MOR will change if it is to be able to formulate a rule that will allow for this change and hit the price-level target, and any failures to allow for changes in the relative price of the MOR will inevitably destabilize the price level. If the government issuer cannot make such an allowance, it then has no alternative but to abandon any attempt to peg the price of the MOR if it wishes to ensure a stabilized price level. The odd thing is that it is never clear in Fisher's work why he wanted to peg the price of the MOR in the first place. The obvious alternative, as suggested by Newcomb (1879) or later by Yeager (1985), was to adopt an indirectly convertible system in which the issuer of currency would hand over or take in for each $1 note redemption media of the same market value as some stipulated commodity (or commodity-basket). The nominal price of the MOR would then have been free to fluctuate, and changes in its relative price could have been easily accommodated without the damaging consequences that arise with a rule that determines the nominal price of the MOR.

10 The term 'brassage' is however somewhat misleading. It suggests a minting charge, but as Fisher's discussion makes clear, the purpose of the charge was to protect the government against speculation rather than to cover minting costs. The brassage charge also needs to be distinguished from what Fisher regarded as 'seignorage'. The former is the bid-ask spread, the latter in his system is the difference between the nominal value of a gold coin and the market value of the gold of which it is composed.

11 He went on to argue that such speculation would in case probably be 'no more common that speculation in silver at present' (ibid.), but this argument does not really help him. If silver speculation was not much of a problem when he was writing, it was presumably because the market price was relatively free to fluctuate, and agents did not anticipate any significant government-induced changes in silver prices. The comparative absence of speculation in the silver market gives little indication one way or the other about speculation in the gold market under Fisher's system.

12 Fisher appears to have overlooked this problem. After discussing why an additional restriction was needed against upward changes in price, he dismissed the danger of speculative attack when prices were expected to fall:

> No similar precaution need be taken against the opposite form of speculation – for a fall in the price of bullion. Such speculation would not injure the Government reserve, but rather strengthen it by the temporary addition of stocks of bullion which dealers can spare for a time and so sell to the Government at present high prices . . . . Moreover, it could be shown that such speculation, besides being harmless, would be unimportant, for the reason that the stock of gold bullion outside the Government vaults available for such operations is never likely to be large.
>
> (Fisher 1913c: 387)

This argument is uncharacteristically weak. It is true, but irrelevant, that the government's stocks temporarily rise, and the illustration in the text proves wrong Fisher's claim that such speculation would be harmless. Fisher is then left with the argument that the amount of gold available for such operations is limited, but limited as they are, private stocks of gold were (and are) still large in absolute terms; and would be larger still under Fisher's scheme because the possibility of this profit opportunity would create an additional incentive to hold gold. Even a government that held a large proportion of the world's stock of gold would still stand to lose a lot from arbitrage operations based on the stock that remained outside its control.

12 Money and the market: what role for government?

This chapter was first published in the *Cato Journal*, vol. 12, no. 3, Winter 1993: 557–76. I thank Charles Goodhart, David Greenaway, George Selgin, and Peter Boettke for comments on an earlier draft.

1 The text should not be misunderstood. It states that the unit of account is different in a particular, albeit important, way because of network economies. It does not suggest that currency is subject to the same network economies as the unit of account. The issue of currency denominated in a particular unit of account is in many respects much like the bakery discussed in the text, and one would expect major benefits from it. It is the only provision of the unit of account that is different.
2 Again, to anticipate any misunderstanding, let me state that I fully support the removal of legal restrictions on competing private currencies, and I have nothing against the introduction of new units of account. However, it seems to me that advocates of new currencies or currency competition have never come to terms with network factors, and the failure to do so would appear to be an important reason why so many (otherwise relatively) market-friendly economists have been so lukewarm about competing currencies.
3 There is no point reiterating here the arguments for free banking that are covered in detail by White (1984, 1989), Dowd (1989), Glasner (1989), Selgin (1988), Horwitz (1992), Sechrest (1993) and others.
4 Convertibility is superior to a Friedman-type monetary rule in various respects: it has a far better track record; it has an automaticity that the monetary rule lacks, and therefore avoids the public choice and other problems of discretionary management; and it avoids the slippage between target and performance that can occur when the meanings of monetary aggregates change, and which in practice has plagued monetary rules whenever they have been tried.
5 The evidence also indicates that these reforms were not followed by the chronic unemployment problems that Phillips-curve analysis would predict. In Poland and Germany, for instance, unemployment actually fell following the monetary stabilization (Sargent 1986: ch. 3), and so too did unemployment in France after 1926. There are apparently no figures available for Hungary or Czechoslovakia, and the only country where unemployment actually rose is Austria, where it was rising already. It is hard to extrapolate from these experiences to predict what would happen to unemployment if comparable reforms were carried out today in the former Soviet bloc. My own guess is they would be followed by relatively rapid recovery once markets could start operating properly – remember Germany in 1948 – but it seems to me that these economies are so messed up anyway that their governments have no real option but to press ahead and hope for the best.
6 See, for example, Carrington (1992), Hanke and Schuler (1991a, 1991b), Schuler and Selgin (1990), and Schuler, Selgin, and Sinkey (1991).

7 From the government's point of view, the main expense of the system would be the operating cost of the board – the government would provide the board with its assets, but would still get the return it would have obtained from them minus the operating cost of around 1 per cent. Such costs can hardly be considered excessive, especially in view of the monetary stabilization benefits they would bring. The only problem in practice might then be for the government to obtain the foreign securities to set up the currency board in the first place, but one would imagine that a credible commitment to embark on such a reform would produce increased confidence on which the government could rely for loans of the securities it would need. This would be especially so if the monetary and banking reforms were carried out in conjunction with privatization, price liberalization, and fiscal reforms to revive economic life and put government finances on a sound basis. For any government committed to genuine reform, the currency board would be pretty much self-financing.

8 Adequate safeguards are essential if the reform is to be credible, and credibility is critical if private agents are to build the new regime into their expectations of the future and adjust in the least costly way. If private-sector agents do not believe the reform will last, they will continue to anticipate continuing inflation and act accordingly, and many of the benefits of the reform would be lost. Agents would still be reluctant to commit themselves for the future, they would be reluctant to supply goods to the market because they anticipated further price rises, they would still have difficulty reading price signals, and so on. A reform that lacked credibility might still be able to deliver price stability, or something like it – if it managed to last – but it would do so at a potentially much higher cost.

9 For more details on how the currency board might operate, see Schuler, Selgin, and Sinkey (1991) and Hanke and Schuler (1991a, 1991b). The latter also provide a draft law for Bulgaria on pages 28–9 that could provide the basis for legislation anywhere else. My only reservation is that the legislation should explicitly eschew any monopolistic privileges on the part of the currency board, and that it should stipulate a sunset clause that would provide for the board to be liquidated when there was no longer any need for it. The reasons for these provisions will become apparent later in the text.

10 Such a provision would prevent the government from running up debts in the domestic currency, and then being tempted to avoid repayment by intervening later to devalue the currency or abolish its convertibility. The historical monetary reforms discussed earlier all incorporated such measures, and it would be most unwise to omit them. Even if later governments turned out to be 'well-behaved' – and one cannot assume they would – such measures would nonetheless contribute to the success of the reform by strengthening its credibility.

11 If the country concerned picked the currency of its major Western trading partner, it would also obtain the benefits of maximizing the stability of its real exchange rate in international trade. The main trading partner of any Eastern European country once it has adjusted to free (?) international trade would be Western Europe, and given the exchange-rate bounds of the Exchange Rate Mechanism (ERM), picking the mark would promote real exchange rate stability with the whole European Community (EC). Picking the dollar or the yen instead would stabilize real exchange rates with the United States or Japan, but those gains would be more than offset by the losses from the instability of the real exchange rate *vis-à-vis* Western Europe.

12 One common objection is that these governments may not have the initial assets with which to endow the currency board in the first place, but as noted already, the

government can always borrow the necessary assets if its overall reform pro-gramme is credible. If it lacks the credibility to do that, then its real problem is its own reform programme, not its current lack of assets as such, and it will continue to face severe finance constraints until it gets its act together.

13 In the US, for instance, the dollar used to be defined as a particular weight of gold. A dollar note was then only a claim to a dollar (i.e. the amount of gold just spec-ified), and not a dollar *per se*. Under the system proposed here, the unit of account would be initially defined for legal purposes in terms of a specified amount of for-eign currency, but as the text goes on to explain, its legal value would eventually be market-determined.

14 While this arrangement might sound unfamiliar, it only appears so because we are used to thinking in terms of a single monopoly issuer of currency. Under a typical historical free banking system, each bank took the commodity-defined unit of account – usually some amount of gold – as given, and issued convertible exchange media denominated in that unit of account. There were (external) economies of scale-network economies – to use the term in the text – in the use of the unit of account, but there was no indication of any tendency toward natural monopoly in the provision of financial instruments denominated in that unit of account.

15 It is in each bank's own interest to replace competitors' currency with its own, so it will always hand out only its own currency over the counter. At the same time, a bank will also accept the currency of other banks (provided they are considered sound) and then return it to the issuer. Doing so not only enables it to replace the other banks' currency with its own, but the historical experience also suggests that competitive banks would find it in their mutual interest to accept each other's notes and arrange for returns via a formal clearinghouse (see White 1984 or Selgin and White 1987).

16 The monetary system would therefore be an indirectly convertible one in which the banks redeemed their currency with a redemption medium that was something other than the good (or basket of goods) whose nominal price is held fixed. Indirectly convertible systems are perfectly feasible, but the reader is referred elsewhere to more detailed discussions of how they work (see e.g. Coats 1989, Yeager and Woolsey 1991 and Dowd 1995b). If the objective is to maximize price-level stability, the best anchor whose price should be stabilized is one based primarily on the basket of commodities and services of which the CPI represents the price. This anchor would have an almost perfect correlation with the CPI itself, so stabilizing its nominal price should yield a very stable price level (see espe-cially Dowd 1994b). For our purposes here, it merely suffices to establish that the preferences of currency holders win out, and if they want price level stability max-imized, then that is what the banks will provide. How the banks actually do so is then a technicality, albeit a very important one.

17 A new brand must have the same value as the old when it is introduced, but it would imply a different rate of price-level change over time. One that did not have the same initial value as the existing brand would be incompatible with its net-work, and that network would therefore function as an entry barrier against it.

18 Some writers have argued, however, that the public would prefer deflation to price-level stability. Friedman (1969) suggests that the optimal path is a rate of deflation roughly equal to the rate of interest, and Selgin (1988, 1990, and elsewhere) advo-cates a 'productivity norm' by which the price level would move inversely with changes in productivity. It seems to me that neither of these norms is as good as price stability, but what is really important is that the system should cater to the public's desires (i.e., and provide them with the price-level norm they want).

One counter-argument raised by Jerry Jordan in his discussant's comments is that the public may have no preference for any particular inflation rate, and he points to opinion polls that suggest that members of the public have different preferred inflation rates. I am inclined to the view that people do want zero inflation, or something close to it, and I am sceptical of opinion polls that often ask inappropriate questions and have no safeguards to ensure that people give consistent, economically rational answers. To give but one example, polls typically suggest that the current rate of inflation is too high, but that the public also wants lower interest rates in the short run, which usually requires higher monetary growth and higher inflation in the longer run.

19 In effect, any bank would be committed to buy and sell its currency at a fixed price on demand. Any excess supply would therefore come back to the issuer for redemption. The only circumstance where the value of a bank's currency could deviate significantly from this level would be where the bank itself failed, but even in that case, we would still expect other banks to pick up the failed bank's market share, and the value of most of the currency stock would still be at the normal equilibrium level.

20 Xenophobic reactions to foreign investment are nothing new, but very misguided. As Selgin, Schuler, and Sinkey (1991: 17) point out, 'For more than a century after independence, British investments in the United States were so large that some Americans feared British economic domination. Nothing of the sort happened; in fact, British investment sped America's rise as the world's greatest industrial nation.' American and European Japan-bashers would do well to take note.

13 Two arguments for the restriction of international capital flows

This chapter was co-authored with K. Alec Chrystal and was first published in the *National Westminster Bank Quarterly Review*, November 1986: 8–19.

1 See Tobin (1978) and Dornbusch (1986).
2 For a full explanation of this point, see Chrystal (1985).
3 See Labour Party (1985) and Hattersley (1985).
4 This proposition is rigorously demonstrated by Hemmings (1981) and King (1983).
5 See Dornbusch (1976).
6 For a detailed discussion of this episode, see Chrystal (1984).

14 Monetary policy in the twenty-first century: an impossible task?

This chapter was first published in the *Cato Journal*, vol. 17, no. 3, Winter 1998: 327–31. I thank Dave Cronin from the Central Bank of Ireland for his helpful comments.

1 In the UK, for example, minimum reserve ratios were abolished in August 1981. The Bank of England had originally wanted to maintain them, but bowed to pressure from the commercial banks who argued that they would otherwise lose Eurocurrency business to non-UK jurisdictions (Hall 1983: 171).
2 For example, banks could settle inter-bank debts by transfers of mutual-fund shares instead of writing cheques against deposits at the central bank. The banks would then earn the return on the portfolios in which the mutual funds invest, instead of the (usually much lower) interest on central bank deposits.
3 Among other things, it means the central bank must estimate the demand for base money and then make monetary management decisions conditional on those esti-

mates, and therefore conditional on errors in those estimates. At the same time, it would also have to take account of the estimated demand for monetary base while continuing with the interest-rate, price-level or exchange-rate targets it already had. The central bank's monetary policy task would therefore become considerably more difficult than it already is under a fiat money regime.

4 In the limit, the central bank would have to buy back most if not all of its currency issue. In most countries, these amounts clearly exceed the value of central bank assets. Most central banks would therefore need their governments to bail them out if they are to avoid bankruptcy.

5 An interesting analogy is with the historical gold standard, where the price level was vulnerable to changes in any factors that affected the supply of gold. Changes in the technology of gold extraction could and did then have significant effects on the price level. A notable case in point was the development of the cyanide extraction process in the late nineteenth century, which helped fuel major price-level increases in the period between 1896 and 1914.

6 The details are explained further in Dowd (1994b, 1995a). Briefly put, the central bank would create a new type of financial instrument – a kind of price-level futures contract – and periodically peg its price at some par value. Arbitrage forces would then ensure that any resulting equilibrium was one with zero expected inflation. Adherence to this regime would therefore ensure that the price level was expected to remain roughly constant over time. The actual price level would then remain roughly constant, give or take a relatively small random error from one period to the next. This type of system would deliver the benefits of the gold standard (i.e. the benefits of an automatic discipline on the issue of currency), but without the potential disruptions that inevitably arise when the price level is tied to the vagaries of the gold market.

7 If the demand for central bank currency fell to zero, the convertible regime would ensure that the supply of central bank currency also fell to zero in an accommodating manner. The potential nightmare of hyperinflation would not arise because the value of the currency would no longer be determined by the supply of central bank currency, but by the nominal anchor to which the new system was tethered. Provided the anchor was suitably chosen, the demand for central bank currency could then be allowed to disappear without any noticeable inflation.

15 Reflections on the future of gold

This paper was first published in the *Review of Policy Issues*, vol. 1, no. 2, Summer 1994: 45–55. I thank Peter Curwen for helpful comments.

1 The consequences of which have been catastrophic. With the removal of the discipline against the over-issue of currency that the gold standard previously provided, central banks the world over have embarked on an inflationary binge the like of which has never been seen before in world history. For more on the failure of fiat money and the disastrous effects of these policies, see, for example, Dowd (1996b) or Leijonhufvud (1981).

2 These stocks also usually make up very large proportions of the relevant central bank's total reserves. In 1992, for example, stocks of gold made up no less than 59 per cent of US reserves, 56 per cent of French reserves, 51 per cent of Belgian reserves, and 46 per cent of reserves in the Netherlands and Switzerland (GFMS 1993: 34). For once, the UK comes out fairly well in relative terms, with gold making up only 18 per cent of reserves (ibid.).

3 Figures for individual central bank holdings of gold for 1993 do not appear to be

readily available, so the figures quoted refer to central bank holdings in 1992 (GFMS 1993: 34). There is, however, unlikely to be much difference between holdings in one year and holdings in the next.

4 On this issue, central bankers' motives appear to be even more inscrutable than usual. Presumably they continue to hold gold for a combination of reasons. They appreciate full well that if they all sold it then the price would fall considerably and they try to hold up the price by tacitly refraining from selling it. The closely-knit nature of the central bankers' club presumably helps to keep individual central banks fairly 'loyal' to the tacit agreement not to sell. Central banks also remain considerably removed from genuine commercial reality, and so are not too bothered by the costs of gold-holding. At the same time, they are also able to disguise the true costs of their gold-holding in their accounting procedures, which, by and large, have never been exposed to proper scrutiny. One also suspects that in the background is a vague feeling that by getting rid of their gold holdings the central banks would be seen to be admitting to the fraud perpetrated on the public by the abandonment of the gold standard and the inflationary policies that followed. On this latter point, I can only say that the fraud was committed whether they admit to it or not.

5 There is already considerable evidence of a more commercially rational approach by central banks. Thus, *Gold 1994* notes a wider trend towards 'more active management of reserves, including gold' (ibid.: 34), which leads to a more critical evaluation of portfolios in terms of their cost and return. In some cases, central banks have also introduced commercial benchmarks to assesss their holdings of all assets.

6 Indeed, there is already some evidence of central banks reviewing their gold holdings. During 1993, for example, the Bank of Canada sold 121 tonnes of gold until the Canadian Department of Finance announced in April 1994 that no further sales would take place (GFMS 1994: 33).

7 The nervousness of the markets in the face of even relatively small central bank sales of gold lends further support to this scenario. For example, *Gold 1994* reports that official-sector disposals of gold have played a significant role in the market despite their fairly small size (ibid.: 31). The same publication also notes how Dutch Central Bank sales of 400 tonnes in 1992 'may have raised fears of further official disposals but did not induce panic sales from the private sector' (ibid.: 33), but the very fact that they regard it as significant that Dutch sales did not produce panic is eloquent evidence of market nervousness. This conclusion is confirmed by the 'fears of massive disposals from [European] central banks' in the aftermath of the Dutch sales, and again during the 1993 ERM crisis (GFMS 1994: 33).

8 The defining characteristics of a bimetallic system were that that the currency unit (for example, the pound) was legally defined as x units of gold or y units of silver, and a debtor had the right to choose whether to use gold or silver when settling his debt. Consequently, gold and silver were both used for monetary purposes, and not just as tokens. The bimetallic system was the historical norm for many centuries until it was displaced relatively recently, in historical terms, in the early 1870s. For more on this system, see for example, Friedman (1990).

9 If there was too much of one metal relative to the other, the market price of the metal in excess supply would fall relative to the market price of the other metal. Everyone would then want to pay in the cheaper or more abundant metal, and so coins in the other metal would disappear from circulation. If one metal disappeared from circulation, then the bimetallism would function as if it were a monometallism (i.e. depending on the metal, a gold standard or a silver standard).

10 Figures based on those in Jastram (1981: tables 16 and 18).

16 Long-Term Capital Management and the Federal Reserve

This chapter was first published as no. 52 in the Cato Institute *Briefing Paper* series, on 23 September 1999. I thank Dave Campbell, Jim Dorn, Jacobo Rodriguez and an anonymous referee for their useful comments on earlier drafts.

1 *World Economic Outlook* (IMF 1998), chap. 1: 4. Further details can be found in Eichengreen *et al.* (1998).
2 The most vocal have been the repeated calls by the Malaysian Prime Minister, Mahathir Mohammad, for greater controls over the activities of international 'speculators'. Indeed, Mahathir went on to blame hedge funds for causing the recent economic meltdown in South East Asia and repeatedly singled out George Soros in particular as being personally responsible for many of the region's problems. See for example, 'Mahathir Blasts Speculators', *CNNfn:* 30 January 1999, available at cnnfn.com/worldbiz/europe/9901/30/davos_mahathir/. These claims cannot be taken seriously, and one suspects that Mahathir is seeking scapegoats to cover up his own policy failures.
3 For more on hedge funds, see also Brown *et al.* 1999 or Webb 1998.
4 These figures are derived from those given on page 4 of the testimony of David Lindsey, the Director of the SEC's Division of Market Regulation, before the House Committee on Banking and Financial Services on 1 October 1998, when the Committee was hearing evidence on the activities of hedge funds. This testimony is available on the web at http://www.hedgefunds.net/testimony.htm.
5 A detailed account of the rescue is given in the testimony of the President of the New York Fed, William J. McDonough, to the House Banking and Financial Services Committee on October 1. This is available at the New York Fed's website, http://www.ny.frb.org.
6 Since LTCM insiders have still to reveal their side of the story, one can only speculate on why the management of LTCM rejected the Buffett offer. However, they would have been confident at this point that another offer would be forthcoming, and there are good reasons why they might have expected this second offer to be more generous than the first. For one, Buffett had a fierce reputation for buying up firms at rock-bottom prices and was clearly driving a very hard bargain. In addition, they could reasonably infer from its recent behaviour and record in past crises that the Fed was determined to prevent the firm failing, and if it was to do so, it needed to give them some incentive to co-operate. In other words, they had some bargaining power with the Fed, which was clearly desperate to prevent the failure of LTCM, but they had no such bargaining power with Buffett. If they turned Buffett down, the management of LTCM could therefore be fairly confident of getting a better deal shortly afterwards. From their point of view, rejecting the Buffett offer would have made good sense – but only because they could expect a better offer later.
7 So what did Federal Reserve intervention actually achieve? The answer depends on what offers would have been forthcoming for LTCM in the absence of Federal Reserve intervention. There would have clearly been an offer from the Buffett consortium, because that consortium was operating independently of the Fed. However, it is not clear whether the consortium led by the Fed would have come together and made an offer in the absence of the Fed's involvement. If it had, the outcome would have presumably been substantially the same as the outcome that actually occurred, but without the Fed involvement. However, if there had been no other offers, the management of LTCM would probably have accepted the Buffett offer as the only way to avoid failure. In that case, the net effect of the Fed

intervention would have been to get a better deal for LTCM's shareholders and managers, at the expense of Buffett and his associates who were thereby deprived of an opportunity to make a profit from LTCM's difficulties. This leads one to wonder whether Buffett has a case against the Fed for loss of income.

8 For more on these developments in risk management, see for example the readings in Carol Alexander (1998) or Dowd (1998: 3–37).

9 Firm-wide risk management guidelines include the Group of Thirty Report (1993), a report by the General Accounting Office in May 1994, and a number of other reports by other interested parties (see for example Dowd 1998: 16). Stress-testing and scenario analysis are explained in Dowd 1998: 121–31, and credit-enhancement techniques are explained in Wakeman (1998: 255–75). For more on the use of credit derivatives, see Tavakoli 1998.

17 The Financial Services Act

This Chapter was written in 1998 and co-authored with Jimmy M. Hinchliffe, who was then completing his Ph.D. on the Financial Services Act at Sheffield Hallam University. We thank Mark Billings, David Campbell, David Goacher, and the various policy-makers and industry executives interviewed in the course of this research for their invaluable inputs. For obvious reasons, we are obliged to protect the identities of our interviewees, and so cannot thank them by name.

1 Quoted in *Money Marketing*, 2 November, 1995: 30.

2 Public choice theory maintains that politicians, bureaucrats and regulators will tend to follow their own interests, and do not promote the broader 'social interest' as such, despite their fiduciary obligations to do so. There is a mountain of evidence to support public choice theory, particularly from case studies of public policy in the United States. For more on public choice, see for example Buchanan *et al.* (1980) or Mueller (1989).

3 For over two centuries, these products have been bought and sold on a legal basis of *uberrima fidei* and *caveat emptor*. *Uberrima fidei* meant that contracts were regarded as void if one or other party could be shown not to have acted in utmost good faith. Given this basis, *caveat emptor* then meant the parties involved in contracts were presumed to be responsible for looking after their own interests. In plain English, it was a case of buyer (or seller) beware, but sharp dealing was not to be allowed on either side.

4 This case generated a lot of publicity because the victims included members of the rock group Pink Floyd, but was unusually sensitive because it made both the Bank of England and the DTI look particularly incompetent. The Bank of England had sacked a number of people after exchange controls were abolished in 1979, and in doing so had advised them to invest their redundancy money in Norton Warburg. The DTI was embarrassed because it had renewed Norton Warburg's registration to practice despite the fact that Norton Warburg's auditors had qualified their report and so warned them of their doubts about the firm. It was not for nothing that the satirical magazine, *Private Eye*, used to refer to the DTI as the Department of Timidity and Inactivity.

5 In our opinion the Government was quite right to reject a 'super-regulator'. Such a regulator would almost certainly have been even more costly than the FSA regime, and the record of the SEC is hardly one to be admired. As a plethora of studies have concluded, the SEC has served private interests and, according to the most famous study, SEC disclosure requirements have not 'saved the purchasers of new issues one dollar' (Stigler 1964: 87).

6 To his credit, Gower was also engagingly frank, and famously commented that he had rejected the use of cost–benefit analysis partly because he was not competent to conduct one!

7 Indeed, his only explicit objective was to invoke the legal notion of the reasonable man and suggest that regulation 'should be no greater than is necessary to prevent reasonable people being made fools of, but should not protect fools from their folly'. However, this objective does not take us very far.

8 In addition to commissioning Gower, the Government also set up two other committees to make recommendations on a new regime. One committee was established by the Governor of the Bank of England in May 1984 and comprised the City elite, and the other represented the eighteen trade associations. Both groups reported secretly in August 1984, but neither of the reports was published or even officially acknowledged. Gower mischievously comments that 'GAG, the acronym by which the Governor's Advisory Group was known, was singularly apt' (Gower 1988: 11).

9 The behind-the-scenes horse-trading was also complicated by the looming Stock Exchange deregulation – Big Bang – which eventually took effect in 1986. The Big Bang reforms were to make life more competitive for the stock market: they were to open up share trading to a wider range of institutions, abolish cosy arrangements (e.g. such as the distinction between brokers and jobbers) and put downward pressure on commissions. To some extent, the establishment of self-regulation was part of a trade-off between the Government and major powers within the City: the City would submit to Big Bang, and in return the Government would promote 'self-regulation' and go easy on retail financial regulation.

10 One of our industry interviewees had fond memories of these debates: 'the Parliamentary debate at the time was fascinating. I remember one debate in the House of Lords, on whether the Act was going to catch the chap who had a chat to another chap at the golf club and said "I've got some promising Far Eastern Units". Was the Act to cover this type of advice as well? I mean, oh God!' Debates also raged as to whether collectible stamps and coins should come within the purview of the regime as well.

11 The Act itself makes fascinating, if difficult, reading. Gower notwithstanding, the legislation had every conceivable objective: investor protection, efficiency, fairness, competitiveness, promotion of confidence, flexibility, transparency, simplicity, vigorous law enforcement, self-regulation, etc. etc. The reality, alas, is that most of these 'objectives' were put in to placate critics who could see all too clearly that industry interests were the dominant influence on the design of the new regulatory regime.

Gower himself was dismayed by the Act, and strongly criticized it afterwards. As he wrote later,

> The Act started in December 1985 as a modest bill drafted as well as one could possibly have hoped for . . . [Subsequently] it grew, mainly as a result of government amendments put down to placate powerful pressure groups and drafted in unseemly haste . . . The result, not surprisingly, is an Act of great complication and frequent obscurity.
>
> (Gower 1988: 20).

12 These mergers (and other subsequent changes which we do not go into) also illustrate the structural weakness of the regime. FIMBRA was merged with Lautro in part because it was on verge of financial collapse and had in fact been subsidized by Lautro members (i.e. banks and insurance companies) since March 1991. However, a second reason for the merger into the PIA was to paper over the cracks: both regulators had

become severely tarnished by the plethora of scandals that had occurred in the early years of the regime, FIMBRA in particular being widely (and correctly) perceived as a trade association rather than a regulator. As a senior industry director commented to us, the attitude of FIMBRA was that 'we mustn't swing our arms around too much and cut too many heads off because we rely on these people to pay the bills for regulation'.

13 The Act also introduced the principle of polarization, which required that those giving advice must choose to be either tied advisers and only advise on the products of the company to which they are tied, or be independent advisers, in which case they would be the agent of the investor and would have a duty to advise on the whole range of products in the market. The principle was later described by the then-Chancellor, Nigel Lawson, as an 'extraordinary doctrine' (Lawson 1992: 401), a muddled alternative to full transparency which has reduced choice, impaired competition and contributed significantly to the costs and bureaucracy of the regime. We shall have more to say on this principle later on.

14 This 'best advice' requirement was very clear-cut for an independent adviser. An independent adviser had to conduct a comprehensive review of the client's circumstances, needs and future prospects, and then recommend the best product available on the market to meet the client's needs. The 'best advice' rule applied somewhat differently to a tied adviser, who was obliged merely to recommend the most 'suitable' product from within the range of products that were available from his company. Ironically therefore, 'best advice' from a tied adviser could be a wholly unsuitable product for the consumer, but the adviser would satisfy the 'best advice' duty if the product was the most suitable from the potentially very narrow range of products on which he could advise.

15 SIBRO was a notable exception, lacking any powers to fine its members. The SIBRO regime was lax even by the standards of the other regulatory agencies. One of our interviewees described it as 'happy valley' because members could get away with almost anything. Not surprisingly, perhaps, many of the worst offenders in the subsequent mis-selling cases were SIBRO members, and there were suspicions that they had joined SIBRO precisely because of its powerlessness.

16 There were no requirements as far as training and competency were concerned – despite vociferous calls from consumerists and from some professional bodies. When educational requirements were eventually introduced, they were abysmally low and, even then, too difficult for many salesmen, who resorted to cheating aided and abetted by their employers. As one former employee later said,

> The licensing exam was a joke. You learned your stuff from a computer programme and then you were supposed to take a multiple choice test from the programme. But people were going in and out of the room, and the branch manager would look over your shoulder and if he saw you putting a finger on the wrong answer he would tell you the right one. Everyone was doing it.
>
> (*The Whistle* 1996: 13).

17 Naturally, all firms publicly deny that their managers knew these sorts of abuses were taking place. However, in private a number of them freely acknowledged that senior management did know but chose to turn a blind eye. After all, if the contracts were coming in, it did not pay to ask too many awkward questions. To have intervened to stop these practices would have undermined sales. Branch managers who were too conscientious would have missed their sales targets and lost their bonuses, and compliance officers who were too efficient would have made themselves pariahs.

18 As another ex-salesman subsequently revealed,

> We should not have worried about passing exams, though. When testing time came, the trainers left the room so that we could consult our manuals and sort

out the answers by committee. I often wonder how many of my class of 1990 are still giving 'expert' advice to the public after that training course.

(*The Whistle* 1996: 13).

19 Another instance of the regulators' willingness to give in to industry pressure was their handling of the polarization issue. Polarization required that those offering advice on investment products choose to be either independent advisers (i.e. and act as the agent of the client) or to be tied advisers (and act as the agent of the insurance company to which they were tied). Ostensibly, therefore polarization was introduced to enable investors to identify whether an adviser was working as their agent or the agent of a financial institution. In reality, by contrast, polarization was a means for the larger assurance companies to prevent competition on the commissions paid to salesmen. To prevent such competition, the large life companies desired Government backing for a commission-fixing agreement. However, this would be unpopular with the 15,000 or so independent advisers because it would place a cap on their earnings. To get the agreement through, the regulators offered the polarization principle to the independent advisers as compensation. They liked polarization because it protected their market niche and stopped the larger institutions from giving pseudo-independent advice. Polarization therefore arose out of a deal between the regulators and the independent arm of the industry to allow the life companies to fix commissions!

20 As one consumerist told us,

If you look at life assurance figures, the number of life assurance policies that are surrendered within the first three years is still enormous, and they are obviously being sold to people who oughtn't to be buying them – if it were at sort of 1 per cent or even 5 per cent, you'd reckon that's probably within the level of people who every year become unexpectedly unemployed. But with levels of 15 up to 20 per cent, there are a lot of people who are still being sold to who could never afford it in the first place.

21 Another industry executive interviewed was engagingly frank about attitudes within the industry towards legislation and regulation:

I'd never seen so many sleazy backrooms in my life; it was grievous. I remember one guy, saying to me a few months before the FSA was due to come into force. 'What Financial Services Act?' and so I briefly explained to him about the Act and about compliance. He said, 'Oh yes. *You* can do all that stuff. I can tell you that once my salesmen are in the front room with the punter, they will say anything to get them to sign. And it doesn't matter what the law says!' This attitude was extreme, but . . . it was not unusual.

22 One former salesman later admitted,

I never fully completed a Factfind at the client's home because it seemed to be a common practice to fill in the missing details on return to the office. Everyone was doing it. The attitude was 'Get the business! Fill in the paper work when you get back to the office.' Factfinds were being manipulated to suit the sale you wanted. If you wanted a big sale then write the Factfind to make that look like Best Advice. It was more commission for us.

One of his former colleagues later acknowledged that 'These [Factfinds] were little more than a waste of time to some of the "old hands" who worked the system to suit themselves' (*The Whistle* 1996: 16).

23 Again, our interviewees were sometimes extremely candid about what went on, and what they said was not at all flattering. One of them said to us:

> Well, I personally always conformed to the proper rules . . . but some people would just fill facts and figures in! . . . I've seen it throughout my life, and even with very, very reputable companies. . . . I would phone someone up and it would be on the Factfind that they'd made a will, that they get X amount of earnings, that they had a house, and so on, and then when you chased them up, it turned out they'd got nothing. No will, no house, no job, nothing. . . . Its still happening. . . . Its got to the stage where I write on the Factfinds that another so and so has made it all up.

24 Senior management have always claimed that it is very difficult for them to control their sales staff and even to know what they were doing. One of our executives said to us:

> the big problem . . . was that what was going on out there with the end customer was very, very different from what the people who sat in the boardrooms thought was happening. I mean these organizations are populated by actuaries and very worthy people who all knew each other in the City and so on . . . but had no idea how their policies translated through to sleazy brokers in somewhere like Dagenham saying anything that came into their mind to get the customer to sign. They just didn't know what was happening.

We find this sort of argument unpersuasive. Controlling sales staff is not easy, but that is exactly what senior management are paid so much to do. However, the real issue, more often, is that senior management did not want to know what was going on because they already had a very good idea. As one industry bigwig said to us, 'Everybody knew what was going on in the late 1980s. I came across it myself. We all knew that life assurance salesmen were bloody awful people, who were to be avoided at all costs.'

A number of other industry people confirmed this view. Management knew what was happening, but it paid not to ask (i.e. they preferred to appear fools rather than knaves). Not asking also gave management what they thought was plausible deniability.

25 *Financial Times*, 11 June 1994, 'When he dies my dear, all this will be yours: How the life assurance industry, with such a strong position in society, became accused of a breach in trust' (Peter Marsh).

26 The *Economist*, December 1993, 'Disillusioned with life: Mis-selling British pensions'.

27 Even then, the regulators did not intervene of their own accord. They only intervened when Government ministers started getting a lot of political heat and began publicly criticizing regulators for doing nothing. Once again, it took political intervention to get anything done.

28 Those in the better pension schemes received guaranteed, inflation-adjusted benefits, in part because of the benefits of employers' contributions. Administration costs were also lower for these schemes. People who transferred from such schemes lost guaranteed benefits and employers' contributions, frequently lost additional benefits (e.g. of sickness cover) and paid higher administration/commission costs. It was therefore practically impossible to make out a good case that people in such schemes would be better off transferring to personal pensions.

29 We would not wish to say that the Government's intentions were totally indefensible. Opposition parties had never liked the Financial Services Act and wanted a much tougher, more powerful and more aggressive regulatory agency – something like the SEC in the US. Ministers were therefore reluctant to admit to the flaws of

the FSA system in part – in small part, admittedly – because doing so would have played into the hands of the opposition who wanted an alternative system that could have turned out to be even worse – and still might.

30 The FSA quotes are all taken from its press release on Prudential Assurance, dated 16 December 1997.

31 This did not stop industry people complaining about the damage the pensions scandal was doing to their reputation. However, in private many of them acknowledged that the industry deserved the damage and that they had poor reputations to start with. As one industry executive said in an interview: 'I've got at least a metre and a half of files in my office on pensions mis-selling. . . . The industry always had a crap reputation; now it's just crappier than it was . . . Have you seen *Groundhog Day?*'

32 We do not have much time for this excuse. The industry view was well put by one of our industry contacts:

> The review has been . . . the biggest product recall in history. Normally with a recall, you get your Volkswagen and your brakes don't work or whatever, so you go to a Volkswagen dealer, he puts new brakes in, you drive away and that's the end of it. And they've got the brakes sitting there and they've probably got a bloody great pile of brakes sitting there so you're alright. But with this product recall, you've got to redesign the whole [expletive deleted] car! And on parameters which the car won't drive on anyway! As if that weren't bad enough, the regulators keep on changing the parameters as well.

However, the plain fact is that firms knew that they had record-keeping and other obligations under the FSA, and many of them did not take these obligations seriously. There was a product recall situation but it was the firms that issued the unsound products and they knew they were defective when they issued them.

33 Gower (1988: 11).

34 Not surprisingly, perhaps, the one area where the regulators were willing to fight the industry was in protecting their own interest where that was perceived to be threatened. One of our interviewees put this delightfully:

> we have now invented a civil service [reminiscent of] the science fiction film where a chap invented a computer that not only knew how to defend itself, but also hit back whenever something tried to attack it. That's what the PIA's like now. I mean, the Legal and General last week put out a paper saying, 'Yes, we can do stakeholder pensions but you'll have to cut out this amount of regulation – it's costing us a fortune.' . . . God, did they get knocked over the head by the PIA! 'How dare you ruin our careers!' basically.

35 Another of our industry interviewees was very clear on this point, and on what it implied: the industry are

> still not scared enough of the regulators to worry about them too much. . . . They'll say all sorts of [different] things in public, but that's the reality of it. And even now there are some companies who are out there mis-advising, with their managements knowing perfectly well that's what's going on. They don't give a damn.

36 The FSA regime was also a disaster when judged on its costs. While the estimates made at the time that the Act was passing through Parliament suggested that the total costs would be around £100 million, the actual costs have been much greater.

In a recent study, Bannock and Peacock estimated the total costs of the regime to be £330 million per annum (Bannock *et al.* 1995). It is ironic that a number of piffling scandals in the early 1980s – the most serious of which causing losses of £12m – should have led to a regime costing so much. To add insult to injury, the regime has not even prevented the scandals that it was supposed to do; and, indeed, the scandals have been far more serious after the FSA than before it!

References

Alexander, C. (ed.) (1998) *Risk Management and Analysis, Volume 1: Measuring and Modelling Financial Risk,* and *Volume 2: New Markets and Products,* Chichester and New York: Wiley.

Ball, L. and S. G. Cecchetti (1990) 'Inflation and Uncertainty at Short and Long Horizons', *Brookings Papers on Economic Activity* 1: 215–45.

Bannock, G. and A. Peacock (1995) 'The Rationale of Financial Services Regulation: Is the Current Structure Cost-Effective and Working?' discussion document, Graham Bannock and Partners Ltd.

Barro, R. J. and D. B. Gordon (1983a) 'Rules, Discretion and Reputation in a Model of Monetary Policy', *Journal of Monetary Economics* 12: 101–21.

—— (1983b) 'A Positive Theory of Monetary Policy in a Natural Rate Model', *Journal of Political Economy* 91: 589–610.

Benston, G. J., R. A. Eisenbeis, P. A. Horvitz, E. J. Kane and G. G. Kaufman (1986) *Perspectives on Safe and Sound Banking: Past, Present, and Future,* Cambridge, Mass.: MIT Press.

Benston, G. J. and G. G. Kaufman (1988) *Risk and Solvency Regulation of Depository Institutions: Past Policies and Current Options,* New York: Salomon Brothers Center, Graduate School of Business, New York University, monograph 1988–1.

—— (1995) 'Is the Banking and Payments System Fragile?' *Journal of Financial Services Research* 9: 209–40.

—— (1996) 'The Appropriate Role of Banking Regulation', *Economic Journal* 106: 688–97.

Bernanke, B. S. and M. Woodford (1997) 'Inflation Forecasts and Monetary Policy', *Journal of Money, Credit, and Banking* 29: 654–84.

Bresciani-Turroni, C. (1937) *The Economics of Inflation,* London: George Allen and Unwin.

Brown, S. J., W. N. Goetzmann and R. G. Ibbotson (1999) 'Offshore Hedge Funds: Survival and Performance, 1989–95', *Journal of Business* 72: 91–117.

Browne F. X. and Cronin, D. (1997) 'Payments Technologies, Financial Innovation, and Laissez-Faire Banking: A Further Discussion of the Issues', 153–65 in J. A. Dorn (ed.), *The Future of Money in the Information Age,* Washington D.C.: Cato Institute.

Buchanan, J. M., R. D. Tollison and G. Tullock (1980) *Toward a Theory of the Rent-Seeking Society,* College Station: Texas A&M University Press.

Butlin. S. J. (1961) *Australia and New Zealand Bank: The Bank of Australasia and the Union Bank of Australia Limited, 1821–1951,* London: Longman.

Cameron, R. (1967) 'Scotland, 1750–1845', 60–99 in R. Cameron (ed.), *Banking in the Early Stages of Industrialization: A Study in Comparative Economic History*, New York: Oxford University Press.

Cantor, R. and F. Packer (1994) 'The Credit Rating Industry', Federal Reserve Bank of New York *Quarterly Review* 19 (Summer–Fall): 1–26.

Carrington, S. (1992) 'The Re-Monetization of the Commonwealth of Independent States', *American Economic Review* 82 (*Papers and Proceedings*): 22–6.

Chant, J. (1992) 'The New Theory of Financial Intermediation', 42–65 in K. Dowd and M. K. Lewis (eds), *Current Issues in Financial and Monetary Economics,* London: Macmillan.

Chrystal, K. A. (1984) 'Dutch Disease or Monetarist Medicine? The British Economy Under Mrs Thatcher', Federal Reserve Bank of St. Louis *Review* 66 (May): 27–37.

—— (1985) 'Have High Capital Flows Overseas Harmed Britain?' *Economic Review* 3 (September): 24–8.

Clark, J. A. (1988) 'Economies of Scale and Scope at Depository Financial Institutions: A Review of the Literature', Federal Reserve Bank of Kansas City *Economic Review* (September–October): 16–33.

Coase, R. H. (1937) 'The Nature of the Firm', *Economica* 4: 386–405.

Coats, W. (1989) 'In Search of a Monetary Anchor: A "New" Monetary Standard', mimeo, International Monetary Fund, Washington D.C.

Cothren, R. C. (1987) 'Asymmetric Information and Optimal Bank Reserves', *Journal of Money, Credit, and Banking* 19 (February): 68–77.

Dewatripont, M. and J. Tirole (1994) *The Prudential Regulation of Banks*, Cambridge, Mass.: MIT Press.

Diamond, D. W. and P. H. Dybvig (1983) 'Bank Runs, Deposit Insurance, and Liquidity', *Journal of Political Economy* 91: 401–19.

Dornbusch, R. (1976) 'Expectations and Exchange Rate Dynamics', *Journal of Political Economy* 84: 1161–76.

—— (1986) 'Exchange Rate Economics: 1986', paper presented to the Royal Economic Society, 17 July.

Dow, S. C. (1993) *Money and the Economic Process*, Aldershot: Edward Elgar.

—— (1996) 'Why the Financial System Should be Regulated', *Economic Journal* 106: 698–707.

Dow, S. C. and Smithin, J. (1994) 'Change in Financial Markets and the "First Principles" of Monetary Economics', mimeo, University of Stirling and York University, Ontario.

Dowd, K. (1988) 'Is Deposit Insurance Necessary?' mimeo, University of Nottingham.

—— (1989) *The State and the Monetary System*, New York: St. Martin's Press.

—— (1990) 'Does Europe Need a Federal Reserve System?' *Cato Journal* 10: 423–42.

—— (ed.) (1992a) *The Experience of Free Banking*, London: Routledge.

—— (1992b) 'Free Banking in Australia', 48–78 in K. Dowd (ed.), *The Experience of Free Banking*, London: Routledge.

—— (1992c) 'Models of Banking Instability: A Partial Review of the Literature', *Journal of Economic Surveys* 6: 107–32.

—— (1992d) 'US Banking in the "Free Banking" Period', 206–40 in K. Dowd (ed.), *The Experience of Free Banking*, London: Routledge.

—— (1993a) 'Re-examining the Case for Government Deposit Insurance', *Southern Economic Journal* 59: 363–70.

—— (1993b) *Laissez-Faire Banking*, London: Routledge.

—— (1994a) 'Competitive Banking, Bankers' Clubs, and Bank Regulation', *Journal of Money, Credit, and Banking* 26: 289–308. (Also published as Chapter 5 of this book.)

—— (1994b) 'A Proposal to End Inflation', *Economic Journal* 104: 828–40. (Also published as Chapter 8 of this book.)

—— (1995a) 'A Rule to Stabilize the Price Level', *Cato Journal* 15: 39–63.

—— (1995b) 'The Mechanics of Indirect Convertibility', *Journal of Money, Credit and Banking* 27: 67–88.

—— (1996a) 'The Case for Financial *Laissez-Faire*', *Economic Journal* 106: 679–87. (Also published as Chapter 2 of this book.)

—— (1996b) *Competition and Finance: A Reinterpretation of Financial and Monetary Economics*, Basingstoke: Macmillan/New York: St. Martin's Press.

—— (1997) 'The Regulation of Bank Capital Adequacy', *Advances in Austrian Economics* 4: 95–100.

—— (1998) *Beyond Value at Risk: The New Science of Risk Management*, Chichester and New York: Wiley.

Eichberger, J. and F. Milne (1990) 'Bank Runs and Capital Adequacy', mimeo, University of Melbourne.

Eichengreen, B. (1994) *International Monetary Arrangements for the 21st Century*, Washington, D.C: Brookings Institute.

Eichengreen, B. and D. Mathieson, with B. Chadha, A. Jansen, L. Kodres and S. Sharma (1998) 'Hedge Funds and Financial Market Dynamics', *Occasional Paper* 155, Washington, D.C.: International Monetary Fund.

Engle, R. F. (1982) 'Autoregressive Conditional Heteroskedasticity with Estimates of the Variance of United Kingdom Inflation', *Econometrica* 50: 987–1007.

Evans, M. (1991) 'Discovering the Link Between Inflation Rates and Inflation Uncertainty', *Journal of Money, Credit, and Banking* 23: 169–84.

Feldman, A. (1998) 'Investment Titan's Fall', *New York Daily News*, 28 September.

Fisher, I. (1911) *The Purchasing Power of Money: Its Determination and Relation to Credit, Interest and Crises*, New York: Macmillan.

—— (1913a) 'A Compensated Dollar', *Quarterly Journal of Economics* 27: 213–35.

—— (1913b) 'A Remedy for the Rising Cost of Living: Standardizing the Dollar', *American Economics Association Papers and Proceedings* 3-4: 20–8.

—— (1913c) 'Appendix: A Compensated Dollar', *Quarterly Journal of Economics* 27: 385–97.

—— (1913d) 'Reply [to Objections]', *American Economics Association Papers and Proceedings* 3-4: 46–51.

—— (1914) 'Objections to a Compensated Dollar Answered', *American Economic Review* 4: 818–39.

—— (1920) *Stabilizing the Dollar*, New York: Macmillan.

—— (1935) *Stabilised Money: A History of the Movement*, assisted by H. L. Cohrssen, London: George Allen and Unwin.

Friedman, M. (1960) *A Program for Monetary Stability*, New York: Fordham University Press.

—— (1969) 'The Optimum Quantity of Money', 1–50 in M. Friedman (ed.), *The Optimum Quantity of Money and Other Essays*, Chicago: Aldine.

—— (1990) 'Bimetallism Revisited', *Journal of Economic Perspectives* 4: 85–104.

Gallarotti, G. M. (1993) 'The Scramble for Gold: Monetary Regime Transformation in the 1870s', 15–67 in M. D. Bordo and F. Capie (eds), *Monetary Regimes in Transition*, Cambridge: Cambridge University Press.

Garrison, R. W. and L. H. White. (1997) 'Can Monetary Stabilization be Improved by CPI Futures Targeting?' *Journal of Money, Credit, and Banking* 29: 535–41.

General Accounting Office (1994) *Financial Derivatives: Actions Needed to Protect the Financial System*, Washington, D.C.: General Accounting Office.

Gilbert, R. A. (1984) 'Market Structure and Competition: A Survey', *Journal of Money, Credit, and Banking* 16: 617–45.

Girton, L. and D. Roper (1981) 'Theory and Implications of Currency Substitution', *Journal of Money, Credit, and Banking* 13: 12–30.

Glasner, D. (1989) *Free Banking and Monetary Reform*, Cambridge and New York: Cambridge University Press.

Goldberg, S. (1958) *Introduction to Difference Equations*, New York: Wiley.

Gold Fields Mineral Services (1993) *Gold 1993*, London: Gold Fields Mineral Services Ltd.

—— (1994) *Gold 1994*, London: Gold Fields Mineral Services Ltd.

Goodhart, C. A. E. (1987) 'Why Do Banks Need a Central Bank?' *Oxford Economic Papers* 39: 75–89.

—— (1988) *The Evolution of Central Banks*, Cambridge, Mass.: MIT Press.

—— (1989) *Money, Information and Uncertainty*, 2nd edn, Basingstoke: Macmillan.

—— (1991) 'Are Central Banks Necessary?' 1–21 in F. Capie and G. E. Wood (eds), *Unregulated Banking: Chaos or Order?* London: Macmillan.

Gorton, G. and D. J. Mullineaux (1987) 'The Joint Production of Confidence: Endogenous Regulation and Nineteenth-Century Commercial Bank Clearinghouses', *Journal of Money, Credit, and Banking* 19: 457–68.

Gower, L. C. B. (1984) *Review of Investor Protection: Report: Part I*, London: HMSO, Cmnd. 9125.

—— (1988) 'Big Bang and City Regulation', *Modern Law Review* 51: 1–22.

Greenspan, A. (1998) 'Private-Sector Refinancing of the Large Hedge Fund, Long-Term Capital Management', yestimony before the House of Representatives Committee on Banking and Financial Services, 1 October (available at the Board of Governors website, www.bog.frb.fed.us).

Group of Thirty (1993) *Derivatives: Practices and Principles*, Group of Thirty Global Derivatives Study Group, New York: Group of Thirty.

Hall, M. J. B. (1983) *Monetary Policy Since 1971: Conduct and Performance*, London and Basingstoke: Macmillan.

Hanke, S. H. and K. Schuler (1991a) 'Teeth for the Bulgarian Lev: A Currency Board Solution', *International Freedom Foundation Issue Briefing*, Washington, D.C.: International Freedom Foundation.

—— (1991b) 'Currency Boards for Eastern Europe', *Heritage Lectures* 355, Washington, D.C.: Heritage Foundation.

Hasan, I. and G. P. Dwyer (1988) 'Contagion Effects and Banks Closed in the Free Banking Period', 153–77 in *The Financial Services Industry in the Year 2000: Risk and Efficiency. Proceedings of a Conference on Bank Structure and Competition*, Chicago: Federal Reserve Bank of Chicago.

Hattersley, R. (1985) 'A New Exchange Control System', *Fiscal Studies* 6 (August): 9–13.

Hayek, F. A. (1976) *Denationalisation of Money*, Hobart Special Paper no. 70, London: Institute of Economic Affairs.

Hemmings, D. B. (1981) 'Exchange Controls, Security Prices and Exchange Rates', *Bulletin of Economic Research* 33: 82–90.

Hillier, B. 'Some Unpleasant Budgetary Arithmetic of a Proposal to End Inflation: A Comment', *Economic Journal* 106: 628–34.

Horrigan, B. R. (1987). 'The CPI Futures Market: The Inflation Hedge That Won't Grow', *Federal Reserve Bank of Philadelphia Business Review* (May–June): 3–14.

Horwitz, S. (1992) *Monetary Evolution, Free Banking, and Economic Order*, Boulder, Colo.: Westview.

Howitt, P. W. (1990) 'Zero Inflation as a Long-Term Target for Monetary Policy', 67–108 in R. G. Lipsey (ed.), *Zero Inflation: The Goal of Price Stability*, Toronto: C. D. Howe Institute.

Humphrey, D. B., Pulley, L. B. and Vesala, J. M. (1996) 'Cash, Paper and Electronic Payments: A Cross-Country Analysis', *Journal of Money, Credit, and Banking* 28: 914–39.

Humphrey, T. M. (1990) 'Fisherian and Wicksellian Price-Stabilization Models in the History of Economic Thought', Federal Reserve Bank of Richmond *Economic Review* (May–June): 3–12.

—— (1992) 'A Simple Model of Irving Fisher's Price-Level Stabilization Rule', Federal Reserve Bank of Richmond *Economic Review* (November–December): 12–18.

International Monetary Fund (1998) *World Economic Outlook: A Survey by the International Monetary Fund*, Washington, D.C.: International Monetary Fund (May).

Jacklin, C. J. (1987) 'Demand Deposits, Trading Restrictions, and Risk Sharing', 26–47 in E. C. Prescott and N. Wallace (eds), *Contractual Arrangements for Intertemporal Trade*, Minneapolis, Minn.: University of Minnesota Press.

Jastram, R. W. (1981) *Silver: The Restless Metal*, New York: Wiley.

Jevons, W. S. (1875) *Money and the Mechanism of Exchange*, 20th edn, London: Kegan Paul, Trench, Trubner (1920 reprint).

Jones, R. A. (1976) 'The Origin and Development of Media of Exchange', *Journal of Political Economy* 84: 757–75.

Kaufman, G. G. (1987) 'The Truth About Bank Runs', Federal Reserve Bank of Chicago, *Staff Memorandum* 87–3.

—— (1988) 'Bank Runs: Causes, Benefits, and Costs', *Cato Journal* 7: 559–87.

—— (1992a) 'Lender of Last Resort in Contemporary Perspective', *Journal of Financial Services Research* 5: 95–110.

—— (1992b) 'Capital in Banking: Past, Present, and Future', *Journal of Financial Services Research* 5: 385–402.

Keynes, J. M. (1919) *Essays in Persuasion*, New York: W. W. Norton.

Kindleberger, C. P. (1978) *Manias, Panics, and Crashes: A History of Financial Crises*, New York: Basic Books.

King, R. G. (1983) 'On the Economics of Private Money', *Journal of Monetary Economics* 12: 82–90.

Labour Party (1985) *Jobs and Industry: Investing in Britain*, London: UK Labour Party.

Lawson, N. (1992) *The View From No. 11*, London: Bantam.

Leach, J. A. (1998) 'The Failure of Long-Term Capital Management: A Preliminary Assessment', statement to the House Banking and Financial Services Committee, 12

October (available at www.house.gov/banking/101298le.htm).

Leijonhufvud, A. (1981) *Information and Coordination: Essays in Macroeconomic Theory*, New York: Oxford University Press.

Lewis, M. K. and K. T. Davis (1987) *Domestic and International Banking*, Oxford: Philip Allan.

Lindsey, R. R. (1998) 'Testimony' before the House of Representatives Committee on Banking and Financial Services, 1 October.

McDonough, W. J. (1998) 'Private-Sector Refinancing of the Large Hedge Fund, Long-Term Capital Management', testimony before the House of Representatives Committee on Banking and Financial Services, 1 October.

Menger, K. (1892) 'On the Origin of Money', *Economic Journal* 2: 239–55.

Miles, D. (1995) 'Optimal Regulation of Deposit Taking Financial Intermediaries', *European Economic Review* 39: 1365–84.

Minsky, H. P. (1982) 'The Financial Instability Hypothesis: Capitalistic Processes and the Behaviour of the Economy', 13–29 in C. P. Kindleberger and J-P. Laffargue (eds), *Financial Crises: Theory, History and Policy*, Cambridge and New York: Cambridge University Press.

Mueller, D. C. (1989) *Public Choice*, 2nd edn, New York: Cambridge University Press.

Mullineaux, D. J. (1987) 'Competitive Monies and the Suffolk Bank System: A Contractual Perspective', *Southern Economic Journal* 54: 884–97.

Munn, C. W. (1985) 'Review' (of Lawrence H. White's *Free Banking in Britain*), *Business History* 27: 341–3.

Newcomb, S. (1879) 'The Standard of Value', *North American Review* (September): 223–37.

Patinkin, D. (1993) 'Irving Fisher and His Compensated Dollar Plan', Federal Reserve Bank of Richmond *Economic Quarterly* (Summer): 1–33.

Personal Investment Authority (1997) *Third Survey of the Persistency of Life and Pensions Policies*, London: Personal Investment Authority (November).

Radford, R. A. (1945) 'The Economic Organisation of a P.O.W. Camp', *Economica* 12: 189–201.

Rolnick, A. J. and W. E. Weber (1985) 'Banking Instability and Regulation in the US Free Banking Era', Federal Bank of Minneapolis *Quarterly Review* (Summer): 1–9.

—— (1986) 'Inherent Instability in Banking: The Free Banking Experience', *Cato Journal* 5: 877–90.

Sargent, T. J. (1986) *Rational Expectations and Inflation*, New York: Harper and Row.

Schnadt, N. and J. Whittaker (1993) 'Inflation-Proof Currency? The Feasibility of Variable Commodity Standards', *Journal of Money, Credit, and Banking* 25: 214–21.

Schuler, K. (1992) 'The World History of Free Banking: An Overview', 7–47 in K. Dowd (ed.), *The Experience of Free Banking*, London: Routledge.

Schuler, K. and G. A. Selgin (1990) 'A Proposal for Reforming Lithuania's Monetary System', mimeo, University of Georgia (November).

Schuler, K., G. A. Selgin, and J. F. Sinkey, Jr (1991) 'Replacing the Ruble in Lithuania: Real Change versus Pseudoreform', Cato Institute *Policy Analysis* 163, Washington, D.C.: Cato Institute.

Sechrest, L. J. (1993) *Free Banking: Theory, History and a Laissez-Faire Model*, Westport, Conn.: Quorum.

Securities and Investments Board (1993) *Pensions Transfers: A Report for SIB by KPMG*

Peat Marwick, London: Securities and Investments Board (December).

Selgin, G. A. (1988) *The Theory of Free Banking: Money Supply Under Competitive Note Issue*, Totowa, N.J.: Rowman and Littlefield.

—— (1990) 'Monetary Equilibrium and the Productivity Norm of Price-Level Policy', *Cato Journal* 10: 265–87.

—— (1992) 'On Foot-Loose Prices and Forecast-Free Monetary Regimes', *Cato Journal* 12: 75–80.

—— (1993) 'In Defense of Bank Suspension', *Journal of Financial Services Research* 7: 347–64.

—— (1994) 'Free Banking and Monetary Control', *Economic Journal* 104: 1449–59.

Selgin, G. A. and L. H. White (1987) 'The Evolution of a Free Banking System', *Economic Inquiry* 25: 439–57.

—— (1988) 'Competitive Monies and the Suffolk Bank System: Comment', *Southern Economic Journal* 55: 215–19.

Simpson, D. (1996) *Regulating Pensions: Too Many Rules, Too Little Competition*, Hobart Special Paper no. 131, London: Institute of Economic Affairs.

Sloan, A. (1998) 'What Goes Around', *Newsweek*, 12 October (available from www.newsweek.com).

Soros, G. (1994) *The Alchemy of Finance: Reading the Mind of the Market*, New York: Wiley.

—— (1998) *The Crisis of Global Capitalism [Open Society Endangered]*, New York: PublicAffairs.

Sprague, O. M. W. (1910) *History of Crises under the National Banking System*, Washington, D.C.: US Government Printing Office.

Staines, P. (1996) 'The Benefits of Speculation: A Bond Market Vigilante Replies to Will Hutton's *The State We're In*', *Economic Notes* 69, London: Libertarian Alliance.

Stigler, G. J. (1964) 'Public Regulation of the Securities Market', *Journal of Business* 372.

Sumner, S. (1990) 'The Forerunners of "New Monetary Economics" Proposals to Stabilize the Unit of Account', *Journal of Money, Credit, and Banking* 22: 109–18.

—— (1991) 'The Development of Aggregate Economic Targeting', *Cato Journal* 10: 747–59.

—— (1995) 'The Impact of Futures Price Targeting on the Precision and Credibility of Monetary Policy', *Journal of Money, Credit, and Banking* 27: 89–106.

—— (1997) 'Reply to Garrison and White', *Journal of Money, Credit, and Banking* 29: 542–5.

Taussig, F. W. (1913) 'The Plan for a Compensated Dollar', *Quarterly Journal of Economics* 27: 401–16, 23.

Tavakoli, J. M. (1998) *Credit Derivatives: A Guide to Instruments and Applications*, Chichester and New York: Wiley.

Timberlake, R. H. (1993) *Monetary Policy in the United States: An Intellectual and Institutional History*, Chicago: Chicago University Press.

—— (1984) 'The Central Banking Role of Clearinghouse Associations', *Journal of Money, Credit, and Banking* 16: 1–15.

Tobin, J. (1978) 'A Proposal for International Monetary Reform', *Eastern Economic Journal* 4: 153–9.

Tollison, R. D. (1988) 'Public Choice and Legislation', *Virginia Law Review* 74.

Trivoli, G. (1979) *The Suffolk Bank: A Study of a Free-Enterprise Clearing System*,

London: Adam Smith Institute.

Ullman-Margalit, E. (1978) 'Invisible-Hand Explanations', *Synthèse* 39: 263–91.

Wakeman, L. (1988) 'Credit Enhancement', 255–75 in C. Alexander (ed.), *Risk Management and Analysis, Volume 2, Measuring and Modelling Financial Risk*, Chichester and New York: Wiley.

Wallace, N. (1988) 'Another Attempt to Explain an Illiquid Banking System: The Diamond and Dybvig Model with Sequential Service Taken Seriously', Federal Reserve Bank of Minneapolis *Quarterly Review* 12 (Fall): 3–16.

Webb, A. (1998) 'Hedge Fund Fever', *Derivatives Strategy* 3 (October): 33–8.

Weller, B. (1998) 'Betting with Hedges', *The Financial Regulator* 3 (December): 20–3.

White, L. H. (1984a) *Free Banking in Britain: Theory, Experience, and Debate, 1800–1845*, New York: Cambridge University Press.

—— (1984b) 'Competitive Payments Systems and the Unit of Account', *American Economic Review* 74: 699–712.

—— (1989) *Competition and Currency: Essays on Free Banking and Money*, New York: New York University Press.

Wicksell, K. (1935) *Lectures on Political Economy, Volume Two: Money*, ed. with an Intro. by L. Robbins, London: Routledge.

Yeager, L. B. (1985) 'Deregulation and Monetary Reform', *American Economic Review Papers and Proceedings* 75: 103–7.

—— (1992) 'Toward Forecast-Free Monetary Institutions', *Cato Journal* 12: 53–73.

Yeager, L. B., and W. W. Woolsey (1991) 'Is There a Paradox of Indirect Convertibility?' mimeo, Auburn University and The Citadel, Charleston, S.C.

Young, P. (1998) 'Lessons from LTCM', *Applied Derivatives Trading* (October) (available at http://www.adtrading.com).

Index

Printed in the United States
by Baker & Taylor Publisher Services